COMPREHENDING MISSION

For Paula, Tabor, Nathan, and Rebecca
τὸ δὲ καλὸν ποιοῦντες μὴ ἐγκακῶμεν

American Society of Missiology Series, No. 49

COMPREHENDING MISSION

The Questions, Methods, Themes, Problems, and Prospects of Missiology

Stanley H. Skreslet

Maryknoll, New York 10545

Cover illustration: *Codex Sierra,* initial page for the year 1551 C.E. Economics, politics, intercultural encounters, and matters of theology are all evident in this remarkable document, which records the purchase of expensive vestments and other European goods for a mission church on Spain's colonial frontier. More contextually, the account book uses traditional pictographs, an indigenous language (Nahuatl) for an alphabetic text, and a vigesimal Mixtec system of numbering to describe the various sacred and secular items acquired for the community or payments made for services rendered on its behalf between 1550 and 1564. From N[icolas] León, ed. and trans., *Códice Sierra* ([Mexico] Poulat, Litografió, 1906). Public domain.

Founded in 1970, Orbis Books endeavors to publish works that enlighten the mind, nourish the spirit, and challenge the conscience. The publishing arm of the Maryknoll Fathers and Brothers, Orbis seeks to explore the global dimensions of the Christian faith and mission, to invite dialogue with diverse cultures and religious traditions, and to serve the cause of reconciliation and peace. The books published reflect the views of their authors and do not represent the official position of the Maryknoll Society. To learn more about Maryknoll and Orbis Books, please visit our website at www.maryknollsociety.org.

Published by Orbis Books, Box 302, Maryknoll, NY 10545-0302.

Manufactured in the United States of America

Library of Congress Cataloging-in-Publication Data
Skreslet, Stanley H.
Comprehending mission : the questions, methods, themes, problems, and prospects of missiology / Stanley H. Skreslet.
p. cm. -- (American Society of Missiology series ; no. 49)
Includes index.
ISBN 978-1-57075-959-8 (pbk.)
EISBN 978-1-60833-118-5
Missions–Theory. I. Title.
BV2063.S56 2012
266.001--dc23 2011036387

Contents

Preface to the American Society of Missiology Series

The purpose of the ASM (American Society of Missiology) Series is to publish—without regard for disciplinary, national, or denominational boundaries—scholarly works of high quality and wide interest on missiological themes from the entire spectrum of scholarly pursuits relevant to Christian mission, which is always the focus of books in the Series.

By *mission* is meant the effort to effect passage over the boundary between faith in Jesus Christ and its absence. In this understanding of mission, the basic functions of Christian proclamation, dialogue, witness, service, worship, liberation, and nurture are of special concern. And in that context questions arise, including, How does the transition from one cultural context to another influence the shape and interaction between these dynamic functions, especially in regard to the cultural and religious plurality that constitute the global context of Christian life and mission?

The promotion of scholarly dialogue among missiologists, and among missiologists and scholars in other fields of inquiry, may involve the publication of views that some missiologists cannot accept, and with which members of the Editorial Committee themselves do not agree. Manuscripts published in the Series, accordingly, reflect the opinions of their authors and are not understood to represent the position of the American Society of Missiology or of the Editorial Committee. Selection is guided by such criteria as intrinsic worth, readability, coherence, and accessibility to a range of interested persons and not merely to experts or specialists.

The ASM Series, in collaboration with Orbis Books, seeks to publish scholarly works of high merit and wide interest on numerous aspects of missiology—the scholarly study of mission. Able presentations on new and creative approaches to the practice and understanding of mission will receive close attention.

The ASM Series Committee
JONATHAN J. BONK
ANGELYN DRIES, O.S.F.
SCOTT W. SUNQUIST

Acknowledgments

This project began indirectly with an unexpected invitation from editor Jonathan Bonk in 2001 to survey ten years of dissertation research in English on mission for the readers of the *International Bulletin of Missionary Research*. At the time, I had other thoughts in mind about the direction my future research should take, but the topic of missiology as a distinctive field of study proved to be irresistible. Nearly a decade later, the idea-seed planted so long ago has at last come to fruition. For the initial prompting that came my way via the Overseas Ministries Study Center and its much-appreciated journal, I am thankful.

No one could ask for better research support than that provided by the superb collection of the William Smith Morton Library at Union Presbyterian Seminary and the Morton Library's expert professional staff. Librarians Pam Wells, Lisa Janes, and Rachel Perky in particular have come to my aid countless times when I needed to locate and obtain books and articles not in our collection. Without their assistance, invariably offered with a word of encouragement, the finish line for this project would no doubt still lie somewhere over the horizon.

Gratefully, I have also received other forms of institutional and collegial support over the past few years that have most certainly helped to improve my work and to speed its progress. I am indebted especially to the trustees of Union Presbyterian Seminary for their willingness to grant me a sabbatical leave that extended through the 2009–10 academic year. Without the provision of this uniquely precious time for writing and specialized research, I would not have been able to finish this book. On two occasions, colleagues on the UPSem faculty read and graciously responded to draft chapters of the manuscript. Those discussions over lunch were rich moments of critique, challenge, and informed engagement with a number of the most important ideas to be presented in the pages that follow. I remain deeply grateful, too, for the consistent encouragement I have received from several past and current administrators at Union Presbyterian Seminary, including most particularly Louis B. Weeks, John T. Carroll, and Brian K. Blount.

Finally, I wish to acknowledge the many ways that Paula Skreslet has contributed to this volume: as an expert librarian, a keen-eyed copy editor, an experienced missionary, and a supportive spouse whose enthusiasm for this project never flagged. It is to her and our now-grown triplets—each of whom has been and continues to be an inspiration to us both—that this book is dedicated.

Abbreviations

1–2 Apol	Justin Martyr. *First and Second Apologies*
ABCFM	American Board of Commissioners for Foreign Missions
BZNW	Beihefte zur Zeitschrift für die neutestamentliche Wissenschaft
CARA	Center for Applied Research in the Apostolate, Georgetown University
CIM	China Inland Mission
Civ	Augustine. *Concerning the City of God against the Pagans* (*de civitate Dei*)
CMS	Church Mission(ary) Society
Diog	*Epistle to Diognetus*
EH	Bede. *Ecclesiastical History of the English People*
Ep	Pliny the Younger. *Letters*
ER	*Encyclopedia of Religion* (2nd ed. 2005)
HE	Eusebius. *The Ecclesiastical History*
IBMR	*International Bulletin of Missionary Research*
IIMO	Interuniversitair Instituut voor Missiologie en Oecumenica, Utrecht
IMC	International Missionary Council
IRM	*International Review of Mission(s)*
LMS	London Missionary Society
NS	New series
QD	Quaestiones disputatae
RPP	*Religion Past and Present*
SNTSMS	Society for New Testament Studies Monograph Series
SVM	Student Volunteer Movement for Foreign Missions
UMCA	Universities' Mission to Central Africa
WCC	World Council of Churches
WUNT	Wissenschaftliche Untersuchungen zum Neuen Testament

1

Who Studies Christian Mission, and Why?

The purpose of this book is to introduce the field of missiology. At first glance that might appear to be a dry task with little promise of relevance for today, especially for those Western Christians whose churches now largely disavow the missionary agendas of their nineteenth-century forebears. Indeed, just thirty-five or forty years ago, it was widely believed that academic missiology had seen its day. As Gerald Anderson (1996, 23) has observed on more than one occasion, the field was perceived to be in "serious decline" in the early 1970s. Theological faculties were losing interest in the subject. In some cases, professorships were simply left unfilled. At many more institutions, chairs of mission studies were reoriented and then connected to more politically correct areas of the curriculum, such as ecumenical theology, comparative religion, third world theology, intercultural theology, or world Christianity.

In part, a need for serious reevaluation had been prompted by the closing of the modern colonial era, which eventually removed from the scene a number of state actors that had lent varying degrees of support to churches and mission societies through the first half of the twentieth century. For some, this geopolitical development was taken to mean the beginning of the end of organized efforts to evangelize the world in the name of Jesus Christ. The explosive growth of secularism in the West at about the same time created an expectation on the part of some that most if not all forms of religion would likewise soon be marginalized. Further, a new awareness of the reality of cultural pluralism within a shrinking "global village" led to an emphasis on dialogue and other attempts to promote mutual understanding across the boundaries of religious difference. In this situation, the idea of mission could appear to be obsolete, if not an outright threat to world peace. And so, as the missionary impulse faded in many of the churches that had led the way in world mission from the late eighteenth century (especially among Protestants), the desire to study mission in those same quarters withered for a season.

We now know, of course, that Christian mission did not disappear. Over the last third of the twentieth century, the number of cross-cultural missionaries seems actually to have grown. Decisions to downsize some longstanding mission programs were more than offset by new or expanded efforts undertaken by other Western organizations (Coote 1995). A shift to shorter terms of service similarly tended to boost the aggregate number of participants in world mission. Over the same period, a growing number of churches outside the West began to respond with vigor to their own sense of call to intercultural forms of mission, pursued on an increasingly global scale (Jaffarian 2004). Many of these have been Pentecostal. Some of the largest are Korean, but no one nationality or regional identity dominates this latest surge of mission energy.

The astonishing and quite unexpected vitality that now marks Christian mission worldwide invites scholarly attention. The diversity of world Christianity brought into being over the past few centuries through modern missions ensures an inherently interesting journey for those drawn to study this phenomenon. It will no longer do to confine oneself to a Western point of view or to assume that the decisions of a few North Atlantic Protestant mission agencies and the magisterium of the Roman Catholic Church could define the universe of present and future possibility for Christian mission. At the beginning of the twenty-first century, it is impossible to ignore the fact that the reality of mission is exceedingly complex, with concealed social processes, political consequences, and complicated organizational dynamics, among many other factors, complementing matters of theology. An accurate description of the field of missiology as currently practiced will need to reflect the highly variegated nature of its subject matter.

MISSIOLOGY AND TRAINING COURSES

Before describing the approach to missiology to be taken here, it may prove helpful to the reader to have some idea about how others have approached this subject area. Introductions to missiology written since the 1960s have generally fallen into two categories, by no means mutually exclusive. One route to our subject has been curricular in nature. That is to say, a number of introductions to the field of missiology were developed in connection with particular courses of study or training programs.

Perhaps the most widely used introduction of this type is the *Perspectives* reader and study guide developed by the Institute of International Studies in cooperation with the U.S. Center for World Mission, both based in Pasadena, California. *Perspectives on the World Christian Movement*, now in its third edition, anchors an elaborate ongoing study program in which tens of thousands of students in a hundred or more locations have participated already, primarily in the United States. Senior editor Ralph Winter has affirmed that the *Perspectives* course is "essentially" an introduction to missiology (Winter 1996, 171), despite a statement in the reader itself that appears to say otherwise (Winter and Hawthorne 1981, xiv).

In terms of approach, Winter and Hawthorne have chosen to divide their collection of readings into four "perspectives" on mission: biblical, historical, cultural, and strategic. This last subject area, by far the largest of the four sections, is the capstone for the whole and provides a key to the ultimate purposes of the text. As Winter has indicated elsewhere (1996), the *Perspectives* course is aimed at lay volunteers and seeks to enlist them in the task of world evangelization, which is described above all as a matter of frontier evangelism among "unreached" people groups. A review of the materials selected for inclusion in the reader leaves one in no doubt that the editors have worked almost exclusively from within a conservative evangelical worldview, albeit on a global scale.

Another example of a basic course book is *Following Christ in Mission* (Karotemprel 1996). This set of essays is presented as a "foundational course" in missiology for Roman Catholic seminarians, religious sisters, institutes of consecrated life, missionary institutes, and Catholic laypersons already engaged in some form of mission work. An international team of editors and contributors headed by Indian academic Sebastian Karotemprel pooled their considerable expertise to create this "guidebook" for study, which has been endorsed officially by the Vatican's Congregation for the Evangelization of Peoples.

Like the *Perspectives* reader, *Following Christ in Mission* also comprises four main sections, but otherwise the two texts barely resemble each other. Karotemprel and his editorial team have emphasized theology over strategy. Two of the four primary headings used in the book are self-evidently theological in nature: "theological foundations" and "theology of religions." A third heading, "paths of mission," is less an examination of missionary methods from a practical standpoint than a serial treatment of theological issues arising in connection with particular ways of entering into mission (proclamation, dialogue, inculturation, liberation, and ecumenism). Missionary spirituality and the figure of Mary are also considered under the "paths of mission" rubric. Not unexpectedly, the other main section denominated "history" emphasizes Catholic experience in mission. *Following Christ in Mission* unabashedly calls attention to the documents of Vatican II (Winter and Hawthorne look instead to the Lausanne process for conciliar pronouncements), while exposing students to more recent debates over the interpretation of these seminal Roman Catholic texts.

One of the contributors to *Following Christ in Mission*, Paul Vadakumpadan, has since produced a textbook of his own: *Missionaries of Christ* (2006). Roman Catholic seminarians in India are the primary audience for whom this concise "basic course in missiology" has been developed, but the proposed syllabus also includes chapters that present Protestant and Orthodox perspectives on mission. Vadakumpadan indicates (5–6) that the structure of his book is based on *Evangelii Nuntiandi*, an apostolic exhortation issued by Pope Paul VI in 1975. Of the several theological topics highlighted in this resource, particular attention is paid to the theme of liberation as an integral aspect of "evangelization."

A final example to be considered in this section does not appear initially to be a course textbook at all. This is the two-volume "missiological encyclopedia" developed for use at Utrecht University in the Netherlands, which was published first in Dutch and then in English under the title *Philosophy, Science, and Theology of Mission in the Nineteenth and Twentieth Centuries*. Author Jan A. B. Jongeneel indicates that his intention was not to dwell on the subject of mission per se (its foundation, purposes, methods, or organization), but to focus on how this phenomenon has been studied over roughly the past two centuries (1995, 2). Along the way, he shows considerable interest in the contributions made by nontheologians to the study of Christian mission. In this handbook, Jongeneel presents a systematic description of scholarly research on the subject of mission, broadly conceived.

The title of Jongeneel's project makes plain his proposed structure for the field. Major sections are devoted to the philosophy of mission, the science of mission (in which empirical studies are highlighted), and the theology of mission. In the first two of these three primary divisions, Jongeneel is at pains to emphasize the academic character of missiology, which he seeks to establish by pointing out the intellectual distance these researchers ordinarily have maintained from their object of inquiry (on this underlying objective, see Jongeneel 1998). Theologians of mission, on the other hand, are expected to be committed to the cause of Christian outreach. By proceeding in this way, Jongeneel makes it possible to portray missiology as a subject fit to be studied in both secular and church-related contexts.

As more than one reviewer of Jongeneel's impressive resource has pointed out (for example, Roxborogh 1996), he has arranged his material in such a way that the presentation responds to a dilemma faced by many European professors of mission who must be able to offer their courses to secular university students, as well as ordination-seeking seminarians. Thus, even if not an actual course book, Jongeneel's "guide through the whole field of missiology" (1995, 13) shows sensitivity to and has perhaps been consciously shaped by a particular set of classroom needs. The same is probably true of the other three introductory textbooks already described, since they, too, were written with particular groups of students in mind. The marked dissimilarity of these widely respected course books on missiology does leave one wondering if the authors are in fact describing the same subject area. It may be that specific curricular objectives have exerted undue influence on one or more of these four introductory texts.

TO MISSIOLOGY VIA THEOLOGY OF MISSION

A second way to introduce missiology is to propose that it is a form of theological reflection. In this case, as Andrew Walls (2002b) has observed, missiology is taken to be a shorthand term for theology of mission, theology of the apostolate, or sometimes theory of mission. Nontheological aspects of mission need not be totally ignored in this approach, but they tend to be made subordinate to theological concerns or considered useful to discuss only to the extent that they illuminate, support, or challenge the adequacy of theological assertions about mission. This kind of introduction to missiology is not so much focused on the training of missionaries or the mobilizing of volunteers as it is on defining norms for Christian missionary activity, whether undertaken by individuals, churches, or other organizations. Theologians of mission not only seek to uncover fundamental principles that might recommend one or another form of Christian outreach, but they also raise questions about the motives that lie behind missionary action, the ultimate significance of other religious traditions, and the theological potential of culture. In order to formulate responses to these and other related questions, missionary theologians are further obliged to determine their positions on matters of revelation, ecclesiastical authority, and the meaning of salvation. In keeping with the universal scope claimed for theology in general, the implicit mandate of mission theology is virtually unlimited, which helps to explain why this mode of missiology continues to exercise broad appeal.

We have already looked at two introductions to missiology that pay close attention throughout to issues of theology: *Following Christ in Mission* and *Missionaries of Christ*. Roughly half of Jongeneel's missiological encyclopedia is likewise focused on theology of mission. If just a few other notable representatives of the genre may be cited, we will have before us a fuller picture of this well-traveled passageway to research on mission.

A good place to begin is with David J. Bosch's book *Transforming Mission*. Twenty years after its much-anticipated publication in 1991, this remarkably comprehensive and influential volume (already reprinted more than twenty-six times including an expanded 20th Anniversary Edition released in 2011,with a new foreword and concluding chapter; translated into fifteen languages, with approximately sixty-nine thousand copies in circulation worldwide [Saayman 2009, 219]) continues to be widely employed as a foundational text, for both beginning and advanced courses in missiology. Bosch (1929–92) devoted substantial portions of his magnum opus to an exposition of mission in the New Testament and to a review of mission history, but his primary emphasis was on theology, as shown by the subtitle chosen for the book: *Paradigm Shifts in Theology of Mission*. Bosch handles the New Testament material in such a way that the reader may be led to discern more than one biblical perspective on mission, a result made possible by the fact that the different gospel writers, the apostle Paul, and his several immediate successors had different challenges to face and a range of kerygmatic accents they wished to highlight. In a similar fashion, the history of mission is shown to be composed of a series of theologically driven understandings of mission, which Bosch characterized as missiological "paradigms," following Thomas Kuhn (1970) and Hans Küng (Küng and Tracy 1989).

Bosch's appreciation for differences in approach to Christian witness and his willingness to draw on an extensive array of historical and theological resources for reflection on mission keep his introduction to missiology far away from any hint of sectarian narrow-mindedness. Even so, Bosch does have preferences, and these begin to surface in earnest once he turns to sketch out what he calls "an emerging ecumenical missionary paradigm" (1991, 368–510). The key word in this formulation is "ecumenical," which Bosch takes to be the particular feature of the coming paradigm most likely to make it "relevant" to the next era of Christian history ("toward a *relevant* missiology" is the subtitle attached to the last third of the book). Also significant is Bosch's decision to ground his final paradigm in ecclesiology rather than another of the classical theological loci often connected to mission (for example, christology, soteriology, or eschatology), a move that may have been inspired by the church-centric methodology of Vatican II. The priority for Bosch is to understand the fundamental nature of the gathered community to whom God's own mission (the *missio Dei*) has been especially entrusted. As he puts it, everything else connected to this emerging postmodern paradigm will be "already present," when the church's role in mission is put under discussion (368).

A book published at about the same time as *Transforming Mission*, which shares to a large degree Bosch's theological predilections, is *Missiology: An Ecumenical Introduction* (1995; a somewhat different Dutch edition was published in 1988). General editor Frans J. Verstraelen and his colleagues also perceive missiology to be a theological discipline, most closely connected to systematic theology (1995, 6). More precisely, they construe missiology as an interlocutor for the rest of theology with respect to the world outside the church. In their view, missiology is responsible for "initiating" and "mediating" the engagement of theology with its new global context (467). What qualifies missiology for this role is its long experience with various kinds of pluralism, which several contributors demonstrate through a series of regional essays and analyses of some selected contextual theologies. For Verstraelen et al., ecumenicity implies a resolve to strengthen Christian unity. Their "ecumenical introduction" to missiology contributes to this objective by self-consciously balancing Catholic and conciliar Protestant viewpoints and authors throughout the book.

Ecumenical commitment is likewise evident in another collaborative effort produced especially for readers of German: *Leitfaden Ökumenische Missionstheologie* (Dahling-Sander 2003). In this case, the World Council of Churches sector of the ecumenical movement receives special consideration (the volume as a whole is dedicated to Konrad Raiser, on the occasion of his retirement from the WCC), but other perspectives are also represented in essays that summarize and reflect on Roman Catholic, Evangelical, Pentecostal, and Orthodox experience in mission. An unusual strength of this book is felt in the attention it gives to methodological issues in missiology, with the historiography of mission receiving substantial treatment. Other areas of emphasis track closely with the mission and ministry concerns of many European churches: migration, globalization, partnership, and dialogue. Contextual developments in mission theology are examined with respect to Asia, Africa, and Latin America.

Similarly hopeful about the promise of an ecumenical approach to the study of mission is Karl Müller, whose *Mission Theology: An Introduction* was published in 1987 (a translation of the original 1985 German edition). In this textbook, two chapters contributed by Protestant missiologist Hans-Werner Gensichen supplement a predominantly German Catholic perspective on mission theology. Throughout the book, conciliar Protestant voices and documents are considered alongside intra-Catholic exchanges over mission priorities. Müller and his colleagues are especially keen to identify the tasks to be assigned to missiology and to underline the cooperative relationships that should link missiology to the rest of the theological disciplines. In particular, Gensichen proposes for missiology a responsibility to promote within "conventional" Western theology the importance of interfaith dialogue, the formulation of contextual theologies, and Christian responsibility for development on a world scale (26–27). The chapters that follow Gensichen's programmatic essay on missiology as a theological discipline then go on to flesh out the implications of this disciplinary program by defining the biblical foundation, goals, and work of mission.

In his own way, Johannes Verkuyl also advocated an ecumenical understanding of mission through his well-known handbook *Contemporary Missiology: An Introduction* (1978; first published in Dutch in 1975). Verkuyl was firmly committed to a postcolonial vision of mission theology that recognized its new historical context (xiii; 309–40). He explored with sensitivity the role that might be played by dialogue in a Christian theology of religions (341–72). Active at a time when the hold of apartheid in South Africa appeared to many to be unbreakable, he was eager to articulate a public *missio politica oecumenica* that could imagine otherwise. These and other aspects of Verkuyl's point of view would seem to put him in the same camp later to be claimed by the Dutch cohort of Verstraelen, but the situation is not quite so cut and dried as that. Verkuyl's approach to mission theology also lays emphasis on ministries of individual conversion (196–204), raises hard questions about the false promises of Marxism and other ideologies (373–404), doggedly insists on the importance of evangelizing the Jews (118–62), and exhibits a good bit of skepticism with respect to the theological claims of Islam (on this, see Wessels 2002, 90–92). These latter positions in particular have won a hearing for Verkuyl among many evangelicals, with the result that his introduction has been read across a wide theological spectrum of scholars and students of missiology.

An important Catholic contribution to recent debates over the theological character of missiology has been offered by Francis Anekwe Oborji, a Nigerian diocesan priest and professor of missiology at the Pontifical Urban University in Rome. In *Concepts of Mission: The Evolution of Contemporary Missiology* (2006), we find another attempt to forge a theology of mission that is distinctively Catholic but also aware of broader developments in missiological thinking. Oborji treats his subject in three parts: "basic issues," where the development of missiology as a theological discipline is considered; "historical perspectives," which focuses on several classic modes of mission in a manner reminiscent of David Bosch (mission as conversion, church planting/church growth, adaptation/inculturation, dialogue, and *missio Dei*); plus, "new perspectives" on ecumenism and contextual theologies. Oborji shows interest in a wide range of Protestant opinion and research on mission, as he listens not only to conciliar Protestants but also to evangelical, Pentecostal, and Independent voices. Another distinguishing mark of Oborji's approach emerges out of his inclination to read Vatican II on mission through the postconciliar documents of John Paul II's pontificate (including *Dominus Iesus*). The result is a renewed commitment to Catholic particularity and critical support for many of the traditional methods of mission (especially proclamation), balanced by an obvious desire to participate in ecumenical dialogue and to foster a spirit of collaboration in mission.

A final example to be reviewed here is Alan R. Tippett, *Introduction to Missiology* (1987). Tippett's material (much of it published previously) is loosely gathered into four categories, characterized as "dimensions" of missiology (theological, anthropological, historical, and practical). The heart of the book, however, is to be found in the interaction of mission theology with anthropology. A casual reviewer might get the impression that anthropology has the upper hand in this parley of disciplines. After all, most of the historical and "practical" examples adduced here are related in some way to Tippett's large store of anthropological field experience, and many of the theological essays are presented with the kind of charts, boxes, and arrows commonly used to illustrate social science research. A deeper analysis, however, will find in this introduction to missiology a theological point of view that effectively determines what sort of anthropological insights might be admitted into the conversation. Wisdom from applied anthropology that could help missionaries better understand the processes of social and religious change is avidly embraced, especially if this research can throw light on the dynamics of church growth. Less welcome are studies that dare to raise questions about the legitimacy of the missionary enterprise. History is likewise treated as a select repository of data that must be carefully combed in order to illustrate how "certain basic themes" (220) of expansion and growth have recurred in Christian history since New Testament times. A specific contribution of this volume appears in the attention paid throughout to the task of missionary training, a practical concern that hardly appears in most of the other introductions to missiology already surveyed. An exception is the *Perspectives* course reader, whose lead editor, Ralph Winter, was Tippett's one-time colleague at Fuller Theological Seminary's School of World Mission (now School of Intercultural Studies).

A DYNAMIC AND EXPANSIVE FIELD OF STUDY

We have by no means exhausted the riches of mission theology here and a few more course books could certainly be mentioned. Even so, the works already described should be able to stand together as a fairly representative sample of the most widely used contemporary introductions to missiology. As we have seen, the theology of mission dominates as a conceptual framework through which to approach the study of mission, whether from a Catholic, conciliar Protestant, or evangelical Protestant point of view.

This way of going about our missiological business works well in several respects. For example, the theology of mission is unsurpassed as a way to demonstrate commitment to particular motives, methods, and/or proximate goals of mission. The theology of mission has also become an increasingly effective means to connect critical reflection on the church and its vocation with many different kinds of mission experience, which opens up the possibility that more of theology could be infused with missiological insight and energy (on this as a goal for theology of mission, see Guder 2003). In addition, over the past several decades theology of mission has demonstrated a remarkable capacity to become dialogical in ways that can contribute to the strengthening of ecumenical and interfaith relations. This latter aspect of mission theology may well be what most profoundly recommends it to Christians now living in tense situations of religious conflict.

While not disputing any of these gains, I am not convinced that theology of mission is the best avenue by which to approach the field of missiology as a whole. My chief concern is not that a commitment to mission makes it impossible for mission theologians to be objective. In the postmodern intellectual context in which we find ourselves, authors are expected to have commitments and so it has become much harder to make the claim that scientific objectivity is necessarily impeded by religious faith (an effective rebuttal to this claim is offered in Newbigin 1989, 1–65). Without a doubt, one can find in the books reviewed above many examples of competent researchers listening carefully to viewpoints not their own. Ironically, perhaps, this habit seems to be nurtured and reinforced when mission theologians *commit* to an ecumenical posture.

The problem with using theology of mission as the primary frame of reference through which to conceptualize and introduce the field of missiology lies rather in the way this angle of approach tends to obscure the broad scope of contemporary research on mission. We see, for example, that when theological categories are applied to mission activity, certain kinds of data are likely to be privileged, while other information is overlooked or simply not sought. For modern theologians operating in the West, scripture, tradition, and Christian experience are the sine qua non of their craft. To do theology means to apply reason to what flows through these indispensable taproots of Christian faith, using techniques of analysis suggested by the discipline of philosophy. Issues of culture and the existence of other religious traditions may enter into these discussions, but they typically do so in the guise of environmental factors with which the modern theologian is obliged to deal, on a par we might say with urbanization or class conflict.

Thus, mission theologians are often eager to debate colonialism as an intellectual problem but show less interest in the conduct of particular colonial regimes. Or issues of language and discourse may surface with attendant questions raised about the act of translation, but the task of communicating actual messages across known cultural and linguistic boundaries is left relatively unexplored. Or the facts of religious pluralism are posed in order to challenge notions of Christian chauvinism, but the give and take of daily dialogue in living communities and the difficulties involved when attempts are made to share faith on a personal scale may not receive the same level of attention as more theoretical issues.

My point is that mission theologians are prone to share with their close colleagues, the systematic theologians, a preference for the abstract over the particular. In their quest for general principles, the material aspects of mission experience may be neglected. This way of looking at missiology may also predispose one to relate first and foremost to the work of other theologians, to those scholars who are likewise attempting to define norms for Christian attitudes and practice, instead of historians, anthropologists, sociologists, and other nontheological experts who also focus their scholarly attention on the subject of mission. And quite naturally, when theological interests are paramount, the study of mission can easily become just another front for entrenched theological opponents to wage yet one more round in their ongoing ideological battles (see, for example, the modernist and fundamentalist debates over mission in the 1920s and 1930s).

Leading journals in the field of missiology routinely publish or give recognition to nontheological research on mission. The book review sections of such noted periodicals as the *International Bulletin of Missionary Research*, *Missiology*, *Missionalia*, *International Review of Mission,* and *Mission Studies*, just to name a few of the major English-language journals in the field, regularly include descriptions of books and articles produced by social scientists, area specialists, religious studies scholars, and a wide variety of historians. The obvious implication of this fact is that these experts are themselves functioning as missiologists or at least are conducting research that reputed scholars in the field consider directly relevant to their own work.

Current patterns in dissertation research, reported in many of these same journals, point in the same direction. A significant portion, if not a majority, of younger scholars working in the field today, are approaching the study of mission primarily from nontheological perspectives, if the findings of my own research on English-language dissertations in missiology between 1992 and 2001 still hold true and give an accurate indication of global trends more generally (Skreslet 2003). These younger scholars, together with their advisors, appear to be pushing the boundaries of missiology ever wider.

Finally, when the most important bibliographic projects in the field are taken into consideration, the expansive scope of missiology becomes impossible to miss. A bellwether in this regard is the classified bibliographic structure that regularly appears in the *International Review of Mission*. Since 1912 this feature of the journal has functioned as a major conduit of information about published research in the field. Thousands of articles, books, and conference reports, among other materials, have been brought to the attention of the journal's readers by means of this bibliographic tool. At the same time, the classification system used by the editors can tell us something about their understanding of missiology and how they think mission ought to be studied. Unmistakably, as this conceptual structure for the field has been modified over the years, the profile of nontheological research on mission has grown, so much so that theology of mission as a formal category now represents a very small part of the overall scheme (Skreslet 2006a, 173–87). A similar result is obtained when major alternative bibliographic frameworks for missiology are examined. The *International Mission Bibliography* may be taken as a prime example (Thomas 2003; see also Skreslet 2006a, 187–89). In this project, conducted over eighteen years under the auspices of the American Society of Missiology and in consultation with the International Association for Mission Studies, the interdisciplinary character of missiology is clearly illustrated. Fewer than half of the twenty subject areas that make up this bibliographic structure are theologically oriented. The social sciences and cultural studies receive special attention.

MISSIOLOGY REDEFINED

Thus far, my intention has been to describe the typical means scholars have used over the past few decades to describe the field of missiology. As we have seen, theological approaches predominate, regardless of denominational background or doctrinal bent. Having provided a selective review of the introductory literature, I then put forward a very brief account of current trends in mission research, based on a general impression of what is now being published in many of the field's leading journals, buttressed by more detailed analyses conducted on a fairly large sample of recent dissertation research and several officially sanctioned bibliographic projects. Without question, secular research focused on Christian mission has grown in recent years to such an extent that it now constitutes a significant portion of the scholarly activity taking place in this subject area. It would appear that the current crop of introductions on offer (with one important exception) has not kept pace with the emerging character of missiology as actually practiced in the postcolonial era. What we have today, by and large, are many introductions to mission theology but very few treatments of missiology as a whole.

Jongeneel's "missiological encyclopedia" is the one introduction to missiology that has acknowledged structurally the contributions of secular research to the field. He does this by giving formal recognition to philosophy of mission and science of mission as co-equal branches of missiology next to theology of mission, as pointed out earlier. Jongeneel's reconceptualization of the field represents, in my view, a proposal that must be taken seriously. I am not persuaded, however, that his solution is entirely satisfactory, because his framework for the field differentiates theological from nontheological research on mission in a way that may be artificial or confusing. In fact, Jongeneel has difficulty finding much research at all to fit under the heading of philosophy of mission and most of what he cites is quite dated. Much more can be said about the science of mission, especially since history and the social sciences fall into this category, but it is certainly significant that theology of mission remains by a considerable margin the largest segment of the three (more than twice as many pages are devoted to this branch of missiology than to the other two combined). Thus, the tripartite structure Jongeneel presents to describe missiology is far less balanced in the end than his theoretical approach would at first seem to suggest.

Additional questions arise when we scrutinize the subcategories of Jongeneel's schematic framework. Does it make sense, for example, to separate "axiology of mission" (studies on the value of mission conducted from within the philosophy of mission sphere) from "missionary ethics" or "missionary diaconics/service" (subbranches listed under theology of mission)? What is the result when the "science of translation" and related treatments of missionary discourse are handled apart from "missionary apologetics"? Such fine distinctions as these threaten to obscure the integrative character of missiology, which may be one of its most distinctive marks as a discipline (on this, see below and Skreslet forthcoming).

This introduction will proceed on the assumption that missiology includes but is not limited to mission theology. In doing so, I will be heading in a direction similar to that mapped out by Jongeneel, but I do not propose to sequester mission theology from the rest of missiological research as he has done. My working definition for the field is based on a second description of missiology supplied by Andrew Walls (2002b): "the systematic study of all aspects of mission." Accordingly, missiology is understood here to be an intersection point among the many disciplines that take an interest in mission-related phenomena. Some of these disciplines are more often than not reckoned among the theological sciences, but others would not normally find their way into the standard seminary curriculum. Put in another way, missiology has two distinctive "publics" to which it now relates directly, as Mika Vähäkangas (2010) has observed: those who do mission and university academics.

There is a cost that comes with this decision. Allowing for the possibility of more than one methodology makes it difficult to establish missiology as an independent discipline in its own right. If missiology means simply to apply the methods of other academic specialties to a common subject matter, then it may not be a discipline at all in the usual sense but merely an area of inquiry where different scholarly interests happen to overlap. For this reason, as Walls (2002b) has noted, some scholars prefer to use the more general term "mission studies" in place of missiology. To be sure, when its hybrid character is emphasized, missiology would appear to resemble strongly a number of other composite academic fields, such as medieval studies, Renaissance studies, or Middle Eastern studies, more than it does any of the classical disciplines, including theology.

A case for the distinctiveness of missiology as a scholarly field must be constructed on grounds other than the possession of a singular, trademark methodology. One way to do this is by recognizing some of the factors that consistently mark the work of scholars who are recognized as or call themselves missiologists. This approach suggests that missiology is an enterprise carried on by a discernable "community of practice." As Wenger (1998, 152–53) explains with primary reference to nonmissiological endeavors, communities of practice take shape to the extent that their members acknowledge a common identity, engage mutually with a degree of accountability to each other in a joint project, and draw from a shared repertoire of social practices. The practices I have in mind are the particular scholarly habits that together seem to distinguish missiological study from other kinds of academic activity.

The first of these constants is the specific interest of missiologists in the *processes of religious change*. Whether or not personally involved in efforts to share the Christian faith with others, missiologists recognize that religious boundaries are shifting and porous, not static or impermeable. They know that conversion into and out of Christianity has been a persistent element of the church's story from the beginning. Their shared goal is to understand better what these demographic changes might mean, how factors of culture have shaped patterns of religious affiliation, and the various means by which Christians have sought to engage people outside the church with the claims of the gospel. Missiologists have also shown an abiding interest in the reverse effect mission experience has had on missionaries and their sponsors. In other words, missiologists also want to know about how contact with cultures, social traditions, and religious convictions previously outside of the church's experience has led to the transformation of sending communities and their emissaries alike. The idea of religious change I am describing here is similar to the theme of "crossing boundaries" that some missiologists have chosen to highlight recently as a distinctive feature of the field (see, for example, Ustorf 2001, 75–76, and Phan 2003).

Another enduring characteristic of missiology is the respect generally given by its practitioners to *the reality of faith*. Respecting faith in this case means more than conceding a measure of sincerity to those who hold religious beliefs. It also implies an unwillingness to begin one's study of mission with the premise that religious convictions can never be anything except a matter of illusion or deception. This is not to say that missionaries have never been deluded, misguided, or wrong-headed, either in their self-understanding or practice of mission. The point is rather that this discipline consistently demands from its scholars a substantial degree of critical empathy with their object of inquiry. They are asked to be critical, which means subjecting every aspect of mission (including theologies of mission) to rigorous analysis. At the same time, it is assumed within this community of practice that the sharing of Christian faith with others can be an honorable undertaking, whatever flaws and misconceptions might be discovered in the course of one's investigations. By extension, students of mission must also be willing to take non-Christian faith seriously. Only so could one hope to understand the enormous implications involved in religious conversion. If faith did not really matter, neither would the possibility of conversion or movements of religious change mean much, except as generators of sociological data.

A thoroughgoing *integrative impulse* further defines the practice of missiology today. Obviously, a need for integration is to be expected when the study of mission is conducted with multiple methodologies potentially in play. If nothing else, missiologists must be prepared to evaluate the results of theological and nontheological approaches to the study of mission and to bring them into conversation with each other. The many possible bases, methods, and purposes commonly associated with mission likewise beg for comparative analysis. The complex nature of mission as an intercultural activity pushes in the same direction. Christian mission is a social phenomenon that encompasses an unlimited number of local contexts, each of which may be affected by global trends. Every layer of culture—from the material to the conceptual—may be engaged when faith is shared across national, ethnic, and linguistic boundaries. Additionally, in the study of mission not only does theology meet culture but one also finds the religious systems embedded in the world's many cultures coming into direct contact with each other in a variety of ways, ranging from sharp confrontation to cooperative service. Indeed, next to the interplay of theory and practice one would expect to find subtly expressed in all forms of mission, the deep levels of cultural complexity that attend nearly every attempt at Christian outreach make the integrative task an indispensable aspect of this still emerging field of study.

My characterization of missiology as an integrative, multidisciplinary academic field resembles in some respects the position taken by Louis J. Luzbetak, a leading scholar of missionary (or missiological) anthropology. Following Tippett (1974), Luzbetak (1988, 14) emphasizes that missiology is not "a *mere conglomeration* of disciplines but a network of disciplines that systematically interact with one another" (emphasis in original). This indicates to Luzbetak that missiology is a field rather than a discipline, where all the dimensions of mission demand to be examined carefully.

I find myself only partially agreeing with Luzbetak, however, regarding the relationship of theological and nontheological scholarship on Christian mission within this sprawling collection of studies. Luzbetak's position on this point is nuanced but clearly expressed: secular research on mission is "essential" but only "supplementary" to theological reflection on the nature of mission and its normative character. "What counts in missiology above everything else," Luzbetak insists (1988, 14), "is what *God* regards as genuine salvation activities and what *God* means by 'the Kingdom of God'" (emphasis in original). For this reason, Luzbetak concludes that missiology is "basically" a theological field, in which theology "holds the place of honor" among all the disciplines involved.

To be sure, the setting of standards for Christian mission in a *pedagogical, prescriptive* sense is the business of theologians, not secular scholarship. So are questions about the appropriateness of specific mission practices and the assessment of missionary fidelity to the teaching of scripture and church tradition. But the *study* of such norms, including the processes by which they have been or are now being determined, is a topic of interest to a broad variety of researchers. Missiology, I believe, properly encompasses every kind of scholarly inquiry performed on the subject of mission without necessarily subordinating any group of studies to any other. Perhaps the closest analogy to missiology to be found is the field of ethics, which includes but is not restricted to the study of theological ethics (issues of theory and practice also arise in similar ways in these two fields). Education as an academic field might constitute another parallel worth considering, so long as that large-scale scholarly enterprise is understood to encompass the particular concerns, source materials, and methods of Christian *e*ducation and theological education.

OBJECTIVES AND APPROACH OF THIS BOOK

The supply of data at our disposal for the study of mission is huge. This is to be expected, given the encompassing definition of the field with which I am committed to work ("the systematic study of all aspects of mission"). Consideration of more than one disciplinary methodology likewise threatens to extend our collection of potentially relevant information far beyond the bounds that an introductory text could reasonably be expected to handle.

To these considerations of method should be added the fact that Christian mission as a subject has become a much more complex undertaking than at any time previously, with an expanding number of actors and types of organizations involved for many different purposes. The flow of mission no longer moves exclusively or even predominantly from North to South or from West to East, which means that it cannot be conceptualized as a North Atlantic project. A few large-scale organizations do not monopolize the conduct of this activity, as they seemed to do in centuries past. Mission now is truly "from everywhere to everywhere." It involves many laypersons and a relatively few full-time professionals, who share faith and give witness in their own neighborhoods and around the world. The profound complexity of mission today also derives in part from the deep diversity that now marks a global Christian community.

To help solve the problem of scope necessarily implied in my task, I intend to use the five analytical criteria indicated in my subtitle as a means to sift and prioritize what can be known about the study of Christian mission. The first of these criteria I have designated *questions*. That is to say, what sort of things do missiologists want to know about the phenomenon of mission? Are their questions much different from those posed by other researchers? To answer their own inquiries, missiologists then employ a selection of appropriate scholarly *methods*. As indicated already, the interdisciplinary character of missiology is partly reflected in the fact that many of its most important research techniques were first developed for use in other disciplines. Even so, it may be helpful to describe how such methods are typically applied within the realm of mission studies. *Themes* denotes the major results produced so far by these investigations. What are the primary findings that now define missiological knowledge? Do certain trends stand out in current research? *Problems*, on the other hand, are unresolved issues in the study of mission, meaning areas of research still waiting for more adequate treatment. Ongoing arguments over the interpretation of critical data pertaining to the study of mission would also fit under this rubric. *Prospects* then looks ahead to the future of mission studies. If there are inklings of new directions to be taken in research, these will be explored. On more than one occasion, I will indicate topics or questions that have not yet received much attention at all, which nevertheless seem to me to hold promise as subjects worth pursuing.

Readers may recall from the survey of introductions presented above that these works used various terms to indicate the primary divisions of missiology. Winter and Tippett, for example, proposed that the field of missiology could be approached by means of multiple "perspectives" or "dimensions" of mission. Oborji and Jongeneel preferred to describe missiology in terms of a few primary "concepts," although they may not have used this word in exactly the same way. Bosch, for his part, wrote about a series of "elements" that constituted the ecumenical mission "paradigm" he saw emerging toward the end of the twentieth century. The lack of a common vocabulary to use when talking about the structure of missiology points to a larger problem of conceptualization. It is simply not possible at this time to claim that any particular configuration of the field reflects a scholarly consensus among all or even most missiologists. This fact prompts me to say something now about the layout of the chapters to come.

I have chosen to divide the body of my presentation into six chapters. Each of these sections represents a grouping of research around a common theme. To a certain extent, this arrangement of material is the result of a practical decision. One cannot talk about everything at the same time and expect to achieve any measure of coherence. More substantively, the chapter headings used below indicate, in my view, the major topic areas to have arisen within missiology since it began to take shape as a formal academic pursuit in the nineteenth century. In other words, when modern-era scholars past and present have engaged in missiological analysis, they have tended to congregate around the following set of major themes or subjects: Bible and mission, history of mission, theology and culture, interreligious encounter, means of mission, and missionary vocation. An advantage of this approach to the study of mission is that it provides a structure within which theological and nontheological research can be considered next to each other. I have chosen not to have a separate chapter on women and mission, in order to avoid giving the impression that this topic can be isolated from the other six chapter headings I propose to use here. Alert readers will find that feminist perspectives and gender issues have affected the study of mission in nearly every part of this evolving field.

Ultimately, decisions on methods depend on the objectives one hopes to achieve. For this book, three aims have remained paramount. The first is a desire to describe an academic field of study. Accordingly, I have not set out to explain what mission is or ought to be. Indeed, in the research to be discussed there are many different definitions of mission employed. My intent is rather that readers will discover here a competent description of missiology as a form of scholarly inquiry. I want them to know what is distinctive about this field and how it might overlap with other disciplines and scholarly projects. In the course of this discussion, the literature of missiology will be introduced, with substantial attention given to widely acknowledged classics alongside a selection of books and essays that illustrate more recent trends in mission scholarship. With regard to late modern scholarship on mission, special emphasis will be given to materials that have appeared since Bosch and Jongeneel in the 1990s published their comprehensive treatments of the field. In fact, more than half of the works to be cited in this book will date from 1995 or later. While I do hope to represent missiology as fairly as I can by means of this sample of material, it is not my intention to be comprehensive in every possible area of research (an aim that would compromise readability). Thus, many other fine resources that could have been cited will not be referenced here. Throughout, English-language materials will predominate, in large part because this is the primary linguistic medium through which a truly global community of scholars is best able to interact with each other. A successful presentation of this literature, it seems to me, has to reflect not only the international character of missiology but also something of our guild's theological diversity. For this reason, I do not intend to privilege material produced primarily within or for one part of the church. Others, of course, will have to judge whether or not this aspiration has been achieved.

A second objective of this book is to show how the field of missiology has developed over time. I have chosen not to lay out a history for the entire field in a single chapter, preferring instead to explore how thinking and methods of analysis have changed in relationship to particular subtopics. At the same time, one has to keep in mind the fact that the study of mission as a whole entered a completely new phase in the nineteenth century, as Gustav Warneck and other pioneering university researchers put the study of mission on a more scholarly basis. In the premodern era, missionaries and others studied mission, too, but they usually did so with ad hoc approaches and implicit methodologies. By the late nineteenth century, these investigations tended to be more scientific and explicit with respect to scholarly procedures. Precritical reflections on the processes of mission and modern studies will both receive their due in the pages that follow.

A third object in mind for this venture is to communicate enthusiasm for missiology as a field of study. I am convinced that many more students and scholars will find the intellectual challenge of missiology attractive, once they come to know better its various dimensions. The remarks made above about the integrative character of missiology are particularly relevant to this purpose behind my project. The dynamic of specialization that threatens to overwhelm and atomize so many academic disciplines today is partly offset in missiology by an equally strong impulse to make connections among the different aspects of the field and to allow knowledge about mission gained in one sphere to inform the work of others. At one point, I had in mind an alternative subtitle for this study of missiology, which characterized it as "an interpretation and invitation." The interpretive element so indicated no doubt remains. I still have hopes, too, that many readers will find here a compelling invitation to learn more about this fascinating and complex subject.

STYLE POINTS

Most of this chapter has been concerned with matters of content, which meant asking about the limits of the topic to be covered, the points to be emphasized, and how one intends to structure the overall argument. A select review of current literature on missiology as a field of study was also provided in order for the reader to have a sense of the most important scholarly context within which the present work should be evaluated. Still to be considered very briefly is the issue of writing style or the manner of expression that ought to be used. To formulate a response to this question, another one has to be raised with respect to audience: for whom is this book written?

Some readers will have noticed already that this chapter has no footnotes. Nor will those to come. This is not an ideological choice but primarily an aesthetic preference. For some readers, footnotes can be a major distraction, however useful they might be to authors as a way to shore up support for one's position or to add explanatory side comments to an argument (or, it must be admitted, sometimes to squeeze in extraneous material that a researcher just cannot bear to leave behind in the file). Since my hope is to lay out a relatively uncluttered, coherent description of the field of missiology and to aim this discussion, first of all, at readers just becoming acquainted with the discipline, technical footnotes seemed inappropriate. But readers at every level of expertise and background have a right to know the basis of one's assertions and conclusions, especially when these rest substantially on the work of others, and so a spare system of citation has been incorporated directly into the text.

Next to beginners, I have also written with some fellow academics in mind, in particular those specializing in fields other than missiology, who nevertheless share an interest in this subject matter. The prediction of Andrew Walls (1991, 154) that an explosion of demand for mission studies was about to take place has largely come true, with new journals and chairs devoted to missiological research having since been founded, a surge of interest in missionaries and their work expressed among nontheologians in particular (on this, see Sanneh 1995 and Noll 1998), new regional scholarly initiatives focused on the study of mission (for example, the Central and Eastern European Association for Mission Studies), plus a growing cadre of young scholars in evidence around the world (Skreslet 2003). Yet there still seems to be widespread confusion about what exactly missiology entails as an academic enterprise. Thus, a third audience for whom this book is intended is comprised of my fellow missiologists, who might be expected to want as much clarity as possible when it comes to defining the objectives, methods, and scope of our common profession. Many of these colleagues will immediately recognize that a new proposal for envisioning our field has been put on the table. I look forward to whatever discussion about the future of our labors together might be prompted by the appearance of this book.

2

Bible and Mission

If it is true that missiology includes but need not be limited to the theology of mission, as argued in the previous chapter, then it becomes possible to identify more than one way to relate the study of mission to the Bible. Three fundamentally different connections will be examined here. The first considers the historical record of faith-sharing that may be discerned in the canonical scriptures of the Christian community. A second kind of relationship emerges when these same writings are scrutinized theologically, in order to identify biblical norms for Christian mission. A third way to connect the Bible and mission is to consider carefully the career of this seminal text in mission, including its function as a particular means of Christian outreach.

MISSION IN THE BIBLE

To look for evidence of missionary activity in the Bible is to take up a part of the historical task implied by exegesis. Even if one hopes ultimately to apply ancient insights and scriptural principles to contemporary circumstances, it is necessary first to consider what the sacred texts may have meant in their own day. A preparatory step in the exegetical process is to understand the historical situation of the writings in question. Who was the author and what can be known about the text's presumed audience? Are there extrabiblical personalities, ideas, and events to which this part of scripture makes reference, either directly or indirectly? Does the form of the text tell us anything about how the people of that time and place communicated with each other or otherwise constructed their social relationships? Questions like these probe into the background of a given text, in an attempt to lay bare contextual details that may not be readily apparent to twenty-first-century readers. They might also lead one to uncover historical data embedded in the biblical texts that could be evaluated quite apart from hermeneutical considerations or apologetic concerns. When this happens, the Bible becomes an indispensable source of information needed to describe and analyze the earliest stage of Christian mission history.

We should not expect all the books of the Bible to contribute equally to our understanding of mission history. Many missiologists who study the biblical record are naturally drawn first to the Acts of the Apostles, since that book most obviously focuses on the initial efforts of Jesus' followers to share his message and story with new groups of hearers after the crucifixion. The letters of Paul, because they come from the pen of the most famous evangelist who ever lived, likewise attract their fair share of attention from mission historians but have to be reconciled with the portrait of the apostle offered in Acts. Compared to these two all-important sources of biblical data pertaining to the mission activities of the early church, the other nongospel writings in the New Testament are only marginally relevant to the historian of mission.

The Gospels themselves are important for two reasons. To the extent that the early Christians consciously emulated the missionary example of Jesus, the Gospels can add depth to our knowledge about that shared methodology. Further, as documents finally produced not in Jesus' time but at least a generation later, the Gospels may be expected to reflect something of the church's circumstances as these developed in the subapostolic era. Serious exegetes will use all of the historical-critical tools at their disposal to differentiate the life situation of Jesus depicted in the Gospels from that of the various communities for whom these narratives were initially produced.

By definition, the Old Testament will not bear witness to the history of *Christian* mission, although it often figures prominently in more theological investigations. In contrast, some of the noncanonical Jewish literature of the late intertestamental period (for example, Josephus and Philo) has proved to be quite valuable to scholars of apostolic-era missions. These writings afford another, rare window through which to look at a remote historical milieu, while also documenting an alternative set of outreach patterns with which early Christian missionary practices may be compared.

Unfortunately, references to first-century Christians in the secular Roman literature of the same period are relatively few and tend to be indistinct. As a result, such sources are not able to tell us much about how the earliest generations of Christians went about sharing their postresurrection faith in Jesus, but they can shed light more generally on the status of the Jews in the Roman Empire. Insofar as Christianity began as a minor sectarian group within Judaism, some of that background information is bound to prove useful to anyone attempting to reconstruct the first chapter of Christian mission history. Finally, to what has been mentioned so far by way of historical source documents may be added a number of noncanonical books that circulated widely within the sphere of the early Christian movement. Where these overlap chronologically with some of the New Testament literature, as seems to be the case with the Didache, for example, or the first letter of Clement and perhaps a few of the apocryphal second-century Acts and Gospels, they provide the historian with yet one more set of resources from which to extract potentially relevant information about the earliest phase of Christian mission.

For much of the past century, Adolf Harnack's *Expansion of Christianity* (1904–5) was widely regarded as the classic scholarly synthesis of early mission history. Harnack sought to apply a rigorous scientific method to all of the source materials outlined above. In a profound way, he showed how a deep understanding of first-century diaspora Judaism could illuminate and provide a crucial context for the literary data presented in the New Testament. After Harnack, no serious scholar of early mission history could be unconcerned about how factors in the environment (for example, transportation and communication patterns within the Mediterranean world), the development of nascent church structures like the episcopate, or Roman attitudes toward the many different religious traditions contained within the empire may have aided or otherwise shaped the spread of Christianity in New Testament times.

Harnack believed the eventual success of Christianity was due, above all, to its transition from a narrow national religious tradition on the model of Judaism to a universal worldview more like the intellectual culture of Hellenism. Even if some scholars now question the extremely sharp contrast drawn in Harnack's work between Jesus and Paul, his assumption that Christian mission was a continuation of vigorous Jewish efforts to proselytize Gentiles in the intertestamental period, or the robust confidence he maintained in the natural affinity of "true" Christianity with the assimilative spirit of Hellenism, Harnack's fundamental insight on the cultural dimensions of mission history cannot be ignored. No contemporary analysis of early Christianity and the manner of its propagation in the first century would be complete without proper attention being paid to all the material and social forces at work in its broader environment. A simple harmonization of the New Testament's stories of gospel proclamation and apostolic itineration will no longer suffice for the missiologist seeking to understand early mission history.

A second comprehensive study with which all students of mission in the New Testament will want to become familiar is Eckhard Schnabel, *Early Christian Mission* (2004). In this formidable two-volume work, Schnabel revisits the documentary, epigraphic, and geographical ground covered so carefully by Harnack. Even more remarkably, Schnabel also attempts to engage a whole century's worth of subsequent scholarly activity on his subject, including a huge collection of secondary literature related to mission in the Bible, and he largely succeeds. Schnabel's focus is almost entirely on the first century. He is not, therefore, so concerned as Harnack to connect the New Testament's account of early Christian mission with its subsequent course of development up to the time of Constantine. For Harnack, this longer story was the point of his work. In his view, only by the middle of the third century had Christianity fully come to terms with its Mediterranean environment. Paul had initiated a turn to Greek culture that the generation of Origen brought to a satisfying conclusion (Harnack 1904, 391–97). It was this form of Christianity that soon thereafter became established throughout the Roman Empire and Harnack's study attempts to explain how this surprising outcome came to pass.

A leading concern for Schnabel is to establish the historical value of the New Testament data pertaining to mission. He is especially keen to defend the author of Acts as a trustworthy historian (20–35) and to make a case for Jesus as the ultimate source of the Great Commission in Matthew 28:18–20 and parallels (348–82). In Schnabel's analysis, Jesus of Nazareth does not stand in opposition to or apart from the ensuing history of Christian mission. Instead, Jesus is portrayed as the initiator of a universal missionary movement that encompassed both Jews and Gentiles from the start. According to Schnabel, the broad extent of Jesus' missionary vision is demonstrated initially by his readiness to interact with a number of individual non-Jews as they approached seeking his help and then through those disciples whom he dispatched to the ends of the earth after the resurrection. Along the way, he surveys an extensive list of specific locations where the Jewish-Christian and then Gentile disciples of Jesus were evidently active in the first century, from Jerusalem and Antioch to Rome and Spain and even India. In this way, Schnabel reinforces and illustrates his conclusion that "the universal and international mission of the followers of Jesus . . . was initiated, inaugurated and established by Jesus of Nazareth" (386).

Already in this brief discussion of sources and surveys of mission in the Bible, several leading research questions have been identified. The most fundamental of these concerns the nature of the New Testament and the value of its various writings for historical investigations. As noted above, Schnabel exemplifies a scholarly approach that seeks to establish the New Testament as a dependable source of reliable data with which the story of early Christian mission can be reconstructed with some confidence. Other researchers, following in the modern tradition of critical New Testament scholarship defined by innovators such as Hermann Reimarus (eighteenth century), Ferdinand Christian Baur (nineteenth century), and Rudolf Bultmann (twentieth century), more often tend to cast doubt on the narrative claims of the New Testament documents. At the center of these debates is the book of Acts, a self-conscious work of history writing (cf. Acts 1:1–2) that is nevertheless also infused throughout with the author's theological point of view. A generation ago, Martin Hengel (1980) offered a deliberately provocative defense of Luke as a responsible historian and in doing so nicely framed a number of the most essential historiographical issues at stake in this discussion. More recent treatments by Fitzmyer (1998, 124–28) and Dunn (2009, 68–98) bring us nearly up to the present with respect to New Testament scholarship on the historicity of Acts.

A second group of scriptural studies likely to be of high interest to many missiologists studying mission in the Bible clusters around the topic of Jewish mission in the New Testament period. There can be no doubt that the early Christians avidly sought converts from among Jews and Gentiles alike. To what extent were they merely imitating the already established missionary practices of Hellenistic Judaism?

Following Harnack, it was largely assumed that the early church had learned how to do mission from the Jews, whose tradition seems to have been passing through an expansionist phase in the Greco-Roman period. How else to explain the presence of proselytes and "god-fearing" Gentiles in Jewish assemblies (for example, Cornelius in Acts 10), first-century rites of conversion for Gentiles seeking to join the Jewish fold, the demographic growth of diaspora Judaism in the Second Temple era, and evidence from Josephus (especially *Antiquities* 20:34–48) that seems to point to an eagerness on the part of Jews to commend their faith to others? Harnack's view has been vigorously challenged by Martin Goodman (1994), who argues that while first-century Jews most certainly sought respect for their faith from Gentiles and might have occasionally used some missionary means to gain political or social advantages for their community, the case for a widely embraced Jewish proselytizing mission is too weak to bear much scrutiny. Barriers to admission remained high throughout the Hellenistic and Roman periods. Jewish attitudes toward converts were ambiguous at best. Goodman also highlights the fact that not a single explicit call to first-century Jews to take up missionary activity has yet been discovered in the literature. Thus, despite the assertion of Jesus at Matthew 23:15 that zealous scribes and Pharisees would spare no effort to win converts ("crossing land and sea to make one proselyte"), Goodman insists that the Christian turn to a universal mission embracing all of humanity was, in fact, "a shocking novelty in the ancient world" (105). Subsequently, John Dickson (2003) has argued for the recognition of a strong Jewish "mission commitment" in New Testament times, largely based on a more expansive definition of missionary behavior than that employed by Goodman, Scot McKnight (1991), and others who continue to see little, if any, indisputable evidence of a mission impulse in ancient Judaism.

Arguments over whether proactive Jewish missions existed in the New Testament era are related to a larger conceptual problem that hovers over much of the shared research space claimed by New Testament scholars and missiologists. Simply put, what kinds of activity encountered in the New Testament should be reckoned as mission? Analyses that focus primarily on the verbal proclamation of a distinctive message by the apostles and their closest co-workers tend to highlight theological issues. In the next section of this chapter, such approaches will take center stage. In the meantime, several research perspectives on mission in the Bible that do not begin with theological criteria may be briefly described.

One pathway that some scholars have used to identify mission in the New Testament is based on lexicology. The idea behind this research strategy is that mission, like any defined task or particular concept mentioned in scripture, is likely to have a distinctive set of terms linked to it. Certain verbs, for example, may be expected to recur whenever a biblical figure "does" mission or otherwise engages in some kind of missionary action (for example, "proclaiming," "sending," "gathering," "making disciples," "baptizing," "working," etc.) . Other terms may become associated with those whom the apostles and others hope to share their message ("the nations," "crowds," "world") or come to stand as characteristic metaphors for the church's outreach efforts ("planting, "building," "sowing," "reaping," "fishing"). Schnabel (2004, 36–37), following Rudolf Pesch (1982, 14–16), has drawn together a carefully screened list of terms he understands to constitute the "semantic field" of mission in the New Testament, arranged by category. A much broader selection of terminology potentially related to evangelism is presented in Barrett and Johnson, *World Christian Trends* (2001, 697–738). Technical commentaries and the standard lexical aids must, of course, be consulted for detailed knowledge about specific terms, including the history of their usage in a variety of contexts. An invaluable resource that ought to be consulted in the course of any lexicological investigation of mission-related vocabulary is Ceslas Spicq, *Theological Lexicon of the New Testament* (1994).

Narrative criticism is another methodology to have arisen within New Testament studies that has shown potential for the analysis of mission activity in scripture. In this approach, scholars seek to understand the literary techniques employed in the Gospels and Acts, looking, for example, at the ways authors have constructed their plots and described characters. Also important in this subdiscipline of literary criticism are factors such as tone, pacing, point of view, and the presence or function of a narrator in a given story. Within biblical studies, narrative criticism has become a particularly useful tool for identifying the different roles played in Gospel narratives by "minor" characters, even ones without names or speaking parts. The work of Elizabeth Struthers Malbon (2000) is exemplary in this respect. Working more directly within missiology but with the benefit of a narrative critical perspective, Skreslet (2006b, esp. 79–117) has also sought to increase awareness of the background figures in the New Testament and their often-overlooked contributions to early mission history. Of crucial importance is the capacity of narrative criticism to prompt thinking about the social roles assumed by a variety of minor and major New Testament characters engaged in mission. Thus, in Skreslet, one encounters both well-known and obscure biblical actors who, in different sets of circumstances, might operate primarily in public or private spaces, alone or in concert with others, cross-culturally or within closely knit family networks, while assuming a variety of social postures for Christian witness (for example, "in front of" an audience of strangers as a public proclaimer of the gospel or "beside" a close friend or family member while sharing faith more personally).

Sociologists of religion have also contributed to our understanding of evangelization in the New Testament era. Such scholars pay close attention to the processes of religious change as these can be identified within particular social systems. This might mean, for instance, looking at the church in the first century as an example of what many scholars are now likely to call a new religious movement. An assumption that grounds this scholarly methodology is that whatever differences in doctrine one might discover when comparing newly founded religious groups, certain sociological factors tend to be critical for their successful growth and development. Thus, it becomes a priority to understand how such groups construct social boundaries around themselves in order to reinforce a distinctive identity. The means by which new members are assimilated is likewise a matter of deep interest. As might be expected, sociologists of religion are keenly attentive to broad-based movements of religious conversion, especially as these can be quantified. Large-scale shifts in religious affiliation may indicate new trends underway with respect to values, attitudes, or behavioral norms previously held in common by large numbers of people and so point to profound societal changes. Less important in these analyses are matters of theological conviction or professed motivations for missionary thought and action. A widely read example of a sociological approach to the results of early Christian mission is Rodney Stark, *The Rise of Christianity: A Sociologist Reconsiders History* (1996).

Social scientific methods have also become increasingly important within New Testament studies, beginning in the 1970s. An early contributor was Gerd Theissen, whose *Sociology of Early Palestinian Christianity* (1978) and many other books and articles stimulated considerable thinking along sociological lines with respect to the origins of Christianity. Theissen argued for explanations of Christianity's emergence that took seriously the economic, ecological (geographic), political, and cultural conditions of its first-century Palestinian environment. Other New Testament scholars applied the same logic to Christianity's larger context within the eastern Mediterranean world. Particularly influential has been Wayne Meeks, *The First Urban Christians: The Social World of the Apostle Paul* (1983). In addition to describing Christianity's conceptual transition from the world of the village to that of the city in a particularly vivid way, Meeks examined a number of other social factors that quite likely shaped the character of the scattered but still interrelated local religious communities reflected in the Pauline correspondence. The emphasis in Meeks falls on issues of social status (gender, class, relative social power), the *ekklesia* as a distinctive kind of first-century organizational structure, the "social function" of doctrine, and the methods of socialization (including ritual) used to create and maintain a peculiarly Christian subculture within a predominantly pagan and sometimes hostile Greco-Roman world. Like Stark, Meeks only here and there directly addresses the missionary *processes* by which Pauline Christianity came into being, but his way of writing social history adds much to our understanding of the now quite unfamiliar setting in which Paul and others shared their faith and suggests even more about how such processes might be studied in the future.

BIBLICAL RESOURCES FOR THEOLOGY OF MISSION

Theologians of mission usually turn to scripture for entirely different reasons than historians. Whereas the latter typically seek from the New Testament detailed information about how mission unfolded in the time of Jesus, the apostles, and the generation that immediately followed them, the former are more likely to be searching for enduring principles that have guided or could guide Christian witness across time. Even exegetes, when they operate as investigators of past mission experience need not concern themselves with any contemporary applications of whatever they might learn about mission in the Bible. Mission theologians who decide to feature the Bible in their research, on the other hand, are likely to have at least one eye cast on the future. A common assumption among these scholars is that the Bible can function as a wellspring of inspiration and direction for the church's mission in every age.

More specifically, what mission theologians tend to seek from the Bible are two kinds of help. The first has to do with the legitimation of Christian mission. By what authority does any missionary or church dare to share faith or to invite others to participate in the body of Christ? In other words, where is the ultimate justification to be found for the giving of Christian witness through intentional missionary activity? It is quite possible to assert an extrabiblical foundation for mission, arguing, as many have done especially in the modern period, that missionaries could contribute to human development through their educational and humanitarian efforts. In contrast, theological appeals tend to rely on scripture to make the case that mission is a constituent element of the Christian life, a matter of inner necessity, which does not depend on any other philosophical grounds for its justification.

Theologians also often use scripture to evaluate the conduct of mission. Here a leading issue is the problem of how to prioritize the purposes of truly authentic Christian mission. Equally important is the need to identify the most appropriate means to use in the pursuit of these aims. Marc Spindler has insightfully discussed the different uses of scripture by mission theologians in his essay, "The Biblical Grounding and Orientation of Mission" (1995).

What follows in the rest of this section is a sampling of particular approaches to mission in the Bible, conceived from a variety of theological viewpoints. I am not trying to be comprehensive with respect to this subtopic, which will also receive attention in several chapters to come. My intention rather is simply to illustrate some of the different ways mission theologians have attempted either to anchor their understanding of mission in scripture or to use the Bible to critique specific sets of missionary methods and the proximate goals that lie behind them. The order of presentation to be employed will proceed from what are relatively narrow appeals to scripture to more complex theological analyses of mission in the Bible. I do not propose to conclude with or lead up to a normative definition of mission or evangelization here, preferring instead to survey a range of recommendations already on offer for a biblical theology of mission.

An obvious place to begin is with William Carey's identification of the Great Commission (Matthew 28:18–20 and parallels) as a sufficient basis on which to construct a worldwide program of missionary outreach. Carey, in his famous 1792 *Enquiry into the Obligation of Christians to Use Means for the Conversion of the Heathens*, did not seek from the Bible any specific instructions for how to accomplish his proposed venture. For the apparatus of his mission program (the "means" to be used), Carey looked instead to the commercial trading companies that operated internationally in his day. Mission-minded Christians in England and elsewhere were urged to organize themselves in a similar manner as private voluntary associations, with boards of directors, investors (donors), rational policies regarding the recruitment and training of mission personnel, plus sustainable financial plans. Their cause would be "propagating the gospel amongst the heathens" (86), rather than the pursuit of business profits. Crucially, the whole enterprise rested on what Carey understood to be a biblical principle: "If the prophecies concerning the increase of Christ's kingdom be true, and if what has been advanced, concerning the commission given by him to his disciples being *obligatory* on us, be just, it must be inferred that all Christians ought heartily to concur with God in promoting his glorious designs" (77; emphasis added). For Carey and countless other friends of mission after him, those divine promises and that mandate from Jesus could supply more than enough motive to justify whatever sacrifices might be required from those hoping to extend the reach of the church and its message to the whole world.

Duty is but one of the reasons to be found in scripture that might serve as a basis of mission commitment. Many others have chosen to highlight instead their concern for the eternal fate of non-Christian humanity, based on those passages in the Bible that point to the necessity of Christ's work on the cross in God's plan of salvation. In essence, this is a biblical argument for Christian mission founded on the motive of love. As Paul puts it, "the love of Christ urges us on" in the task of reconciliation (2 Cor. 5:14). God's compassion for the world, which led to the sending of the Son (John 3:16), is taken as a model for those who wish to follow and participate in Christ's mission. In the same way that Jesus showed a willingness to search high and low for lost, precious sheep in his local Palestinian context, some in later generations would sound a call to emulate his example, but on a larger scale. Bosch (1991, 208–9) understands such reasoning to have undergirded much Eastern Orthodox thinking about mission, especially in the patristic period. Johannes van den Berg (1956) has argued that professions of love for God and humanity were a common and perhaps decisive feature of British evangelical pleas for mission involvement in the eighteenth century.

Bosch and van den Berg, among many others, remind us that the love motive (or any other driving force ostensibly drawn from the Bible) can be compromised, even among its most passionate advocates. Worldly interests never rest, with the result that all rhetoric on behalf of mission cast in terms of our love for God or humanity (or dedication to God's glory) has to be interrogated and measured against actions proposed or taken in pursuit of these ideals. Nationalist impulses, for example, or notions of religious territoriality, can easily subvert benevolent intent directed toward humanity and turn it instead into a scramble after patently earthbound advantages. The integrity of the love motive is imperiled whenever it is made subordinate to an ethnocentric worldview that may be able to accommodate pity and the giving of charity but resists genuine empathy. Bosch (1991, 286–91) suggests that the best example in the modern period of something like disinterested love functioning as a basis for mission may have been practiced by the Moravians in the eighteenth century.

Another kind of limited foray into scripture on behalf of mission theology has focused on the means of mission. In these efforts, the Bible is searched carefully in hopes of identifying the signal marks of apostolic mission. Thus, on the example of Jesus in Mark 6:7–9 (and parallels), a group or denomination might decide to send out their missionaries in pairs, perhaps dressed in distinctive ways. The same passage has been used repeatedly as a basis on which to stipulate an ascetic ideal for those aspiring to live as the disciples sent out on mission by Jesus did. The mendicants of the Middle Ages come to mind immediately in this regard, but we also have later Protestant groups like the China Inland Mission in the nineteenth century inculcating among their missionaries a lifestyle of radical dependence on God in response to the instructions of Jesus: "Take nothing for your journey, no staff, nor bag, nor bread, nor money—not even an extra tunic" (Luke 9:3).

At times, different parts of the church have made the performance of miracles a distinctive aspect of their approach to evangelization, in imitation of Jesus and the charismatic itinerants known to have been active in first-century Christianity. Based on their own readings of the New Testament materials, others have insisted on public preaching and/or compassionate service as indispensable elements of apostolic mission practice. A few theorists have fixed on one or another relatively obscure detail in the sacred text in order to promote what they believed to be a biblical norm for mission. An example of this approach is the peculiar polity John Eliot laid down for the seventeenth-century Native American converts he gathered into "praying towns." In Eliot's view, the decision to designate "rulers of ten, of fifty, of a hundred," a scheme of limited self-government modeled on Jethro's instructions to Moses in Exodus 18, proved that his program of evangelization was "expressly conformed to the Scriptures" (quoted in Cogley 1999, 168).

A more elaborate theological appraisal of mission in the New Testament focused on methods that deserves an extended comment because of its wide influence is Roland Allen, *Missionary Methods: St. Paul's or Ours?* (1912). Allen's thesis is remarkably straightforward: Paul had a strategy for evangelization that can be applied directly to contemporary circumstances. The key to the apostle's success, according to Allen, was his willingness to leave the churches he had founded in the hands of the converts themselves, as soon as possible. On the basis of a gospel message simply preached, a set of common scriptures, and a recognition of local leadership that had emerged more or less naturally on its own, these new communities could be trusted to make their own decisions on matters of governance, doctrine, and the details of worship. Allen's approach is a textbook example of exegesis in the service of theology. He examines the book of Acts and Paul's correspondence in order to identify a biblical standard by which to evaluate the mission practices of his day. He is not interested in the small-scale techniques of mission as enacted by the apostles but focuses rather on the larger strategic vision that guided Paul and his colleagues in their choice of tactics.

Similarly concerned to find the right theological basis for mission in order to choose the most appropriate methods is Donald McGavran, whose proposal for a theology of mission based on church growth principles has had enormous impact around the world. A biblical theology of mission, McGavran insisted, will not be satisfied with a good-faith effort to search for converts. God's intention is that as many people as possible who are ready to receive the gospel be found promptly and given the opportunity to respond to Christ's call: "God wants countable lost persons found" (McGavran 1962, 310). This is why Jesus talks about a ready harvest and an immediate need for reapers (Matt. 9:38). It is the reason behind his instructions to the disciples not to waste their time among those unwilling to receive the good news they have to share (Matt. 10:14). Some of the most memorable of Jesus' parables highlight the need to be persistent in one's search for what is lost, not resting until it is found (Luke 15:3–32). And in Acts the apostles are shown to practice this principle, concentrating their efforts first on the Jews. Only when that door seems to close do they turn to the Gentiles, thus fulfilling Jesus' promise that the gospel would be preached sequentially, "in Jerusalem, in all Judea and Samaria, and to the ends of the earth" (Acts 1:8).

Beyond the scope of Roland Allen's work on Paul and Donald McGavran's theology of harvest are those theological treatments of mission in the Bible that attempt to work more thoroughly with the whole of the canon. Several of these will now be described, grouped according to their common themes. No claim is made here that anything like a comprehensive roster of biblical theologies of mission is about to be presented. Still, it may be possible even in this restricted space to give an idea about some of the major biblical way stations visited by mission theology in its journey through the twentieth century.

The Mission of God

A nearly ubiquitous concept in mission theology today is the phrase *missio Dei*. The idea of a single mission rooted in God's nature at the very least stands in heuristic tension with the manifold and often competing ventures launched by churches and other organizations dedicated to missionary outreach. It is customary now to talk about the wide variety of ends to which the term *missio Dei* has been put since it came into general circulation shortly after the 1952 Willingen conference of the International Missionary Council. As we will see, these different applications of the term draw on more than one set of scripture passages, as successive attempts have been made using this or related terms to establish a biblical foundation for the theology of Christian mission. John Flett (2010) has closely examined the origins of the term *missio Dei*. He concludes that the undoubted attractiveness of this formulation in the postcolonial era has obscured its basic incoherence, due to the illusory or nonsubstantial way mission theologians have related this concept to the doctrine of the Trinity.

As originally conceived, "mission of God" language gave theologians a way to connect the churches and their missionary programs to the entire history of divine revelation attested in the Bible. Mission is seen not as something begun by any human organization, but as an eternal reality rooted in God's sending of the Son and the procession of the Spirit from the Godhead. Individual disciples and churches could participate in God's mission, but they were not to presume pride of authorship or claim a right to initiate something that properly fell outside their sphere of competence. Such a formulation allows one to tap into an astonishing array of scriptural resources, including witnesses to the incarnation (God's sending of the Son), biblical accounts of the Spirit's activity, the history of prophecy in ancient Israel (God's sending of the prophets), all of what is known about the efforts of Jesus to establish God's reign through his preaching, demonstrations of power, and crucifixion, plus the narrative materials found in Acts and elsewhere that document the work of Jesus' first disciples. *Missio Dei* language also invites one to conceive of the church itself as a sent community, dispatched by the Triune God for witness in the world. As Basel Mission director Karl Hartenstein observed, Willingen's use of the concept *missio Dei* put the missionary idea "within the broadest imaginable framework of salvation history and God's plan for salvation" (quoted in Richebächer 2003, 590).

Even before the end of the 1950s another application of *missio Dei* language had begun to emerge. To the distinction already made between the mission of God and the missions of the churches (*missio ecclesiae*) was added a suggestion that these two forms of action might in fact be opposed to one another. This could be the case, for instance, if church bodies decided to use mission illegitimately to further their own institutional interests or merely to bolster membership rolls. According to some theologians, active opposition from the churches to the notion that God was working through revolutionary movements in the postcolonial era or the historical processes of urbanization and secularization likewise raised doubts about Christian commitment to the *missio Dei*. In ecumenical circles, the culmination of this theological development came in the World Council of Churches study process on the "Missionary Structures of the Congregation," whose Western European working group made bold to assert that many existing forms of the church may well be "heretical structures" that blocked the way of the *missio Dei* and so should be abandoned (World Council of Churches 1967, 19).

Without a doubt, much sociological analysis of varying quality lay beneath this turn in the fate of the term *missio Dei*, but some solid exegetical spadework had prepared the ground beforehand. A key figure in this regard was Johannes Hoekendijk, whose seminal essay first published in 1950, "The Call to Evangelism," put forward *shalom* as a guiding principle for mission in a post-Christendom world. For Hoekendijk (1950, 168), the idea of *shalom*, understood as "peace, integrity, community, harmony, and justice" not only served to connect the messianic promises of the Old Testament to Jesus and his mission, but also fully described the true objective of the church's work in the present. A church that wants to align itself with the Messiah's mission, Hoekendijk suggested, will heed the call to put *shalom* at the heart of its message (*kerygma*), to find ways to embody *shalom* in community (*koinonia*), and to translate the Christian experience of *shalom* into acts of humble service in the world outside the church (*diakonia*).

The cause of *shalom*, swept up as it was into ongoing debates in the 1950s and 1960s over the meaning of the *missio Dei*, became one of the primary ways in mission theology to talk about salvation. Others promoted humanization over Christianization as the proper goal of mission. From the 1970s, an alternative but still complementary term is met with increasing frequency in the literature of mission theology: liberation. A preference for liberationist rhetoric often leads to a different kind of appeal to scripture. Reduced prominence may be given, for example, to biblical promises of God's future provision of harmony and justice at the end of time in favor of stories that feature God-inspired action on behalf of the poor and the marginalized in real-life circumstances. Thus, with respect to the Old Testament, less may need to be said about an impending Last Day and more about the prophets and figures like Moses who challenged the powerful in their own time. Correspondingly, one should expect fewer citations from Jesus and Paul about the cosmic dimensions of God's coming reign but an intense interest in those situations where Jesus confronted the religious authorities of his generation who blessed the status quo. Within the hermeneutical trajectory defined by liberation, the first sermon of Jesus at Nazareth (as recorded in Luke 4:16–30) and the story of the exodus often function as programmatic texts for this brand of mission theology. The special attention paid in Luke to the situation of the poor (in Mary's song of the Magnificat [Luke 1:46–55], for example, or in certain of the parables) also tends to recommend this Gospel in particular to anyone who believes that salvation is, above all, a matter of liberation from current forms of oppression.

Reconciliation

Yet another grand theme suggested for a biblical theology of mission is the idea of reconciliation. As Schreiter (1997b, 379) has observed, in the context of missiology reconciliation has significance "not only as a way of speaking of God's good news for the world but as a way of doing mission itself." Reconciliation as good news is a widely attested leitmotif in the Bible, even in the Old Testament. It is suggested, for example, whenever radical social estrangement is overcome or a profound experience of injustice is rectified. Peaceful relations between former enemies (when not imposed unilaterally) can be a sign of reconciliation. In the New Testament, one finds numerous places in Paul's letters where the idea of reconciliation seems to define his apostolate and message. According to Paul, not only do Jew and Greek find their essential unity in Christ (Eph. 2:13–22), but the cross of Christ is the means by which humanity and everything else in the created order have become reconciled to God (Rom. 5:8–11; Col. 1:19–20). No wonder then that Paul could sum up his life's work as a "ministry of reconciliation" (2 Cor. 5:18).

Elsewhere in the New Testament, we find the theme of reconciliation powerfully portrayed in the story of the prodigal son (Luke 15:11–32). An ethic of reconciling love, summed up in the command to love one's enemies (Matt. 5:44), may be said to lie at the heart of the Beatitudes. Intriguingly, Schreiter (1998) suggests that all of the resurrection appearance stories in the New Testament could be read as narratives of reconciliation. When Jesus appears, the disciples are confronted with their sense of loss and guilt. At the same time, these encounters are moments of healing, because Jesus implicitly demonstrates his willingness to forgive remorseful disciples while offering them encouragement for the future. In this way, as Schreiter shrewdly observes, acts of reconciliation seem to form the very context in which disciples are transformed into apostles, the specific circumstances of their commissioning. The Risen Lord, himself a victim of violence and betrayal, shows by his actions how reconciliation can permeate the church's mission "as a spirituality, as a ministry, and as a strategy" (21).

Reconciliation as a master-theme within mission theology can be reinforced and broadened by pairing it with related concerns. Peacemaking, for example, is a way to talk about the practice of reconciliation in particular situations of conflict and violence. Likewise, we find some eco-theologians calling for greater efforts to heal the earth as an expression of mission intention put in terms of reconciliation (see, for instance, Langmead 2002 and 2008 on "ecomissiology").

More often than not, dialogue is championed as the means of mission best suited for the work of reconciliation. In this case, Jesus' interactions with strangers like the Samaritan woman (John 4:7–30) or Paul's irenic exchange with the philosophers in Athens (Acts 17:16–34) are likely to be highlighted. A dialogical style of mission and ministry might be promoted either as a way to prepare for reconciliation to take place or to manifest a quality of mutuality in human relationships thought to be appropriate for a people who understand themselves to be reconciled with God. In a recent proposal for the renewal of mission theology, Stephen Bevans and Roger Schroeder (2004, esp. 348–95) have linked together commitments to interreligious dialogue, reconciliation, justice, peace, and care for the environment (plus several other elements) under the rubric of "prophetic dialogue."

Universalism

A biblical theology of mission can also be built around the theme of universalism. This is the path taken, for example, by Donald Senior and Carroll Stuhlmueller

(1983) in their influential introduction to mission and the Bible, *The Biblical Foundations for Mission.* By universalism, Senior and Stuhlmueller mean to indicate the unlimited scope of God's salvific intent as revealed in the Christian scriptures. No part of humanity is left out of God's vision for a redeemed world. Further, all of history and the entirety of creation may be understood to be potential contexts for the revelatory activity of God. Senior and Stuhlmueller reach these conclusions on the basis of a close exegetical analysis of nearly the entire Christian canon, where it seems to them that "every historical event, every layer of the universe, and every human being that shaped the experience of Israel and the early church are part of the biblical story" (347).

The potency of this theological approach to mission in the Bible is demonstrated by the major subtopics it spurs Senior and Stuhlmueller to confront. To claim that the God of the Bible wills universal salvation requires a careful study of mission in the Old Testament, where the election of Israel seems to denote a sense of ethnocentric exclusivity. The assertion of a universal gospel, "capable of embracing and being expressed by all cultures and all peoples" (2), immediately raises questions about how the Bible's message has been and might be inculturated in a variety of cultural contexts. An insistence that the church be universal presses these biblical theologians to consider how communities gathered in Christ's name may be guided by scripture, even as they seek to maintain their distinctive common identity in a world of many religions.

A second study (also written from a Catholic perspective) that likewise grapples seriously with matters of universalism and pluralism is Lucien Legrand, *Unity and Plurality: Mission in the Bible* (1990). Legrand writes less extensively than Senior and Stuhlmueller with respect to individual books in the Bible and their relationship to mission, but his thesis is no less comprehensive than theirs. In both Testaments, according to Legrand, one finds a kind of missional dialectic at work, in which an expansive vision of salvation that encompasses all the nations of the earth is effected through the formation of communities set apart by God. In the Old Testament that special polity was Israel and the exclusive quality of Israel's relationship to God is treated as a paramount consideration, but without totally effacing God's concern for the nations. In the New Testament, the emphasis falls on God's turn to the Gentiles and the world as a whole, but the church is still assigned a special role nonetheless in the divine economy. Universal salvation and election may thus be considered the "twin poles" of mission in the Bible (15–27; 152). On the basis of this finding, Legrand will argue that the ways of mission need not be resolved into a single approach or form. A biblical theology of mission marked by paradox bids one to consider flexible methodologies capable of engaging a world full of ambiguity.

Finally, we have the example of David Bosch, whose *Transforming Mission* (1991) includes a major section on theology of mission in the New Testament. As mentioned in the previous chapter, Bosch finds in the New Testament materials he surveys (Matthew, Luke–Acts, Paul) more than one standpoint for a biblical theology of mission. This diversity in scripture is complemented by the church's experience in evangelization, which over two millennia has encompassed a wide range of normative proposals for how to conceptualize mission (called in Bosch "paradigms" of mission). Not surprisingly, Bosch's description of an "emerging ecumenical missionary paradigm" is also marked by variegation. No single theme is allowed to dominate the collection of thirteen interrelated "elements" that define the new direction in mission theory Bosch wishes to recommend. Mission in the postmodern era has to be multidimensional, he believes, able to embrace aspects of "witness, service, justice, healing, reconciliation, liberation, peace, evangelism, fellowship, church planting, contextualization, and much more" (512). To avoid incoherence, a willingness to tolerate not a little "creative tension" among the different parts of this very comprehensive definition of mission is required, as Bosch has acknowledged (367). Ultimately, pluralism as a challenge to Enlightenment thinking (whether expressed in terms of a rationalist absolutism or hyper-subjective relativism) becomes the defining characteristic of his ecumenical paradigm of postmodern mission.

THE BIBLE IN MISSION

Translations

Legions of missionaries and linguists have worked hard over the past two centuries especially to make the Christian scriptures available in as many of the world's living languages as possible. One indicator of this fact appears in the statistics that sum up the current status of Bible translation activity. The number of different languages in which at least one book of the Bible is already in print now exceeds 2,450, according to an authoritative count provided on the website of the United Bible Societies (*www.ubs-translations.org/about_us*). Included in this number are 438 complete translations and 1,168 more languages in which one or the other of the two biblical Testaments has been fully translated (as of 2007). In comparison, a writing that has recently been recognized by the Guinness world record organization as the "most translated document" in the world is the Universal Declaration of Human Rights, which by the end of 2007 had been rendered into slightly more than 360 languages (the United Nations calls attention to this [erroneous] claim at *www.un.org/events/humanrights/2007/worldtransdoc.shtml*). A vigorous program of Bible translation work continues under the auspices of the United Bible Societies, with some 268 projects currently under way in languages that still lack even one published portion of scripture. Additional work is sponsored by the Summer Institute of Linguistics/Wycliffe Bible Translators and a number of other lesser known organizations.

Evangelistic motives lay or lie behind most of these translation efforts, as missionaries and church leaders have sought either to provide already existing communities of believers with the Bible in their own language or to create a means to share this sacred text with new groups of people outside the church. In either case, it is not unreasonable to conclude, with Jaroslav Pelikan (2005, 213), that for Protestants at least "the Bible translator replaced the monk as the principal agent . . . of their strategy of evangelization and missions" in the course of the nineteenth century.

A warrant for translation is included in the text itself. Even in the Old Testament, where Hebrew overwhelmingly dominates as the assumed best medium of communication between God and humanity, a few chapters in the book of Daniel were recorded in Aramaic. Loan-words derived from a variety of foreign languages (most often Akkadian, Egyptian, or Persian) are sprinkled throughout the Old Testament canon (Ellenbogen 1962), an implicit witness to the dynamic cultural contexts in which ancient Israel conducted its political, economic, and religious affairs. Well before the beginning of the Common Era, the Old Testament as a whole had been translated into Greek and in that version (the Septuagint or LXX) was regarded as an authoritative form of scripture by many Jews living in diaspora throughout the Mediterranean basin.

For the earliest followers of Jesus, some form of the Old Testament also functioned as their Bible. In time, another set of writings generated from within the Christian community itself attained equal status. Curiously, what came to be known as the New Testament was not written in the mother tongue of Jesus and his closest disciples, but in Greek. The Gospels themselves provide a window onto the linguistic transition that quickly ensued after the death of Jesus, as certain phrases are reproduced in their original Aramaic (for example, the cry of Jesus on the cross at Matt. 27:46) and then also translated for an audience presumably in need of such assistance. Had the Christian movement remained a small sect within Palestinian Judaism, a shift to Greek might have been tolerated, since the Jews of that area had also been affected by the cultural tsunami of Hellenization that had swept through the eastern Mediterranean region in the preceding centuries (see Fitzmyer, 1979). An intention to share their message with Jews scattered far and wide in diaspora, and then with Gentiles too, made the use of Greek necessary.

The Principle of Translatability

The subsequent experience of the Christian church in mission soon broke through the tacit limits that encircled the Septuagint. The transition from Aramaic to Greek was followed by other translations of the Christian scriptures, initially into Syriac, Latin, and Coptic. In the case of the LXX, accompanying myths of divine intervention on behalf of the translators (provided in Philo and Josephus) had perhaps been necessary to authenticate the new version and make it acceptable to a community long conditioned to revere Hebrew above every other language spoken on earth. The Christian worldview turned out to be different. According to this understanding of God's linguistic economy, all the world's vernaculars were equally gifted with a capacity to receive the gospel. Christianity did not have to make an exception in the face of exigency and suddenly accept a new rendering of its sacred writings in a foreign script. It had been founded on the principle of "translatability" (Sanneh 1989), a circumstance that would have huge implications for the ensuing history of Christian mission, although not everywhere and at all times to the same degree.

After Constantine, different attitudes toward translation began to develop in the Byzantine East and Latin West. In the realm of Eastern Orthodoxy, where national church cultures were not only recognized but nurtured, the principle of translatability continued to be expressed with verve, whether in missionary outreach or in finely contextualized theological traditions. Thus, we find Ulfila (c. 311–83) devising with colleagues the language tools needed to translate the Bible into Gothic, as they sought to convert this ethnic group to Christianity. In Ethiopia, Ge'ez became a medium of scripture at about the same time that Mesrob (c. 350–439/440) and his students created their acclaimed Armenian translation. In a number of contexts dominated by Islam, established Middle Eastern Christian communities felt it necessary to adopt Arabic for apologetic purposes from at least the eighth century (on this history, see Griffith 2008). And then we have the celebrated example of Cyril and Methodius in the ninth century, who do for the Slavs of Moravia and beyond what Ulfila had done for the Goths when they invent the Glagolitic alphabet as a basis for the literary and ecclesiastical language that came to be known as Old Church Slavonic.

The translation activities of Cyril and Methodius and the stiff opposition in some quarters that rose up against them in Moravia exposed a widening philosophical gap on mission strategy between Rome and Constantinople. Unlike the Orthodox in the East, Roman Catholicism in the early Middle Ages was steadily moving away from the principle of translatability. High respect for the Vulgate translation of Jerome (c. 340–420) ended up suppressing the church's natural impulse to translate its scriptures into other European languages. In a connected development, the wide use of Latin within Western Christianity eventually became an effective symbol of the Roman Catholic Church's claim to universality. Reformers like John Wycliffe (c. 1330–84) and Martin Luther (1483–1546) had to contend with official censure when they broke with tradition over the issue of vernacular translations. The Council of Trent (1545–63) reaffirmed for Catholics the singular status of the Vulgate as inspired scripture and so pronounced against the notion of translatability.

Because early modern Protestants were slow to take up the cause of worldwide evangelization, they left unrealized for a very long time many of the potential benefits of translation for mission. This changed dramatically in the generation of William Carey. From the late eighteenth century, Bible translation and the distribution of the sacred text in multiple languages became for Protestants a major means of mission. Quite soon thereafter, the printed scriptures and other texts became material symbols that effectively represented much of what was distinctive about Protestant missions, including literacy, an educated clergy, and lay access to the scriptures. Focusing on *The Pilgrim's Progress* as a transnational religious discourse, Isabel Hofmeyr (2004) has shown how the principle of translatability could also apply to an extrabiblical text. According to Hofmeyr, the extraordinary success of Bunyan's story only partially derived from Western evangelical confidence in its universal validity. Countless audiences around the world were just as eager to receive this text in translation (Hofmeyr concentrates on eighty translations that circulated in sub-Saharan Africa alone) and to appropriate its message on their own terms. As it happened, the early successes of the Bible societies so captured the imagination of the Protestant Christian public that their activities were interpreted as an apocalyptic sign of divine providence on a par with the great revivals of religion taking place at about the same time in the North Atlantic region (so observed Leonard Woods [1966] in 1812 on the occasion of the ordination of the first missionaries sent abroad by the American Board of Commissioners for Foreign Missions). Writing in 1839, Alexander Duff would characterize Bible translation and the circulation of the scriptures as one of three primary methods of evangelization then in use among Protestants (next to proclamation and education). Indeed, already by his day, some advocates of the Bible Societies and their methods were arguing for the distribution of vernacular scriptures without preaching as the purest expression of the missionary impulse because it was less contentious, a notion that Duff ridiculed (1839, 375–78) as equivalent to sending harps to the deaf or passing out medicine to the sick without the advice of knowledgeable physicians. Steer (2004) has written about the policy of the British and Foreign Bible Society from its inception in 1804 to circulate the scriptures "without note or comment."

So far what I have been summarizing in this section are the largely agreed-upon results of missiological research focused on the role of the Bible in mission. For additional details, students will want to consult William Smalley, *Translation as Mission* (1991). Historical methodologies have figured prominently in these efforts, as scholars have attempted to piece together the record of translation work assembled over the centuries. Exegetical investigations have added to our knowledge regarding the status of Greek and other languages in first-century Palestine, while also shedding light on the evolution of Hebrew during the formation of the Old Testament canon. Some aspects of Bible translation history have raised theological questions. This is evident, for example, in the various stances taken on the principle of translatability among the different families of churches, some of which were argued along theological lines. Yet even here there is not much controversy to be found today among Christians with respect to the advisability of translating the scriptures. Advocates and critics of particular translations or styles of translation may disagree with one another, but after the Second Vatican Council (1962–65) opened the door for Catholics to use vernacular forms of scripture in worship and study, virtually no contemporary supporter of Christian mission would think to ask if Bible translation is theologically justified. Translation is now accepted as an indispensable element of mission. It is a kind of contextualization that the gospel not only allows but seems to require.

Vernacularization and Empowerment

Even outside the church, it was widely assumed until quite recently that Bible translation was always a benevolent activity. Where a language group lacked its own set of scriptures, a new translation provided access to a previously unavailable resource for spiritual growth. In the situation of a language spoken by relatively few people, a translator's choice to commit time and treasure to a minor dialect could be interpreted as a sign of respect for a marginalized social group. Further, the history of mission is replete with examples of pioneer translators whose efforts to create writing systems for oral languages made literacy and the creation of new literary traditions possible, a development that could only add to the world's cultural richness. In a few cases, high-quality translations of the Bible (for example, Luther's German translation) came to be regarded by later generations as particularly graceful exemplars of good literary style.

In his forceful defense of translatability as a cardinal virtue both for mission and theology, Lamin Sanneh (1989) elaborates on most of the arguments briefly noted above and adds a few new points of his own. Sanneh draws attention, for example, to the collaborative relationships engendered by translation, as cross-cultural missionaries find themselves quite unable to cope independently with their task. Native informants and "assistant" translators never get the recognition they deserve, Sanneh acknowledges, but the fundamental issue is what happens next in the history of interpretation, after the translated text has been created. Again and again, the products of Bible translation work demonstrate a capacity to transcend even the most grating of missionary ethnocentrisms. Once the scriptures are rendered into the vernacular, it becomes impossible to keep the Bible in foreign custody. In the wide open seas of interpretation that lie ahead, native speakers rather than foreign missionaries are bound to become the master navigators of the present and future, because they have the deepest understanding of the novel and complex cultural environment in which the text has come to be situated. Sanneh concludes his argument by contrasting the basic orientations to culture displayed within Islam and Christianity (211–38). With its untranslatable Qur'an and mandated formal prayers in Arabic (*salat*), Islam obviously privileges one language and culture at the expense of all others. Its preferred method of mission is diffusion from a defined center in hopes of replicating an ideal seventh-century past, rather than translation. At different points in the church's history, Sanneh observes, Christian propagandists may have behaved similarly, but adherence to the principle of translatability invariably promotes cultural pluralism as a norm within the Christian tradition.

On the basis of the church's experience in sub-Saharan Africa especially, Sanneh goes on to assert that the practice of translation adopted by most Western missions eventually undermined Western imperial interests on that continent. This is perhaps the most unexpected and controversial aspect of his thesis. In Sanneh's view, vernacularization in mission empowered Africans among others to resist the control of foreign agents and metropolitan centers. Even in those situations where missionaries actively supported colonial rule, their evangelization project, when founded on the principle of translatability, represented "the logical opposite of colonialism" (105). In many locations, indigenized scriptures stimulated cultural renewal, which in turn became the basis of an emerging national identity that could be activated in defiance of the colonizer. In the Bible's stories of liberation and God's concern for the oppressed, many African Christians discovered conceptual resources by which they could imagine a postcolonial existence for themselves. Coincidently, schools originally established by the missions to increase Bible literacy also became fertile training grounds for some of Africa's most successful anticolonial leaders. In these and other ways, Sanneh concludes, Christian mission was "deliberately fashioning the vernacular instrument that Africans . . . came to wield against their colonial overlords" (5).

The notion that the Christian scriptures when translated are necessarily a means of empowerment for those being evangelized has been stoutly challenged in recent years. An influential voice in these debates belongs to New Testament scholar Musa Dube, who contends that missionary translations often served to advance colonial interests by stigmatizing aspects of native cultures that might stand in the way of imperial designs. Her case in point is the 1840 Robert Moffatt translation of the New Testament later revised by A. J. Wookey, in which the Greek word for "demon" is translated using the Setswana term for ancestors (*badimo*). She condemns Moffatt's choice of words in this instance as an act of violence, a mistranslation meant to alienate the natives from their own culture (1999, 37–39). Dube finds similar strategies at work in the handling of other vocabulary related to traditional Setswana religion, not only in translations of the Bible but in missionary-produced grammars and dictionaries, too. Thus did missionaries like Moffatt and Wookey plant many "colonial culture bombs" in the midst of the non-Western peoples with whom they shared the Christian scriptures, "minefields" that warned African believers not to reenter their own pre-Christian cultural spaces. Far from empowering local Christians, Dube maintained, missionary translations used local languages to create conceptual structures with which the colonizers could reinforce their physical subjugation of the natives. Scripture in the vernacular did not mark the beginning of the end of missionary dominance. It was instead a potent tool of foreign control, a means by which missionary translators were able to continue to exert their influence even from the grave. Lovemore Togarasei (2009) sees a similar pattern at work in the Shona-language Bible translations produced by missionaries in Zimbabwe during that country's colonial era.

Nowhere in Dube's original essay does the name of Lamin Sanneh or any other missiologist surface. That connection is made later in the course of the contentious debate that took place afterward between Dube and contemporary missionary translator Eric Hermanson. In a provocative unpublished paper delivered in 1999 at Hammanskraal, South Africa, Hermanson argued that the earlier translators cited by Dube were not guilty of the crimes with which she had charged them. They had engaged in an acceptable form of contextualization, he believed, since the *badimo* were commonly held responsible for illness and disease in the nineteenth-century spiritual world of the Batswana (reported in Maluleke 2005, 368–69). Dube (2001) answered back with a sharp rejoinder, suggesting that Hermanson was willfully perpetuating a regime of violent translation by refusing to engage in a proper postcolonial analysis of these missionary writings.

We have here an ongoing scholarly dispute that extends way beyond the fine points of how to translate certain Greek terms into particular African dialects. Each of the parties involved appeals to and seeks to participate in larger interpretive traditions related to mission history. Hermanson invokes a point of view already articulated by Sanneh, John Mbiti (1986), Kwame Bediako (1995, 109–25), and Andrew Walls (1996, 26–42). For her part, Dube is extending the line of reasoning pioneered by historical anthropologists Jean and John Comaroff (1991, 1997), which has also been espoused by other biblical scholars, such as R. S. Sugirtharajah (2001). Missiologists should be interested in every aspect of this conversation, which is largely taking place within the broad disciplinary arena of sociolinguistics. Indeed, to study the Bible in mission is to be concerned about the scholarly *and* social processes by which different translations may have come into being. It means paying close attention to the initial reception of these texts and then also the ongoing history of interpretation that follows with respect to multiple audiences. Even the physical form of the translations distributed by the missions deserves examination, since the books themselves were often treated in special ways, if not reverenced as sacred objects (for one example of this phenomenon, see Kent 2005, 71–72). For missiologists, technical studies focused on the biblical languages and social science research on modern translation theory will continue to be important for these discussions, but so will feminist perspectives, anthropological critique, and postcolonial scholarship, all of which can shed light on the sometimes unintended and often subtle effects of missionary translation activities.

3

History of Mission

The purpose of this chapter is not to provide a synopsis of mission history. Other surveys already exist, and, in any case, a single chapter in an introductory textbook could hardly begin to represent the sprawling narrative of global Christianity that now stretches over nearly two millennia. Instead I propose to consider how the missionary aspect of Christian history has been and could be studied or portrayed.

The chapter will be divided into two major parts. In the first and much longer section, my primary concern will be to identify and describe what I think have been the most commonly practiced forms of mission historiography, reaching all the way back to Luke's account of apostolic history. Along the way, consideration will be given to a number of alternative approaches, including ecclesiastical history, hagiography, early modern ethnography, historical *Missionswissenschaft*, and microhistories of the kind now often produced by secular historians, anthropologists, and other social scientists. My intention is not only to lay bare the variety of historiographical styles that have been employed by mission historians in the past, but also to begin reviewing the different kinds of source material missiologists must be prepared to consult and analyze in the course of their historical work today. What the reader can expect in this section then is not a history of mission but something more like a history of the history of mission.

The second part of this chapter will focus more directly on the particular problems contemporary mission historians are likely to face and the methods most often used in response to these challenges. Questions about sources will again be raised, especially in relation to the task of documenting world Christianity in situations of recent rapid growth. In this regard, one is prompted to think about how to analyze the complex social processes necessarily involved in circumstances of widespread religious change. Another line of inquiry asks how well the various agents of evangelization (especially women and non-Western actors) are represented in the written materials that usually make up the archival record. Of special importance, too, is the matter of perspective or the different points of view that could be adopted by the mission historian. A related concern has to do with the active presence of more than one established historical discourse on Christian mission, a fact that inevitably shapes the intellectual environment within which every self-aware mission historian must operate today. By the end of this chapter, we shall have reviewed a series of more technical issues primarily having to do with data gathering and methods of historical analysis, while also attending to the creative side of history writing.

LUKE THE HISTORIAN

The Acts of the Apostles occupies a singular place within the Christian canon. It is not another Gospel, despite the many significant but subtle ties of language and theological perspective that connect it to Luke's story of Jesus. Nor do we find a counterpart for the Acts of the Apostles among any of the other books that eventually came to be included in the New Testament, whether epistle, exhortation (Hebrews), or apocalypse. In terms of genre, Acts appears to be a presentation of early Christian history, with mission put at the heart of the story. If so, we might rightly regard its author, commonly held to be the evangelist Luke, as the first historian of Christian mission. However, the kind of history Luke has chosen to put on offer is far from self-evident.

One way to begin to assess the historical character of Acts is to situate this work within the universe of exemplars available to Luke in his own time. By virtue of the fact that his community embraced the Hebrew Scriptures, he would have been familiar with biblical history and the idea of God's purposeful action in the midst of human affairs. In Acts, divine guidance is assumed to have taken place at a number of crucial moments in the story of the early church, most often by means of the Holy Spirit. Luke's choice of subject also aligns him with a Jewish historiographical tradition that ultimately concerned itself with God's salvific intentions. He is writing, first of all, about *Heilsgeschichte*, the history of salvation, rather than the political, economic, or cultural circumstances of any particular human society. An omniscient point of view reinforces the impression that Acts is a story about God's aims, since it allows the reader to know things that only God could know and to receive regular assurances that the highest of purposes will be served in the end, regardless of any setbacks that might be reported in the meantime. A brief prefatory remark at the beginning of Luke (Luke 1:1–4; cf. Acts 1:1) indicates that the author writes for and from within his own community (he and his named correspondent, Theophilus, are identified as members of a defined "we"), a detail that further heightens the confessional tone of the book.

The matter of Luke's preface also calls to mind a second historiographical tradition that operated quite apart from the ways of Jewish sacred history. There is considerable dispute over the degree to which Luke may have adopted the habits of ancient Greek historiography, but little scholarly disagreement with the notion that the author of Acts must have been exposed through his formal education to some of that tradition's classical treasures. The speeches inserted into Acts, for example, seem to conform to Greek expectations for effective rhetoric, at least in terms of structure and style (Satterthwaite 1993). In any event, Luke's stated intention in the preface to his Gospel (implicitly reaffirmed at the beginning of

Acts) to compose "an orderly account," using the best evidence available to him (oral tradition and eyewitness testimonies), signals an awareness of historical values and practices not acknowledged anywhere within the canonical corpus of the Old Testament. He writes knowing that his readers (Theophilus may be just one of these or a symbol for all of them) would have access to alternative narratives, a possibility not even remotely considered within the proprietary enclave of the Jewish scriptures. His professed objective to deliver an account that conveys "the truth concerning the things about which you have [already] been instructed" (Luke 1:4) could well mean that Luke has written in anticipation of reader reaction to his work. Tellingly, he does not make a claim for divine inspiration, despite the fact that his subject has everything to do with eternal salvation. To the extent that Luke grounds his appeal to be heard on the plausibility and thoroughness of his narrative and the strength of his evidence, he has stepped outside the strict confines of sacred history writing.

Against this background, we may ask again more directly: what kind of history is Acts? Following Marguerat (2002, 31–34), I consider Luke–Acts as a whole to be a "narrative of beginnings," meaning an attempt to account for the emergence and diffusion of a new religious group. The particular task imposed on the author of Acts is to explain what happened to the Jesus movement after the death of its founder.

Intriguingly, we find at the heart of this story a pair of themes somewhat in tension with each other. On the one hand, Luke is concerned to show how a nascent faith community coalesced around a consistent set of beliefs, some common social values, a small number of defining ritual practices, and a shared sense of evangelistic purpose. Sharp disagreements within the community are muted. Surprisingly little is said, for example, about infighting or struggles over doctrine (in striking contrast to the letters of John, in which readers are warned to be on their guard against false teachers, or Paul's account of his disputes with rival Judaizers and "superapostles"). When irreducible differences are reported over whether the whole of the Torah applies to Gentile converts, an amicable agreement nevertheless is said to have been reached with the assistance of the Holy Spirit (at the so-called Apostolic Council in Acts 15). Likewise, Paul and Barnabas will separate without recrimination, after failing to reconcile their two views of mission strategy (Acts 15:36–41). Luke's picture of the early church is surely idealized. While not entirely uniform, the community depicted in Acts is of one mind on those issues Luke considered essential to its self-understanding.

A second theme running through Acts has to do with the dynamic character of early Christianity. This part of the story is about expansion and growth, about the crossing of boundaries and unanticipated cultural encounters. Luke has the benefit of hindsight and a sense of confidence about God's guidance throughout. Yet his narrative gives witness to a process of development or becoming that takes place in the context of intense missionary activity. Thus, we see the character of the community evolving over time in substantive ways, from tight-knit to far-flung, from exclusively Jewish to increasingly Gentile, from a rural movement to an urban phenomenon. Luke is certainly responsible for the way in which these shifts are portrayed dramatically in Acts. He chooses, for example, to use the stories of certain individuals to show how the early church confronted persecution (Stephen) or the problem of Gentile believers (Cornelius). An extended series of arrests, legal proceedings, and (brief) periods of incarceration in which Peter and Paul are featured demonstrates the community's willingness to submit to imperial authority, even as the reader is given to understand that a power greater than Rome's may also be at work. In short, what we find embedded in the imaginative narrative of Acts is an unfolding story about growth and change that probably has a basis in reality, at least in broad terms.

Mission historians are indebted to Luke for much of what can be known about the processes and patterns of first-century Christian evangelism. For this reason alone, Acts will forever remain an indispensable primary resource for the study of early Christianity, even though only a portion of the details included in Luke's account may be able to withstand scholarly scrutiny. The twin themes running through Acts briefly described above represent another strong incentive for mission historians to pay close attention to this book. Luke's history is a first attempt to explain how the church and its universal message could remain constant in the midst of fundamentally new cultural circumstances. Not a few missionaries to come after the first century, plus those historians seeking to understand their actions and intentions, will find themselves grappling with much the same dilemma.

ECCLESIASTICAL HISTORY

Ecclesiastical history is a way to account for a part of the Christian past that puts a particular form of the church at the center of the story. Mission does not have to be a major component of church history, but it can be and often is when the church of the author's time perceives itself to be in a situation of expansion and flux. In two of the most influential early examples of ecclesiastical history, those produced by Eusebius (260–339) and Bede (c. 673–735), substantial attention is given to missionary matters. Each of these ancient historians writes from within his own context, but the obvious intention of Bede to emulate his groundbreaking predecessor produces an impression of overlapping interests and common approach. A primary concern here will be to consider how the use of this historiographical genre could affect one's presentation of mission history.

At the outset of his most famous work, Eusebius enumerates several specific aims he hopes to achieve. Among these is a resolve to record "the number of those who in each generation were the ambassadors of the word of God either by speech or pen" (*HE* I, 1). This is a patently missionary topic and will lead him not only to recount a portion of the church's story covered by Luke in Acts but also to extend and fill out his received narrative of apostolic history with material gleaned from "other sources" to which he had access besides the "divine writings" (preface to Book II). Eusebius goes on to document the experience of the church in the postapostolic period down to his own time. He shows particular interest in the church's martyrs, hardly a surprise given his own direct experience of persecution under Diocletian. He is also keen to show how unbelief and false beliefs temporarily impeded the advance of the divine Logos, whether by fomenting extramural opposition to the church and its mission or by sowing heresy from within its ranks. His narrative has a conclusion. The *Ecclesiastical History* of Eusebius is ultimately about the triumph of God's Word over all that had threatened to hinder its progress in the world up to the moment of Constantine's complete ascendance to power.

Institutional developments often dominate the narratives of ecclesiastical historians. In the case of Eusebius, his interest is focused on the office of the bishop. Lists of bishops are inserted throughout the narrative and provide a kind of outline structure onto which other information can be grafted. Apostolic succession, however, is much more than a literary technique for Eusebius. In this rendition of ecclesiastical history, the bishop becomes an essential symbol of church discipline and orthodox belief. Indeed, the health of the church depends on and can be measured by the depth of episcopal fidelity that may be in evidence at any given time.

Such a pronounced emphasis on orthodoxy and governance carries with it several implications for the writing of mission history. The first is that long-established centers of church life, those places where powerful bishops are most likely to be able to exercise their authority directly, tend to receive far more attention from the historian than do the peripheries, where active and possibly irregular processes of evangelization might be taking place. Coincidentally, as the metropolitan figure of the bishop looms ever larger within the historian's field of vision, the contributions of more liminal actors tend to be overshadowed.

In Eusebius this seems to have happened with respect to the office of evangelist. The last named person so designated is Quadratus, who lived in the early second century (*HE* III, 37). The prophetic gifts of Quadratus are acknowledged. He and others of his generation are praised for their powerful preaching, for their ability to work miracles, and for having distributed their property to the poor in apostolic fashion before engaging crowds of people "who had not yet heard the word of the faith." In fact, enough is said in this chapter about itinerant evangelists to prove that Eusebius was well aware of this ministry pattern and reckoned it to be a normal part of church life even after the passing of the first apostles. Eusebius indicates that he had access to more information on second-century evangelism than he chooses to provide: "It is impossible for us to give the number and the names of all who first succeeded the Apostles, and were shepherds or evangelists in the churches throughout the world" (*HE* III, 37). He decides instead to concentrate on literary activities: "It was, therefore, natural for us to record by name the memory only of those of whom the tradition still survives to our time by their treatises on the Apostolic teaching." In other words, from this point forward his account of mission will feature (in the words of *HE* I, 1 already quoted) "ambassadors of the word of God" who expressed themselves "by pen" rather than "by speech." Of course, the apologists he will highlight are precisely those whose statements of theology had been found acceptable by the church's highest authorities. With many fewer itinerants in the narrative and a decision to emphasize doctrinal conformity, the charismatic quality of faith-sharing recedes.

Both Eusebius and Bede show a willingness to designate God's choice in the political battles raging around them. When Eusebius expresses his wholehearted preference for Constantine, he sets the stage for the possibility of a Christian nation and the prospect of a joint mission by church and state. Eusebius will commit explicitly to such a program in his later writings, but we can see the germ of this idea already in place when Constantine is praised for having "cleansed the whole world of all the wicked and baneful persons and of the cruel God-hating tyrants themselves" (*HE* X, 4, 60). Bede shows the same inclination as he evaluates in Deuteronomistic terms the various kings whose stories have come down to him. Heading Bede's list of model monarchs are Edwin ("he labored for the kingdom of Christ"), Oswald ("the most Christian king of the Northumbrians"), and Oswy, who "not only . . . deliver[ed] his own people from the hostile attacks of the heathen, but after cutting off their infidel head he converted the Mercians and their neighbors to the Christian Faith" (*EH* II, 20; III, 9, 24).

In their zeal for orthodoxy, ecclesiastical historians are more apt to emphasize the differences they perceive among Christians than did Luke, who downplayed controversy while promoting an image of unity within the body of Christ. Confirmed heretics already delivered over to the service of the devil may be beyond redemption. Confused or misguided Christians, on the other hand, could be corrected and so reclaimed for the one true faith. By such reasoning, ecclesiastical historians created conceptual space in which to treat the reevangelization of "nominal" Christians as a form of mission. For Bede this aspect of his historical task became a major preoccupation, because the type of Christianity he clearly preferred had to contend with established rivals that did not pattern themselves after Rome. There are moments in Bede's history when representatives of Celtic Christianity are dismissed editorially as unbelievers, because they adamantly refused to submit to newly arrived bishops and missionaries authorized by Rome (*EH* II, 2). A larger narrative arc, however, gives witness to an extended process of dialogue and engagement through which British, Pictish, Irish, and English speakers slowly become united in one church under Roman jurisdiction. Thus, we find in Bede a variety of mission initiatives presented together, ranging from pioneer efforts to create a church in the midst of thoroughly pagan Saxons to the conversion of Iona and its Irish monks to Roman liturgical customs.

The issues that most agitated Bede with respect to non-Roman Christianity tell us one more thing about his concept of mission and approach to mission history. Questions of authority aside, the problems that epitomized for him the waywardness of Celtic Christianity were two: the date of Easter they observed and their style of tonsure. From a modern perspective, such differences hardly seem worth the attention Bede gives them (Eusebius, too, worried about getting the date of Easter right), until one realizes that these factors of division were a means to monitor the reception of what this historian considered to be a normative Christian *culture*. Ramsay MacMullen's (1997, 150) observation on the aesthetic deficit of early Christianity suggests something about what had changed since the apostolic era:

> In the opening century or two of their existence as a religious community, Christians lacked a distinctive poetry, rhetoric, drama, architecture, painting, sculpture, music, or dance. . . . They had almost no special language of gestures or symbols in which to expresses their feelings or their wishes to, or regarding, the divine, such as pagans had developed.

By the time of Eusebius, the church had been reconceived as a culture-bearing institution, having finally acquired the means to construct its own religiously defined social world. Bede will be followed by many more church historians similarly eager to consider evangelization primarily to be a matter of Christianization, the spreading of Christian culture.

HAGIOGRAPHY

Bede has been criticized for having turned the history of mission into a political narrative (Wood 2001, 44–45). To be sure, his story of the church is so intently focused on the court of the king that the progress of the gospel in England from Kent to Northumbria seems to depend almost exclusively on royal decision-making and the force of arms. According to this way of understanding the evangelization process, the spread of Christianity normally proceeds from the top down, as missionaries and influential bishops successfully redirect the coercive power of monarchs toward divine goals. At the same time, by including hagiographical material in his account Bede allows the reader to see another level of religious culture at work, where the decrees of the sovereign cannot by themselves determine how Christian identity is formed and expressed. In this realm, saints—not kings—are the central characters in the drama, and sacred biography, rather than dynastic lore, is the chief means by which this part of the story is told. It is to Bede's credit that he made room in his church history for renowned missionary figures not entirely loyal to Rome, such as Columba (c. 521–97) and Aiden (d. 651).

For the premodern period, hagiography contributes in two specific ways to mission history. We have in the *Lives* of the saints, first of all, much material that potentially describes how certain individuals may have been active in the work of evangelism, particularly in Europe. Often, when sainted missionaries are given extended biographical treatment, their *Vitae* expand our knowledge of mission history by recalling the memory of persons otherwise unknown or obscure. An example might be someone like the aristocratic Sadalberga (c. 605–70), who established a convent in a border region of Frankland at Laon. Or the abbot Eustasius (d. 629), the successor of Columbanus (c. 543–615) at Luxeuil, who spearheaded a vigorous regional program of Christianization in which several strategically located convents like that of Sadalberga and a host of associated monasteries were vital institutional elements of a sustained missionary initiative. Frontier monks preached, planted new churches, disputed with pagans, uprooted their shrines, performed miracles, and baptized those willing to forsake the old ways. Pioneering nuns prayed fervently, copied books, served the poor around them, dispensed encouragement through their correspondence, and created cloistered communities into which unmarried female converts from paganism could be gathered and taught (McNamara 1996, 120–47). Other evangelizing saints not tied explicitly to existing Christian institutions have also been identified, as in the work of Andrea Sterk (2010a) on captive Christian women and their role in the conversion of Armenia, Georgia, and Yemen. Had the work of the hagiographers not survived, much less would be known today about such individuals or the processes by which monastic foundations participated in the evangelization of non-Christian peoples.

A second contribution of hagiography to mission history springs from its capacity to illuminate the everyday contexts in which late antique and medieval missionaries operated. Incidental details included in the texts can sometimes prove enormously valuable to the historian, especially when they point to local conditions or idiosyncratic behaviors that fall outside the usual expectations for how a saint's life ought to unfold. A group of *Vitae* produced soon after the lifetime of their subjects, for example, might help the historian to reconstruct with more certainty the political structures with which a generation of missionaries in a particular place had to engage. Other biographical materials might show how cross-cultural missionaries either conformed to or defied the dominant social attitudes and practices of the communities in which they labored, as they interacted with indigenous ideas about family, food, marriage, gender roles, foreigners, literacy, and social class. Considered apart from questions of facticity, reports of miracles performed by the saints can also be utilized to demonstrate how people in that context may have thought about many of life's basic challenges, such as illness, poverty, disability, death, and those phenomena most likely to have induced deep psychological fears (personal and communal).

Hagiography resists facile analysis, which means that reliable information about missionaries and their work is not always easy to recover from these documents. That is why it is necessary to use tentative language about the "capacity" or "potential" of hagiographical source materials to yield solid historical data. Many difficulties are created simply by the fact that these documents were never intended to be straightforward reportage. Hagiographers often wrote out of a desire to promote certain values and behaviors within the church by linking them to respected heroes of the faith. They hoped to inspire their audience to follow the saint's example and to demonstrate their own piety by participating in the cult that had grown up around the saint's memory. The interests of a particular cult center might even shape the telling of a saint's story, as Ian Wood (2001, 57–78, 100–122) has shown with respect to the different *Lives* of Boniface (c. 675–754) produced in Mainz, Fulda and Utrecht.

As with visual forms of iconography, artistic conventions soon developed for written hagiographical discourse that tended to reduce the number of ways in which a missionary saint was likely to be portrayed. Biblical templates (Elijah, Peter, Paul, Stephen, and, of course, Jesus) were perennially attractive. Certain saints like Martin of Tours (c. 316–97), Cuthbert (d. 687), Willibrord (c. 657–739), and Boniface became paradigmatic for succeeding generations, as their reputations broke through the limits of era and region (Breisach 1983, 98–99). Paganism, likewise, often lost its local flavoring when represented in the *Lives* of the saints. It was usually enough to credit the devil when opposition arose to Christian outreach or to fit actual pagan practices into a few familiar categories of superstitious belief and behavior.

Historians have good reason to be suspicious whenever later saints are shown performing the same (or very similar) acts of confrontation and wonderworking that made earlier evangelists famous. But even when proved to be largely fictitious, hagiographical accounts may still have something to contribute to the history of mission. The production of new *Vitae* may be evidence of Christianity having begun to take hold in a new location, since this literature tended to be used to teach the already baptized (Kuznetsova 2000, 125–26). And even when the interests of the hagiographer appear to overwhelm the particular concerns of the subject saint, an extant *Life* can continue to function as a historical artifact if it sheds light on what the writer's generation may have considered proper or normative missionary aims and methods. For a concise but detailed review of current scholarly trends in hagiographical analysis, students can consult Susan Ashbrook Harvey (2008, esp. 608–19).

EARLY MODERN ETHNOGRAPHY

An entirely new phase in the writing of mission history began in the sixteenth century, which should come as no surprise. The circumstances of the Western churches had changed dramatically since the time of the first evangelization of northern Europe. Most obviously, an Age of Discovery had opened up previously unknown worlds to European exploration, creating unprecedented possibilities for interreligious encounter. Increasingly mobile Western Christians found themselves face-to-face with many cultures and social practices not easy for them to understand. The urge to evangelize what was not Christian was immediate, persistent, and strong. The monarchs of Portugal and Spain cooperated with the papacy in a joint project of gospel preaching and church planting that was breathtaking in its worldwide scope. So it was that a burgeoning contingent of religious figures from the West took their places within and just beyond the European colonial infrastructures put together in the early modern period. Henceforth, any attempt to survey the spread and growth of Christianity would have to account for the effects of this decisive turn in the geopolitical situation of Christian missions.

The intellectual context for writing about mission history had also changed. Out of the Renaissance had arisen a humanist tradition of scholarship that searched for truth using nontheological sources and methods. At first, humanists focused their attention on the Greek and Roman heritage of classical antiquity. Thus, in the earliest phase of the Renaissance (fourteenth–fifteenth centuries), an expanding movement of scholars examined a rich trove of manuscripts, extant epigraphy, and (ruined) monuments in order to understand better the languages, literatures, and histories of ancient Greece and Rome. Eventually, the philological techniques developed in the course of these studies were applied more broadly, with the result that many more languages and cultures would take up residence within the disciplinary tent of the humanities. What tied the whole of these efforts together was a lasting ambition to describe the world as it really is, with increasing precision. Once the constant factor of change over time had also been acknowledged, this task necessarily took on a historical dimension.

No one would argue that Renaissance scholarship per se included within itself an interest in the history of Christian mission. Yet it seems incontrovertible that humanist learning shaped the outlooks of countless Roman Catholic missionaries in the early modern period, while also affecting their mission agendas. The influence of Renaissance humanism on the practice of mission is undeniable in the case of the Jesuits. Their schools, part of a sustained program to reevangelize Europe and disseminate Christianity in the regions beyond, were built around a curriculum (the *ratio studiorum*, finalized in 1599) that made the "humane letters" an indispensable foundation for the study of advanced philosophical and theological subjects (O'Malley 1993, 200–264). Jesuit scholastics were encouraged to read the pagan classics of Greece and Rome, in line with the humanist notion that good literature could stimulate the acquisition of virtue. Long years of study in the rhetorical arts, the fruits of which were demonstrated in regular public exercises featuring oratory, disputation, and theater performance, lay at the center of these educational efforts.

Having seriously engaged the secular aspects of European culture through their schooling, scores and then hundreds of Jesuit missionaries soon found themselves immersed in a diverse array of non-Christian contexts around the world.

Not all but many of these missionaries expressed through their actions and writings a resolve to discover values and social practices in their places of service that could be affirmed from a Christian point of view. When it appears in this era, genuine respect for cultural others encountered along the pathways of mission contrasts sharply with typically less generous medieval Christian thinking about pagan identity and belief. One has to go back to Origen and the second-century apologists to find anything remotely similar on this scale. The most celebrated early modern example of this orientation to cross-cultural mission is Matteo Ricci (1552–1610), whose careful evaluation of Confucianism in China is remarkable not only for its openness to a non-Western philosophical system but also for its theological agility and subtle pragmatism. Similarly intentioned, though less well regarded today, was the positive approach taken by Ricci's fellow Jesuit Roberto de Nobili (1577–1656) to the caste system of India and several related cultural traditions that defined elite Brahmin identity.

In the work of José de Acosta (1540–1600), we see the humanist impulse and global Catholic mission experience clearly intersecting with the development of mission historiography. By Jesuit standards, Acosta spent only a modest amount of time on the mission field in Peru (1572–86), but his impact was nevertheless considerable. He was an able administrator of a young province, a wily representative of Jesuit interests in the halls of colonial power, and an innovator in mission theory (Burgaleta 1999, 33–55).

For our purposes, Acosta's most important contribution to missiology is to be found in his groundbreaking 1590 study of the New World and its peoples: *Natural and Moral History of the Indies*. Although the actions of missionaries do not take up much room in Acosta's *Historia*, the subject of evangelization is never far from his mind. As he put it in the initial chapter of Book VII (Acosta 2002, 379–80), his account of the customs or mores (hence "moral" history) of the Indians shows them to be civilized in some respects, even "worthy of praise," and therefore capable of receiving the gospel (a hotly disputed claim in his own time). His expectation is that knowledge of these peoples will prove useful to those whom God has sent to labor in their midst as missionaries, because familiarity with native societies should enable better communication to take place across cultural boundaries. He hopes that readers of his book back in Spain who become better informed about this history will "be able to understand the means chosen by Most Holy God in sending to these nations the light of the gospels of his only begotten son Jesus Christ Our Lord." Even the natural history of the New World can have an evangelical purpose behind it, since learning more about the climate and physical features of the Indies and especially its strange natural wonders might well lead one to contemplate "the Highest and Supreme Artificer of all these marvels" (99).

Anthony Pagden (1982, 146–200) aptly characterizes the *Historia* and Acosta's earlier *De procuranda indorum salute* (1588) as a "programme for comparative ethnology." The comparative aspect of Acosta's project is reflected in the various ways he attempts to classify the native inhabitants of the New World. The most basic comparison he makes is between the Spanish and their newly acquired colonial subjects. Here he follows in the wake of the Dominican Bartolomé de Las Casas (1484–1566), who also argued for the common humanity of Amerindians and Europeans. In keeping with his training in Christian humanism, Acosta also makes reference to the ancient Greeks and Romans. These, he asserts, were "much superior" in "courage and natural intelligence" to the people of the New World, but their own heathen customs could be just as "inhuman and diabolical" as those of the Indians or even worse (Acosta 2002, 251). Acosta adds yet another dimension to his analysis by bringing into the discussion some of what he has learned about the cultures of Japan and China from his fellow Jesuits (for example, 284–85, 335–39). Acosta uses these data to conjecture a developmental scale of non-Christian barbarism that depends heavily on the acquisition of literacy. This conceptual scheme then allows him to differentiate among the various Indian groups of which he has some knowledge—in other words, to compare them to each other.

The Aztecs and Incas seemed to Acosta to be most like the sophisticated cultures of the Far East and so the readiest in the New World to receive the gospel. Their practices of government and social organization, their religious ceremonies and rites ("many of them resemble those of the ancient law of Moses; there are others like those used by the Moors, and others that somewhat resemble those of the Gospel law"; Acosta 2002, 312), their methods for calculating time (331–34), and their ability to record history (albeit using images or figures rather than letters and writing) all suggested to Acosta that a reasoned presentation of Christianity could be successful with these groups. More primitive forest-dwellers or unsettled nomads, in his view, could not become Christians without first being "taught to be men" (381).

Acosta's work put mission historiography on a new footing. He did this by shining a bright light on the physical and cultural environments in which mission takes place. At no point does he question the overriding effect of God's providence on human affairs. This conviction alone is enough to mark him out still as a pre-Enlightenment thinker. At the same time, he is clearly seeking to understand the natural and human variables that could shape evangelistic outcomes and so suggest the use of particular strategies for Christianization in different times and places.

Acosta's ethnographic sensibility would be carried forward into the seventeenth century, most notably by French Jesuits working in North America. These missionaries, too, were straining to comprehend the complex and unfamiliar native societies in which they worked. They recorded their findings in a series of edited annual letters published in France between 1632 and 1673. The letters, now known collectively as the Jesuit Relations, in effect constitute a contemporary running account of mission history. As might be expected, the missionaries highlighted their own efforts to convert the indigenous tribes of New France to Christianity, while also reporting on colonial and other European agents whose actions and agendas seemed either to be helping or hindering the progress of the mission. Mixed in are extended descriptions of cultural practices the missionaries observed during their long years of residence in native societies. Included is precious information about how the Indians hunted and fished, their family structures, social relations, migration patterns, housing practices, clothing, diet, and means of communication, plus their stories, myths, and religious rituals (a representative set of excerpts is presented in Greer 2000). In part, these data are exotica, a surefire way to excite and sustain enthusiasm for the Jesuits' work in North America within the mission's support base back in France. More fundamentally, one can see in this reporting an acknowledgment that mission history could no longer be written without attending to its cultural and physical context. The humanist perspective, applied to the experience of the church around the world acquired in the Age of Discovery, was prompting mission historians to think more deliberately and deeply about the cross-cultural aspects of evangelization.

HISTORICAL *MISSIONSWISSENSCHAFT*

In the aftermath of the Enlightenment, scholars in every field of knowledge came under pressure to demonstrate the scientific basis of their work, its essential rationality. Academic theology rose to the challenge, with a variety of strategies employed to defend the plausibility of Christian faith to publics less inclined than previous generations to accept the Bible as a self-authenticating source of truth. Historians of all kinds, including those focused on mission history, likewise found themselves pushed to adopt new modes of investigation and argument, as their discipline reached for greater precision and the elusive goal of scientific objectivity. Earlier forms of mission historiography continued to be practiced in the post-Enlightenment period, but they now had to compete with more critical approaches that did not assume the probability of divine intervention in history or the active presence of Satan in human affairs.

That Edward Gibbon's *History of the Decline and Fall of the Roman Empire* (1776–88) was a milestone on the way to more modern forms of history writing is beyond dispute. Gibbon sought to explain how a great empire had failed to survive. He wanted to know why a society so gifted in the arts of war, government, law, commerce, and the pursuit of virtue could have been undermined by lesser rivals. Gibbon describes in some detail the eventual success of Rome's barbarian conquerors, but his most fervent and conceptually significant passages are probably those in which the internal causes of the empire's demise are analyzed and deplored.

Gibbon understood the decline of Rome to be closely linked to the rise of Christianity. Thus, as he put it at the outset of chapter 15 in the *Decline and Fall*:

"A candid but rational inquiry into the progress and establishment of Christianity may be considered as a very essential part of the history of the Roman empire." Underlying this part of his investigation is Gibbon's intention to understand the social processes by which early Christianity gained its adherents and spread to new locations, which makes this aspect of his project a study of mission history. In the end, five reasons are advanced to explain the triumph of Christianity within what had been a thoroughly pagan Roman Empire: (1) "intolerant zeal" for orthodoxy, which strengthened the believers' sense of group solidarity; (2) the promise of a future life; (3) the primitive church's reputation for miracle working; (4) the perceived capacity of the gospel to improve morals; and (5) the institutional power afforded the Christian movement by the social organization of the church.

The adequacy of Gibbon's explanation for Christianity's success is not our concern here. The fundamental point lies rather in his proposal that ecclesiastical history (and thus, also, mission history) should be handled just like every other kind of historical study. Momigliano (1966, 52) puts this decision in context when he observes that "Gibbon followed Voltaire in boldly sweeping away every barrier between sacred history and profane history." Gibbon famously credits the "convincing evidence of the doctrine itself" and the "ruling providence" of God for Christianity's victory over the established religions of its day, but only a very naïve reader would take these words (again, in chapter 15) at face value. The whole of the *Decline and Fall* is about what Gibbon demurely suggests were the five "secondary causes" of Christian success named above. After the fact, in his *Memoirs* (1966, 157), Gibbon indicates plainly enough that a chief aim of his epic work was to examine "the *human* causes of the progress and establishment of Christianity" (emphasis in the original).

The overall effect of Gibbon's methodology is to separate history from theology. As a result, this new approach cannot be fitted into any of the categories of mission history reviewed thus far. Becoming more scientific will mean fewer (and then no) appeals to the guiding hand of divine providence to explain the workings of history. A key function of ecclesiastical history will also be lost or at least diminished, as historians of Christianity are relieved of their long-maintained responsibility to locate and illustrate real-life examples of theological norms put into practice. Once the historian dispenses with the metaphysical framework of Christian belief about the "life of the world to come," a need will be felt to supply another overarching narrative structure to take its place. No small number of non-theological candidates will be put forward in the ensuing centuries after Gibbon to encompass the history of the church and its mission. In this way, too, we shall find an increasingly secularized understanding of mission history slowly taking shape.

It turns out to be quite some time before a self-identified historian of mission is willing to commit to the path indicated by Gibbon's methods. Even Gustav Warneck (1834–1910), who may have done more than anyone else in the nineteenth century to put the study of mission on a scientific basis, still found the idea of providence an essential tool of historical explanation. Over long decades of careful research and close argument, Warneck worked tirelessly to raise the academic reputation of missiology, advancing the cause especially by founding in 1874 the discipline's first scholarly periodical (*Allgemeine Missions-Zeitschrift*). Yet in his comprehensive handbook to the field, *Evangelische Missionslehre* (1892–1903), doctrinal considerations clearly dominate, so much so that Jongeneel (1995, 79) will not consider Warneck to be the founder of a *Missionswissenschaft* (science of mission) but of the theology of mission (*Missionstheologie*).

The claims of theology are similarly evident in Warneck's influential history of Protestant missions (1906), where God is given credit for directing the actions of his missionary agents by "divine leadings" (173 and passim) and for choosing the right instruments from among the "explorers, merchants and colonial politicians" of Europe to "open up the doors of the world" for new evangelistic initiatives in the nineteenth century (214). In this way Warneck the historian of mission participates in and perpetuates a venerable tradition of providential historiography that reaches back to the apostolic era.

Closer to Gibbon's outlook and methodology is the history of early Christian mission produced by Adolf Harnack, already discussed briefly in chapter 2. In his approach to mission history, Harnack accepts Gibbon's insight that social factors of various kinds affected the development and spread of early Christianity. This conviction will lead him to describe a number of external and internal "conditions" that contributed to the success of Christianity, either by preparing the way for its reception or facilitating in some respect its rapid and far-reaching growth. Numerous communities of Jews in diaspora, for example, became incubators of small Christian fellowships, while also representing a more or less tolerated monotheistic alternative to official pagan belief. Other religious traditions and the ancient philosophical schools are credited with having cultivated and then failing to satisfy the deepest longings of those living around the Mediterranean basin. Above all, Harnack recognized the importance of the political and cultural context provided to Christianity by the Roman Empire, whose many nationalities were effectively drawn together by a common Hellenistic milieu through which new religious ideas could circulate far and wide: "the narrow world had become a wide world; the rent world had become a unity; the barbarian world had become Greek and Roman" (Harnack 1904, 23). Harnack's particular burden in his mission history was to show how Christianity had fortified itself with the power of Hellenism. This was a process of assimilation that not only enhanced the appeal of the new faith to Greek minds but also hastened the collapse of the old forms: "Christianity has throughout sucked the marrow of the ancient world. . . . The whole of [third-century] Catholicism is nothing else than the Christianity which has devoured the possessions of the Graeco-Roman world" (Harnack 1989, 192).

Like Gibbon, Harnack was also keen to separate history from theology and so establish it as a fully independent discipline. But he did so for his own purposes.

Gibbon's aim had been to free universal reason from the asserted prerogatives of revelation. As a committed Christian, Harnack sought to liberate the gospel from the inertia imposed on it by the accumulated weight of dogma. In Harnack's view, the science of history was the best means available to distinguish the eternal essence of the gospel from all time-bound forms of doctrine (including patristic theology and the historic creeds). For him, the duty of the historian "is to determine what is of permanent value" and what has had only a fleeting association with the gospel (Harnack 1957, 13–15). Harnack, therefore, demanded even more than history's right to a sphere of its own apart from theology. "Dogma," he maintained, "must be purified by history" (quoted in Frend 2001, 91).

At first glance, Kenneth Scott Latourette (1884–1968) might appear to be an unlikely party to the emerging scientific tradition of mission historiography initiated by Gibbon and Harnack. Latourette by no means shared Gibbon's regretful suspicion that Christianity had succeeded at the expense of a virtuously pagan Rome. Nor did he advocate with Harnack for an idea of pure Christianity against all forms of the church on earth and its doctrinal patrimony. But he did seek to write as a professional historian, whose office obliged the modern scholar to differentiate his personal faith views from the requirements of rational inquiry. That he had such convictions and wanted very much to share them with colleagues in the academy is evident from his presidential address to the American Historical Association (Latourette 1949) and from hints sprinkled here and there within the seven volumes of his *History of the Expansion of Christianity* (1937–45; for intimations of Latourette's faith stance in his history of mission, see, for example, vol. 1: xvii–xviii, 240–42, 290–91; vol. 7: 481–82, 504–5). Walls (2002a, 8) recognizes the tension inherent in Latourette's approach, when he observes:

> As a Christian, [Latourette] believes in a divine purpose for the world behind history. He is also by instinct and training a post-Enlightenment Western historian, for whom such factors should play no part in historical discourse.

Latourette's quest for scientific objectivity led to some crucial methodological decisions on his part. One was to affect an indirect manner when referring to the faith claims of Christians. We find this, for example, in the way Latourette handles the issue of Jesus' resurrection. It was not appropriate for modern historians to testify that God raised Jesus from the dead, but they might talk about the confidence of the disciples that such an event had happened (1937, 60). Nor could they substantiate the occurrence of miracles in the time of Jesus or later, but it was possible to demonstrate that believing in miracles was a "normal and persistent feature of Christianity" (1937, 323) until modern times and was often associated in the sources with reports of conversion. Latourette applies the same logic on a larger scale when he asks about the influence of Jesus on succeeding generations of Christians. The "possible cosmic significance" of the "Jesus impulse" is ruled to be an improper subject for the historian (1937, 168), but "the effect of

Christianity upon its environment" could be studied sociologically alongside "the effect of the environment upon Christianity" and its mission. When Latourette decides to put these two interrelated concerns at the heart of his project (they are used to summarize and evaluate each major era of his mission history), he applies himself to the same kind of historical *Missionswissenschaft* project Gibbon and Harnack had pioneered before his time.

CRITICAL ETHNOGRAPHY

For a final category of mission historiography, I have chosen to use the term "critical ethnography." For my purposes, this designation will represent a loose collection of subdisciplines whose late-twentieth-century participants understood themselves to be historians, social scientists, or both. Included in this grouping are students of mission who have used the techniques of microhistory, interpretive anthropology, historical anthropology, and sociology of religion. Ideas and influences from semiotics, feminist studies, and postcolonial literary criticism permeate these approaches to mission history. An emphasis on cultural description links this broad-based community of scholars back to the work of the early modern ethnographers already discussed. Even so, this kind of history writing about mission is a departure from long-established points of view and practices in several respects. Few critical ethnographers today, if any, would presume to occupy value-free zones of scientific objectivity and, in fact, expect each other to account for the social positions from which they write. They are wary of past claims made for human progress in history and insist that the widely assumed benefits of modernity, development, and globalization be scrutinized carefully (less skepticism, on the whole, is applied to the idea of secularism). These experts generally strive to show respect for all cultures, while remaining on guard against every form of ethnocentrism.

Critical ethnography is characterized by several habits of analysis that can affect the practice of mission historiography. One is a preference for intensive research on a small scale, where the rich detail of a local context can be fully appreciated. Instead of a bird's-eye view of human experience gathered over centuries and across continents, these scholars seek to understand how particular groups of people lived in specific historical settings. In this kind of history, culture is defined above all by the ordinary transactions of life that often do not receive explicit attention in the sources, usually because they seemed routine and therefore unremarkable to the people of that time and place.

Corresponding to the microdimensions of critical ethnography is an interest in the less powerful members of the communities under study. From the side of history, these are the twice-marginalized: first, by the economic, political, and other hegemonic forces that produced and maintained their social disadvantage and then through the stories told about their times, in which the losers are not allowed to play any significant part except as foils for the winners, who boldly assert through their narratives what they believe to be immutable standards of orthodoxy and cultural identity. It follows that critical ethnography can be doubly alternative. Not only does it feature those previously considered inconspicuous and of little account, but this fresh perspective "from below" implicitly challenges the veracity and completeness of many received accounts.

How does one do this kind of history? Two trends stand out. The first is a move to identify nonliterary sources of data that can shed light on the lives of the otherwise inarticulate. In the aggregate, for example, the poor and working classes may have left their imprint in the buildings and other structures they used for dwelling and working. Additional aspects of material culture may be revealed when local market economies are studied, if such research is able to show how, when, and with whom people traded and the relative value of items used every day by most people (such as foodstuffs, utensils, and tools). Or, following the lead of interpretive anthropologist Clifford Geertz (1973), one can seek to understand the symbolic world of the common person by analyzing ritual performances and other forms of self-expression. Observable behaviors associated with festivals, games, and burial practices, for example, represent a different kind of window onto the history of a people than that provided by the cataclysmic events and dominant personalities so often memorialized in "high" literary texts and great works of art.

A second way to get at the life of nonelites is to reread familiar texts "against the grain," with an eye for supporting characters and hidden themes. Especially when using materials created by missionaries (or sending organizations) to explain their work to supporting constituencies, one has to consider how the needs of each group may have shaped this literature. Dramatic stories of missionary success in the face of daunting resistance met the expectations of many domestic audiences. There were fewer incentives to highlight native agency and indispensability. Thus, a crucial task for mission historiography undertaken as critical ethnography is to exegete the archives (Sebastian 2003), which involves looking around the narrative periphery of extant reports, journals, diaries, and letters, among other sources, in order to hear suppressed voices speaking from the past. Assistant translators and Bible women, native evangelists and rural catechists, plus a host of unnamed but powerful indigenous witnesses to the Christian faith in countless local contexts, are among the background figures whose roles in the modern missionary movement are not well developed in the standard accounts assembled by missionaries. Similar patterns of under-representation may be observed for earlier periods of Christian mission, stretching back to the apostolic era (Skreslet 2006b, 79–117).

The kind of mission historiography I have been describing in general terms is exemplified in the ethnographic work of Jean and John L. Comaroff (1991, 1992, 1997). Over more than thirty years, the Comaroffs have been writing about the Southern Tswana, a loose assemblage of African people located north of the

Orange River whose lands were incorporated into the Union of South Africa in 1910. Much of this research is focused on the social processes by which the Tswana were brought under imperial control and eventually dispossessed. British Nonconformist missionaries, most of them sponsored by the London Missionary Society or the Wesleyan Methodist Missionary Society, are deeply implicated in the historical account of native subjugation constructed by the Comaroffs. Having begun their work among the Tswana early in the nineteenth century, well before the launching of an irresistible, direct push of colonial power from the south, pioneering evangelists and educators are portrayed in this story as the leading edge of European advance into what had been an isolated realm of premodern African culture. Their role, according to the Comaroffs, was to dominate the consciousness of the Tswana and so prepare the way for physical colonization. The missionaries were thus "vanguards of imperialism" (1991, 36), "human vehicles of a hegemonic worldview" (310), "the ideological arm of empire" (314). Conversion in these circumstances could mean the acceptance of a religious message at some level. It necessarily involved the forced induction of the Tswana into a globalized order of Western modernity (1991, 4; 1997, 407).

The Comaroffs characterize their work as "history in the anthropological mode" (1991, 38). In this analysis, missionary intentions and professed aims are less important to understand than the effects of missionary action. Much attention is paid to how the Tswana are represented in the textual record produced by the missionaries, since this was a way to objectify and assert control over those being colonized (akin to the Orientalist discourse so vividly described by the literary and cultural critic Edward Said). Related to this concern is the question of native agency: To what extent were the Tswana able to determine or affect the terms of their colonization? A dialectic or "long conversation" between two conceptual worlds is proposed as the interpretive device that best explains what was going on in this missionary encounter. Both sides of the ledger depend on missionary-generated texts, but additional materials are needed to reconstruct the Southern Tswana point of view. What the Comaroffs (1997, 53) say about their use of sources could be applied more generally to the methods of critical ethnography:

> Often we have no alternative but to work with a highly distorted, disproportionate documentary record. And so we have to make our own archive by disinterring Southern Tswana gestures and acts and utterances from the writing of non-Tswana; in particular, by reading these orthogonally and against each other. But we do not stop there either. We also look to whatever vernacular traces have been left on the landscape, whether they be narrative fragments or private correspondence, praise poetry or buildings, ritual practices or Tswana-authored history books; indeed any of the manifold signs and artifacts that make their appearance in the three volumes that [will] compose this study.

Critical ethnography tends to disparage the missionary enterprise as a self-interested Western intrusion into the lives of others. The work of the Comaroffs is exemplary in this respect, too. But their perspective is not universally held within the ranks of those who study the history of mission as secular historians or social scientists. John Peel's history of the Yoruba in Nigeria (2000), for example, attends to many of the same issues of power highlighted by the Comaroffs but does not reduce the idea of evangelization to a metropolitan project imposed on unwilling non-Western recipients. Peel puts emphasis on the many ways Yoruba Christians chose to appropriate their new religious identity, rather than concentrating primarily on how missionaries attempted to transform mental and physical landscapes (without denying that they tried to do both). This kind of critical ethnography, organized around the concept of dynamic religious change, invites the researcher to consider the broadest possible set of indigenous responses to a variety of missionary messages (presented on more than one level), without determining in advance which replies might represent steps forward toward a fully human existence and which ones necessarily imply regress.

CURRENT TRENDS IN RESEARCH

Scholarly interest in mission history is remarkably strong today. Forty years ago, when Harvard Sinologist John King Fairbank (1969, 877) called the foreign missionary the "invisible man of American history," few would have predicted this development. At the height of decolonization in the 1960s, mission history seemed a quaint relic of a bygone era, so much so that even church historians were turning away from mission-related topics. A shift of interest back to mission history became possible in the 1980s only after a growing number of scholars began to realize how often missionaries and the cross-cultural work they did were, in fact, intimately connected to a number of subjects these historians were fully committed to study. Most of this section will be given over to a brief description of several such clusters of current research on the history of mission, in order to get a sense of where this part of the field of missiology seems to be headed. Alert readers will notice that the last two centuries of mission history receive most of the attention given in the paragraphs that follow, a reflection not of my own research interests but of what I perceive to be the most intensely studied mission history topics at the present time. A few thoughts on some special problems that bear on the writing of mission history today will round out this chapter.

Missions and Imperialism

The past decade has seen a spate of new publications on the modern missionary movement and its relationship to imperialism. While no one seems to be disputing the fact that active collaboration took place, it is by no means taken as proven that the purposes of European colonialism and Christian mission were essentially in alignment with each other or that missionaries had largely conceded the subordination of their project to the needs of the imperialist system. In this ongoing conversation the position of the Comaroffs continues to exert force and has attracted enthusiastic support from other anthropologists, literary critics, and postcolonial theorists (Etherington 2005b, 4). Many historians, in contrast, have been more cautious. Andrew Porter, for example, argues in his wide-ranging study of Protestant missions and the British Empire (2004) that their relationship was more often than not "ambiguous." He highlights the ever-present need of missionaries to be accepted by the local societies in which they resided long-term, a factor that made them more responsive to indigenous values and desires than colonial officials or settler communities ever wanted to be. Dana Robert (2008) points to the resolve of many missionaries to "convert" colonialism, to make it serve the larger purposes of Christian mission rather than the other way around. A growing number of studies (for example, Brock 2005b) seek to clarify the crucial role played by local evangelists, whose numbers everywhere dwarfed those of workers from abroad and so cast into doubt the capacity of foreign missionaries to control the Christianization process over time. Some of these, it is true, were on the payroll of the missions, but many more indigenous witnesses to Christian faith were not and the lack of direct ties to outsiders may have made them all the more convincing representatives of this new religious point of view.

The Spread of Western Science

A second group of studies takes up the question of modern missions and their role in the spread of a Western scientific worldview. The Jesuits in China continue to figure in some of this research, since the "Learning from Heaven" they promulgated among the elites of Chinese society included teaching on scientific subjects (Brockey 2007, 46). The most eminent of the Jesuit mathematicians and astronomers earned respect for their religious order at the court of the emperor and through their publications and conversations with Confucian scholars gained a limited hearing for the Christian message in academic circles. This was an instrumental use of scientific knowledge, a matter of creating access for other work and enhancing the reputation of the Jesuit enterprise as a whole.

Following the Enlightenment, another kind of relationship between Western science and Christian mission slowly emerged, one in which modernity itself became an ingrained aspect of the missionary message being proclaimed by word and deed. Thus, we find missionaries in the nineteenth century beginning to borrow heavily from the language of the Enlightenment (a trend already evident within eighteenth-century Evangelicalism) to explain their purposes and engage audiences. They eagerly incorporated into their missionary propaganda the latest news of technological advancement in the West, in order to demonstrate the vigor and generative power of Western cultures. For some, mission would be entirely reconceived as a civilizing venture, with education and the improvement of social conditions put at the center of their efforts. Many missionaries in the nineteenth and early twentieth centuries saw great promise in the relentless power of modernity to break down resistance to Christian outreach within traditional non-Western cultures and religious systems.

David Bosch can be given credit for stimulating the latest round of missiological research on the Enlightenment. His fresh and substantial treatment of "mission in the wake of the Enlightenment" (1991, 262–345) shows how the modern missionary movement was profoundly a "child of the Enlightenment" (274). Another landmark in this discussion is the set of essays edited by Brian Stanley under the title *Christian Missions and the Enlightenment* (2001). The contributors to Stanley's volume essentially reaffirm Bosch's argument that modern Protestant evangelical missions were deeply influenced by Enlightenment emphases and axioms, often in ways not fully understood by the missionaries themselves or the leaders of the broader movement in which they participated.

Subsequent studies have explored a variety of themes related to the worldwide diffusion of modern ideas and mores by means of Christian mission. An example is Eliza F. Kent's study of book culture and clothing norms promoted by British missionaries in colonial South India (2005). Next to this we might put John M. MacKenzie's work on the aesthetics of the mission station in southern Africa (2003), where landscapes and social arrangements were mapped out according to what were thought to be scientific principles. Yet another direction has been taken by Heather J. Sharkey (2008), who has examined some missionary contributions to a global modern discourse on human rights that developed over the course of the twentieth century. In each of these three cases (and many, many more not mentioned here), mission history has shown itself to be a fertile environment indeed for the study of modernity and its manifold effects around the world.

Gender Studies and Mission Research

A third cluster of recent work within mission history has revolved around gender issues. Some of this research has been biographical in nature, as scholars have sought to unearth the hidden history of evangelism undertaken by missionary wives, Catholic women religious, and legions of Protestant single female missionaries. A first step has been to tell more of these stories in order to supplement and fill out the master narrative of mission history that until recently had been defined almost exclusively by the actions and decisions of men. Next to this desire to encompass more foreign missionary voices within the archive has been a strong push to know more about non-Western Christian women and their participation in the modern missionary movement. Prominent within this group of studies on female missionary agents is the figure of the native Bible woman, who did much of the daily work of Christian outreach (especially in rural settings) for which others often took credit in their official reports and journals. A recent issue of *Women's History Review* (September 2008) dedicated to the topic of "transnational Biblewomen" demonstrates the salience of this subtopic within contemporary scholarship on the history of women in mission.

As the treasury of biographical materials related to missionary women became larger, the conceptual tools needed to analyze both new and old data have also been revised. Intense interest has been focused on the question of gender roles in mission. It is established beyond doubt that many foreign women missionaries found in their work abroad unprecedented opportunities for stepping outside the professional constraints placed on them back home. In certain circumstances, women missionaries preached, itinerated as evangelists, and produced new translations of the Bible (Robert 1993). Some were able to lead congregations (Grimshaw and Sherlock 2005, 188). Many more served as professional educators and administrators, with some founding their own schools or institutes. Others practiced medicine. Equally clear is the fact that exposure to literacy and other forms of mission-based training and education enabled countless indigenous women to reenvision their professional and personal identities.

Of course, new roles for women in mission did not develop in isolation from everything else taking place under the banner of cross-cultural evangelization. Some male missionaries and mission executives, for example, were motivated to reconsider their own conceptions of the missionary task in the light of women's mission experience, as Rhonda Anne Semple (2003, esp. 206–28) has shown with respect to a select group of British missions in the Victorian era. In North America a rising tide of female candidates after the Civil War prompted the creation of autonomous women's mission organizations that to some degree cooperated with but also competed against male-dominated denominational structures. A slogan developed at the time—"woman's work for woman"—lent conceptual coherence to this departure from earlier patterns of mission practice, which had tended to feature ordained male missionaries, the planting of local churches, and aggressive conversionist tactics. As the cadre of female missionaries from the West grew, a turn was also made to address more directly the particular needs of women and girls in traditional societies, especially by devising ways to visit women kept in seclusion (so-called *zenana* missions), establishing orphanages, and increasing access to female education. In this approach to mission, mothers and future homemakers were thought to be the critical hinge on which the Christian conversion of any society absolutely depended.

In fact, "woman's work for woman" was just one of the ways that female perspectives were applied to mission theory over the nineteenth and twentieth centuries. An earlier formulation centered on the ideal "Christian home" that missionaries and their wives were encouraged to establish in non-Western societies as an object lesson for the curious. "Woman's work for woman" was centrifugal in nature, an impulse that sought to engage the woeful realities of women and children outside the missionary compound. Antebellum notions of the "Christian home," on the other hand, assumed that missionary wives would be too busy caring for their own families in primitive circumstances to be able to function as full-time professional missionaries. Theirs was to exhibit for all to see what a model evangelical home looked like, in hopes that indigenous neighbors would be attracted to the underlying religious philosophy of what was in truth an amalgam of Western domestic cultural practices and faith-based commitments.

The work of Dana L. Robert (1993, 1997, 2008, esp. 134–65) is foundational for an understanding of women and their role in the crafting of mission theory in the modern era. Beside her observations on "woman's work for woman" and the "Christian home," Robert has identified a third theory of mission grounded in female experience: "world friendship" (1997, 255–316). In this approach to mission, developed after the devastations of the World War I, issues of justice, world peace, and internationalist concern received priority. The idea of sisterhood continued to be vital but was reinterpreted in terms of mutuality and reciprocity rather than resting on a sense of maternal responsibility to lift mission daughters up out of the cultural degradation that was their unfortunate lot. The new watchword for mainline Protestant women in mission became "partnership." A strengthening ecumenical movement in the early twentieth century reinforced this shift toward the theme of world friendship.

FORWARD IN MISSION HISTORY

The mass of research surveyed in this chapter brings to mind several problems that pertain to the writing of mission history today. The first has to do with perspective. If one accepts the expansive definition of missiology with which we began ("the systematic study of all aspects of mission"), then it should be expected that those contributing to mission historiography will bring more than one point of view to this task. There will be proponents of Christian mission among these historians as well as diehard critics. Some scholars may have actual mission experience in their background, which raises again the old conundrum about whether insiders or outsiders are better positioned to write objective history. Competent historians, in any case, will have to sort out the usual questions of agency and causation in history, about what might constitute an objective fact and the need to differentiate between perceptions of an event and the actual occurrence itself.

Mission history can be controversial, especially when ideological or theological convictions are put into play. Apologetics on behalf of Christian mission, as a rule, cannot be substituted for serious historiography. Strident secularism, likewise, can impede understanding by deciding for others what religious beliefs and behaviors necessarily signify. A challenge for the near future is to expand the dialogue among scholars of mission history, so that it will continue to grow into something more than an intramural squabble over cultural values among Westerners. As Tinyiko Sam Maluleke (2000) has observed, what is required for the next stage of mission historiography is much more than a matter of including new voices from the past. Old frameworks of interpretation and established discourses about mission (both positive and negative, in my view) also have to be interrogated. This means including in the conversation historians of mission from around the world who identify as Christians or even as converts to Christianity, along with others in those same societies who write critically about the history of mission from outside the churches.

Another set of needs pressing hard on the agenda of mission historiography has been created by the unprecedented growth that has taken place in world Christianity. Thanks to the work of Andrew Walls (2002a, 3–71), Lamin Sanneh (2008), and others, it is now a commonplace to observe that precipitous twentieth-century declines in North Atlantic Christianity have been offset by significant additions elsewhere. These gains cannot be attributed to the natural growth of existing Christian communities. Especially in China and sub-Saharan Africa, movements of conversion to Christianity seem to have taken place in response to fervent and sustained evangelistic appeals. That the rate of growth has been so strong in these particular places over the past half century has come as a great surprise to many. As noted at the beginning of this book, it was widely believed at the end of the colonial era that newly established churches outside the West would quietly disappear once the coercive power of imperial rule had been withdrawn, bringing the latest phase of missionary expansion to a firm and decisive close.

Writing about the history of mission since decolonization has just begun, but already several new problems associated with this endeavor have become evident. Chief among these is the situation of the archives. With what resources will scholars in the future write this history? Unlike the previous few centuries, when relatively few mission organizations accounted for much of the activity taking place at any given moment, we now have a plethora of groups spearheading a polycentric array of projects and initiatives. The number of languages employed is virtually unlimited. Few of these organizations have the wherewithal to keep good records of their work and, increasingly, documents are not published on paper any more but kept electronically for uncertain periods of time. If we can be sure of one thing, it is that scholars of postcolonial mission will not have at their disposal the same kind of documentation and archival resources on which those studying the history of modern-era missions have come to depend.

Whatever the challenges might be, the prospects for mission historiography are nevertheless bright. One reason to be hopeful is grounded in the capacity of the Internet to provide wider access to existing archival holdings. Mission photography, for example, is increasingly available in digital formats, with many collections now posted on the website of the University of Southern California's Internet Mission Photography Archive. We can expect considerable numbers of current and future images of mission to be preserved in this way. Many libraries are likewise acting to digitize older manuscript materials and other documents, a move that will reduce the need of some researchers to travel to collections.

New ways for scholars around the world to collaborate on historiographical projects are also beginning to emerge. The Dictionary of African Christian Biography (DACB)—multilingual, open-ended, and presented entirely online—has already rendered invaluable service to the study of Christianity and mission in postcolonial Africa. An accompanying program (Project Luke) to train historians as regional consultants to the DACB is another model worthy of emulation. Finally, mention should be made of the Documentation, Archives, Bibliography, and Oral History Study Group (DABOH) of the International Association for Mission Studies. Most recently, DABOH has focused on the difficulties involved in documenting world Christianity in the twenty-first century. Consultations organized through DABOH have enabled librarians from around the world, plus historians, mission professors, and others, to share information and experience regarding the collection of oral history materials, to seek new ways to increase international cooperation among institutions, and to advise each other about how best to organize and manage the next generation of mission document depositories in support of future scholars and their research.

4

Theology, Mission, Culture

Within the realm of missiology, culture becomes a primary conversation partner with theology, on a par with philosophy or science. Cross-cultural missionary encounters especially invite questions about how faith convictions interact with cultural realities. At issue is not just the need to recognize the inevitable effects of culture on the practice of theology or on the performance of faith in community. Missiologists also want to know about the communication of religious (and other) messages across linguistic and cultural frontiers, the role of missionaries as agents of social change, the complex processes that shape the formation of new churches, and how nascent communities of faith work out their own theologies in a variety of local circumstances.

Since no culture is static, one can assume that even established theological positions have to be in constant conversation with matters of culture, whether explicitly or not. In the context of mission, this dialogue speeds up and often takes on a sense of urgency. What may have been contemplated only in the abstract now confronts the would-be evangelist in an embodied form. Submerged values and taken-for-granted assumptions about Christian norms may be brought to the surface and demand to be examined. In some cases, mission experience completely transforms the messengers, with the result that initial or received views on proper belief and appropriate ritual practices or the evaluation of particular faith cultures, including one's own, undergo radical revision. At other times, evangelistic encounter is ultimately about the effect of missionaries and their organizations on others. Persistently, the global scale of Christian mission and the thoroughly international character of the worldwide community produced by these efforts push theologians to consider ever larger slices of human experience as they reflect on universal questions of meaning and truth.

The aim of this chapter is to explore how missiology relates both to theology and the study of culture. I propose to begin by considering several classical topics connected to systematic theology with proven relevance for the conceptualization of mission. At several points, this discussion will expand on material initially presented in chapter 2 (Bible and Mission). A second major section will consider culture studies as an aspect of missiology. Emphasis here will fall on the capacity of such research to explain what might be taking place in the midst of missionary encounter besides a contest of beliefs. The ground having been prepared, we will then look at several kinds of missiological analysis that self-consciously build on the work of theologians and cultural scholarship at the same time. A brief concluding section will suggest how this part of missiology might pertain to students of theology and culture more generally.

THEOLOGY AND THE STUDY OF MISSION

Salvation

Some notion of salvation lies at the base of every theology of mission. In fact, it could be said that this aspect of theology is more likely to determine the character of one's mission practice than any other doctrinal consideration. Biblical thinking about soteriology presupposes the active participation of God in the salvation process, since it assumes that human beings cannot save themselves. Within the smaller circle of the New Testament canon, a similar consensus has formed around the idea of Jesus Christ as God's indispensable mediator of saving grace. Beyond these two basic convictions, the Christian scriptures offer support for multiple understandings of salvation as a theological construct.

Through the centuries, debates within the church over the meaning of salvation have typically revolved around a series of key questions. Some of these ask, for example, about the nature and scope of salvation. Is salvation about human fulfillment, unity with God, eternal life for believers, or some other end? Who or what might be involved when God acts to save: the souls of individuals, a community of faith, all of humanity, the entire cosmos? Equally perplexing is the issue of timing. Is salvation something that essentially takes place in the past, the present, or the future (or outside of time altogether)? All at once or in stages? Theologians also wonder about the mechanisms of salvation. How is it accomplished? Can human beings participate in God's saving activity? The various metaphors invoked to represent the idea of salvation in biblical theology give vivid witness to its many possible facets. Salvation has been portrayed as a matter of deliverance from danger, redemption from judgment, victory over the powers of evil, the making of friends among enemies.

When an attenuated understanding of salvation becomes a primary lens through which to view mission, the set of practices adopted to express this conception may appear to be eccentric or unbalanced. Some world-denying gnostics in antiquity, for example, picturing salvation in terms of escape from a created order altogether compromised by evil, made it their mission to find a few worthy candidates to initiate into the mysteries of their select and insular company. What then to make of the command to love one's neighbor (an alternative approach to mission widely embraced by the early church and then enacted through many works of compassion) or the joyous declaration of Jesus that God's rule had already begun to transform the creation? Oddly skewed, too, was the behavior of the first missionaries with Columbus in the New World, who rushed everywhere to baptize quickly as many children as possible in the midst of the Amerindian genocide going on around them (Las Casas 1992, 48–53). Sometimes the future aspect of salvation receives undue emphasis in missionary preaching. The result can be a reading of current events that too confidently fits them into precise apocalyptic scenarios and then makes those scripts the content of the church's message to the world. Christian proclamation based on this kind of soteriological foundation may end up reducing the community's missionary mandate to little more than a matter of disseminating speculative information about a largely unknown near-term future.

In Bosch's view (1991, esp. 393–400), the story of mission theology since the Reformation can be summed up as a long struggle to generate more comprehensive models of salvation. The first challenge was to break free of entrenched medieval atonement theories that supposed salvation to be a kind of metaphysical transaction, as in the formulation of Anselm (c. 1033–1109) where Christ's expiatory sacrifice on the cross is thought to have satisfied the wounded honor of God. Alternative approaches developed through the modern era increasingly emphasized the human ethical response to whatever God may have accomplished in Christ. Salvation, seen from this perspective, is more about the attainment of well-being in the here-and-now than it is a future state, and human beings are given substantial responsibility for the realization of God's promises. Liberationist proposals developed from the 1960s represent one form of this aspiration, with justice made the standard by which the achievement of salvation could be measured. More expansive yet is the concept of salvation put forward by Johannes Hoekendijk (1950), noted earlier, which features the biblical value of *shalom* as its primary motif. For Hoekendijk, *shalom* stands not only for the divine future vision of an ideal social order but also for God's desire that peace and harmony be restored throughout the creation now. Mission initiatives based on the ideas of Hoekendijk or some form of liberation theology tend to be socially activist in their orientation. A premium is put on doing the will of God as exemplified in the earthly career of Jesus, who identified with the poor and addressed their most urgent human needs, while opposing the religious and civil powers that oppressed them. This is quite a different agenda for mission than that usually assumed in premodern times, when most missionaries thought it their particular task to inform new groups of non-Christians about what God had done on their behalf elsewhere and to offer an effective means (preeminently baptism) by which the transcendent benefits of divine action could be transferred to sinners.

Calls to integrate the "horizontal" and "vertical" elements of salvation within mission theology intensified over the last quarter of the twentieth century. Bosch's own contribution to this effort (1991, 511–19) was to juxtapose "six salvific events" portrayed in the New Testament (incarnation, cross, resurrection, ascension, Pentecost, and parousia) that, together, suggested to him the direction in which mission theology should go next. Bosch insisted that no theology of mission could be truly comprehensive unless it encompassed and reflected the whole of what God had done (or promised to do) through Christ on behalf of a fallen creation.

The inchoate nature of Bosch's proposal reflected his sense of an "emerging" postmodern paradigm for ecumenical mission theology that hadn't yet coalesced by the end of the 1980s. Writing over the following decade, Robert Schreiter (1992, 1996) and others made a case for reconciliation (the biblical roots of which have already been briefly described in chapter 2) as the integrative metaphor for mission and ministry that spoke most directly to the circumstances of the church in a rapidly changing global environment. The end of the Cold War, the fall of apartheid in South Africa, and the return of democracy to several Latin American countries previously under harsh military rule were all welcome developments that pointed to the possibility of a fresh start in geopolitics. But what should be done with the unpleasant residue left behind in each of these situations: legacies of violence that continued to haunt the survivors, histories of collaboration with unjust regimes, and the lingering hope of countless victims to be made whole? The New World Order in no time also bore on itself the tragic marks of savage interethnic conflicts in the former Yugoslavia and Rwanda. Brutal acts of destruction carried out in the name of Islam soon became another distinguishing characteristic of the new age.

Reconciliation is a response to suffering that yearns for more than the punishment of past crimes. It presupposes the establishment of justice, according to Schreiter (1992, 18–25, 65), and then asks about how to heal societies and human relationships disfigured by violence. Reconciliation requires a truthful accounting of the past, in order to lay bare the need for genuine repentance. Here salvation is a matter of repair, an intention to rebuild or restore what power and coercive force have battered and damaged. Christians cannot claim to be the world's only possible human agents of reconciliation, but Schreiter reminds us (1992, 61) that they bring to this task a singular asset: a foundational narrative in which violence, suffering, and the profound difficulties standing in the way of reconciliation are honestly faced. On the basis of this story (perhaps *only* on these grounds), it becomes possible to construct a "theology of embrace" (Volf 1996) strong enough to withstand the unforgiving logic of retaliation. At its last quadrennial meeting (2008), the International Association for Mission Studies chose to focus on "the gospel of reconciliation" and the problem of human identity. The continuing appeal of reconciliation as an organizing concept for mission theology is further reflected in the recent call to recognize this form of peacemaking as the "heart of mission" (Langmead 2008, 18).

Ecclesiology

Sooner or later, every discussion of salvation in Christian theology is obliged to take up the topic of ecclesiology. By the same token, many theologians have found it difficult to understand the nature of the church fully without also considering its relationship to mission. Thus, it often happens that the concepts of salvation, church, and mission are bound up together in systematic theology, although not always with the same result.

When Jesus sent his disciples out to proclaim the reign of God and to heal (Luke 9:1–2), he initiated the church's mission. Subsequently, an experience of the Holy Spirit compelled the followers of Jesus to speak in many languages about "God's deeds of power" (Acts 2:11). Within the first generation after Pentecost, the church's efforts at outreach extended far beyond the territory of Palestine, resulting in the establishment of congregations from Damascus to Rome. The particular gifts of apostles and evangelists were recognized within the company of believers, but the need for corporate witness was nonetheless maintained. Even Paul, perhaps the most independent of the apostles, made it clear in his correspondence that he expected the churches he founded to partner with him in preaching the gospel. In fact, we might well conclude that Paul had the freedom to decide to work where there were no churches (a preference announced in Rom. 15:20 and 2 Cor. 10:15–16), only because he could count on the effective witness of already existing congregations, as in Thessaloniki: "For the word of the Lord has sounded forth from you not only in Macedonia and Achaia, but in every place your faith in God has become known, so that we have no need to speak about it" (1 Thess. 1:8).

Reflecting on this experience, the early church concluded that mission was one of its constituting marks. This conviction was memorialized in the Nicene-Constantinopolitan Creed of 381, in which the essential nature of the church is defined in terms of four fundamental attributes: not only "one, holy, and catholic," but also "apostolic." Henceforth, any expression of church that did not follow Jesus into mission ceased to be itself in a full sense. The other side of the coin also became an article of faith within early Christianity quite soon after the age of the apostles and itinerant evangelists had passed. This was the idea that evangelization *depended* on the church, which is to say that it was not just one of several instruments of mission but a *necessary* means of salvation. Cyprian's (d. 258) influential dictum, endlessly repeated within Western medieval Christianity and afterward, cast this theological conclusion into its most memorable form: *extra ecclesiam nulla salus* ("no salvation outside the church").

A collective decision to understand the church as the exclusive locus of salvation had profound implications for mission theology. The integrity of Augustine's position on the visible and invisible churches notwithstanding, most Christians fell into the bad habit of identifying the physical church, as it existed in the world, with the kingdom of God on earth. Priests and bishops, the church functionaries who controlled access to life-giving sacraments, were commonly regarded as the guardians of salvation too. Once the interests of states and the church became substantially intertwined after Constantine, the possibility also arose that political realms might be divinized alongside the church. Byzantium and the Holy Roman Empire are the two most famous examples of this mindset, but these great imperia were emulated by a number of regional actors, who likewise sought to increase their legitimacy through religious sanction (Hungary in St. Stephen's time is one example of this phenomenon; the promotion of Moscow as the "Third Rome" is another). In the worst-case scenario, repeated far too many times for comfort today, missionaries and their political sponsors justified the use of force to compel submission to Christian social norms (including the acceptance of baptism) by appealing to the perceived capacity of the church alone to secure salvation for sinners.

Ecclesiological issues continue to be discussed vigorously within mission theology today. Critical studies of past practices are largely agreed that territorial definitions of the church—the notion of Christendom—cannot fail but to distort the nature of the gospel by subordinating the church's saving message to its institutional interests. Likewise, one will search in vain today for proposals that favor the use of violence on behalf of the church and its mission, although some may be willing to consider the use of "soft" power to create openings for Christian evangelism within resistant cultures (particularly those dominated by Islam). Wide open is the question of whether the church is a proper object of mission. Many mission organizations still see church planting or the extension of the church's hierarchical structures as a primary goal of mission. Others worry about the danger of taking the needs of the church too seriously and so emphasize ministries of service and witness not necessarily intended to lead to the creation of new congregations or church bodies. Overall, the degree to which the missionary identity of the church has been reaffirmed over the past two generations is remarkable. The declaration at Vatican II that the church is "missionary by her very nature" (*Ad Gentes* 2) finds deep resonance within Orthodoxy (Anastasios 1989) and among Protestants all across the theological spectrum.

Some Attempts to Relocate Mission Theologically

Johannes Hoekendijk was among the first to sound the alarm on the dangers of ecclesiocentrism in mission theology. Talking about mission as an activity initiated by older churches that culminates in the establishment of new ecclesial bodies seemed to him to be entirely misguided: "Church-centric missionary thinking is bound to go astray, because it revolves around an illegitimate centre" (1952, 332). Hoekendijk's greatest fear was that a genuine desire on the part of God's people to give obedient witness to the gospel would be subverted by the church's organizational needs. Such motivations had relentlessly driven missionaries into questionable arrangements with European colonizers, he believed. With the passing of that era, was it also not time to renounce every kind of ecclesiastical colonialism? Denominational competition, rife in the first half of the twentieth century, indicated to Hoekendijk the waywardness of most mission programs. The usual supporters of mission rallied enthusiastically when the goal was to replicate existing church structures or to extend the limits of Christendom. Where was their passion for the radical, disinterested venture of faith announced by Jesus?

From another perspective, Karl Barth (1886–1968) also cautioned against church-centric theologies of mission. The presenting problem for Barth was not so much the church's pursuit of worldly advantage (such disappointing behavior was to be expected from every human institution) as it was a matter of the Christian community losing sight of its essential and constituting task. When other worthy projects are allowed to interpose themselves between the church and its primary calling, "faith in the Gospel degenerates into religiosity, love becomes devotion to certain 'ideals,' hope becomes confidence in all kinds of social and individual progress" (Barth 1948, 70). Barth's corrective response to this situation is to remind the church that its singular function is to proclaim the word of God. It was created for just this work and has no other reason to exist (Barth 1962, 795–801). Seen from this perspective, the church appears to be less an initiator of mission than it is the recipient of a special vocation. Barth urged that God be recognized as the one who both calls the community into being and sends it into the world for the purpose of witness.

Hoekendijk's critique and Barth's constructive proposals prepared the way for new approaches to mission theology in the second half of the twentieth century that did not begin with the church and its standard missionary agenda. What ties most of these efforts together is a common desire to put mission into a larger theoretical context than that provided by ecclesiology or the practical concerns of applied theology. Thus, we have Barth in the *Church Dogmatics* deciding to locate the topic of mission (and his treatment of the church) within an extensive discussion of justification or atonement ("the doctrine of reconciliation"), which he considers to be the work of God alone. Carl Braaten (1977, 29–36) observes that mission theology in this period more generally takes a turn in the direction of eschatology, with a resulting emphasis on Kingdom of God imagery to explain the goal of mission. In addition, we can see in the widespread adoption of *missio Dei* language, beginning in the 1950s, a sign that many now wished to treat mission as an aspect of the Trinity rather than as a function of the church. One particularly influential example of mission theology developed on the basis of a Trinitarian framework is that offered by Lesslie Newbigin (1978). Building on the ideas of Newbigin and others, Timothy Tennent (2010) has gone on to argue for a Trinitarian understanding of both mission and missiology, in order to keep the *missio Dei* and the mission activities of the churches linked together.

Emerging alongside more fully Trinitarian systems of thought are theologies of mission that give special emphasis to pneumatology. These approaches, too, seem to have arisen at least in part as alternatives to more ecclesiocentric thinking about mission. The explosive growth of Pentecostalism in the twentieth century has raised the profile of pneumatology within missiology, not only with respect to mission theology but throughout the field. Pentecostal theologies of mission consistently highlight gifts of the Spirit, especially as these are manifested in sudden outbreaks of ecstatic speech or instances of healing. When new hearers of

Christian proclamation exhibit evidence of these spiritual gifts, their presence may be taken as a sign that successful evangelism has occurred (above all, baptism in the Spirit). Since testimonies about such events having taken place in the past are often featured in Pentecostal preaching, the phenomena of tongues-speaking and miraculous healing are also usually considered in these circles to be among the ordinary means of missionary outreach.

Until quite recently, Pentecostal theologies of mission tended to be implicit and performative, a matter of "theology acted out" (Anderson 2004, 197) instead of written down. Of course, such theologies of mission, when put into writing, would have to be rational in order to be understood but they still might resist the impulse to systematize knowledge of the Spirit and its unpredictable effects. Nevertheless, mention of a few recurring elements can give a sense of the approach to mission theology suggested by a pneumatological perspective. One is the expectation that spiritual rebirth should include an extraordinary physical experience of some kind, in contrast to more noetic conceptions of conversion that emphasize assent to doctrinal statements or the recitation of creeds. The power of the Spirit is also acknowledged in the assertion that the promised "latter rain" of prophecy and tribulation have already begun (Wacker 2001, 251–65). A sense of impending calamity spurred legions of twentieth-century Pentecostal believers to set out in mission, sometimes without much advance planning. Confidence in the Spirit's guidance could likewise make formal training and official ministries seem beside the point. In exchange for a "low" ecclesiology that deemphasized order and lines of institutional authority, Pentecostals gained an appreciation for lay ministry and the spiritual gifts of women rarely matched until recently by mainline Protestants, Catholics, or Orthodox.

SOCIAL SCIENCE AND THE STUDY OF MISSION

As we have seen (in chapter 3), not a little early modern ethnography took place in the context of Christian mission, with the Jesuits leading the way. Some missionaries also played active roles in the development of the discipline of anthropology. Henri Junod (1863–1934), Wilhelm Schmidt (1868–1954), and Edwin W. Smith (1876–1957) are among those missiologists still remembered today for having successfully bridged the professional worlds of anthropology and mission in the early twentieth century, while contributing substantially to each (Anderson 1998, 347–48, 600–601, 625–26). Even so, a strong majority of anthropologists would eventually turn against Christian missionary activity in principle, believing that cross-cultural evangelism, however intended, inevitably hastens the destruction of primitive cultures around the world, the very subject matter of anthropological science, classically understood (Stipe 1980; a trend toward partnership is asserted in Bonsen et al. 1990).

Whatever hostility may have come to missionaries and their supporters from the direction of anthropology over the years, the fact remains that the social sciences are relevant to the study of mission. Anthropologists, sociologists, and other social scientists have made it their business to study culture, which is the natural workspace of Christian mission. While it may be possible to discuss mission in the abstract or strictly from a theological point of view, neither methodology is equipped on its own to explain everything that happens when faith is shared cross-culturally in the midst of actual life circumstances. Missionary encounters are necessarily shaped by a variety of crucial factors specific to each social setting and historical moment. For example, the perceptions of those involved and how they interpret their experience may be limited or enabled in particular ways by cultural determinants. These same individuals participate in complicated social networks, which in part define their personal identities and outlooks. No way has yet been found to avoid the effects of large-scale social forces at work in one's environment, whether fully understood or not. To comprehend these and other matters of context, missiologists need the help of the social sciences.

Quite soon after the emergence of missiology as a distinct field of study in the late nineteenth century, room was made within its precincts for social scientific data. Influential in this regard was the work of Commission V at the 1910 World Missionary Conference held in Edinburgh. After conducting an exhaustive, unprecedented two-year investigation into missionary training with substantial input from missionaries serving around the world, executives of sending agencies, and many scholarly experts, the commission concluded (World Missionary Conference 1910 [V], 155–79) that "sociology" was an integral part of the missionary syllabus, one of five "necessary subjects" that should be studied by all candidates for mission service (along with "the science and history of mission," "world religions," "pedagogy," and "the science of language"). Training in sociology and world religions was meant to furnish mission workers with the analytical tools they would need to understand their fields of service. It was no longer thought enough that evangelists and other missionaries should be spiritual exemplars and well versed in the Christian message. To be truly effective, they also had to grasp the full complexity of their social setting. Programs of missionary preparation that had already begun to incorporate such ideas, in particular at Yale under the leadership of Harlan Beach, were held up at Edinburgh as models to be replicated elsewhere (the Yale missions curriculum for 1910–11 is fully described in an appendix to the report of Commission V). The recommendations of Edinburgh on missionary training were most fully implemented at Hartford, where Commission V chairman William Douglas Mackenzie served as president. What soon became known as the Kennedy School of Missions at the Hartford Seminary Foundation put the study of anthropology, linguistics, sociology, and world religions at the heart of its educational program (Capen and Hodous 1936). A related effect of Edinburgh is felt in the inclusion of social scientific topics within the

"International Missionary Bibliography" section of the *International Review of Missions*, a scholarly periodical founded in 1912 (Skreslet 2006a, 171–80).

Thus far, I have been writing in general terms about the social sciences and their importance for the study of mission. In the next few subsections of this chapter, a selection of this research (regrettably, very limited) will be discussed, in order to show in more detail the kinds of social scientific scholarship most often encompassed within missiology after Edinburgh 1910. To be sure, missiologists did not necessarily get from social science what many of them expected a century ago, when it was widely believed that secular studies of religion and culture would "prove" the superiority of Christianity. Such was the assumption of James Shepard Dennis, whose influential study *Christian Missions and Social Progress* (1897–1906) earnestly expressed the expectation of many social gospellers committed to foreign missions that a better understanding of social problems and world religions would naturally lead one to appreciate how Christianity is best suited to meet the needs of modern men and women worldwide. Others looked to the emerging discipline of comparative religion (or history of religions) to support their argument that Christianity stood at the evolutionary apex of ethical and social development among all the world's religions (discussed in Masuzawa 2005). While these early missionary hopes for social science were not realized over the course of the twentieth century, missiology has nonetheless been enriched by a wide range of social scientific studies, many of them focused on matters of culture.

Linguistics

Since language is a primary building block of human culture, the field of linguistics has been an indispensable part of the social sciences. Students of mission have had more than one reason to be on alert for advances in linguistics scholarship. First of all, missionaries and their sending agencies have looked to language experts for help in the development of better methods of foreign language instruction. At a theoretical level, this interest might include consideration of basic research on the biological and behavioral processes by which human beings acquire language. More immediately relevant to missionary training are those investigations that examine the practical challenges involved in teaching foreign languages to adults. Near the beginning of the twentieth century it was hoped that the emerging science of phonetics might provide a comprehensive framework for efficient language learning by newly commissioned missionaries. We see this aspiration reflected, for example, in the respect shown at Edinburgh for the ideas of Carl Meinhof, professor of African languages at the Colonial Institute in Hamburg (appendix X in the report of Commission V is a lengthy communication from Meinhof that sets out the advantages of language learning methods based on phonetics). Later in the century, language instruction for missionaries and others began to incorporate new forms of audiovisual technology developed with the assistance of language scholars. In addition, many missiologists over the years have paid close attention to what linguists have had to say about the best use of native speakers in language teaching, the proper ordering of skills to be taught (oral, aural, reading, composition), and the advantages of inductive learning.

Scripture translation is a second area of impact for modern linguistics on missiology. Linguists are not prepared to answer the theological questions that inevitably arise when the Bible is translated, but their work has clarified some of the social issues that surround the task of translation. Biblical research informed by linguistics, for example, has contributed to a better understanding of the material to be translated. This has meant not only helping translators to recognize the different literary genres possibly embodied in the sacred writing that sits in front of them, or the history of composition that molded it into canonical form, or the underlying grammatical structures of the source language, but also to grasp the probable functions of the text in its own time. The point of these exegetical labors has been to understand as fully as possible what this part of scripture may have meant in its original cultural context.

At the other end of the translation project is the audience into whose idiom the text is being rendered. Perhaps the most important insight to be gained from modern studies of language in this regard concerns the active role necessarily played by those on the receiving end of translation work. Corresponding to the best efforts of the translator to recast an existing message into a different language medium are acts of decoding that have their own integrity. In this way of looking at the hermeneutical process, translators cannot reserve to themselves the right to assign final meanings to texts. They must expect interpretation to continue even after the finished written product has been created and distributed. Concern for the insider's (emic) perspective on language is evident in the work of Kenneth L. Pike (1912–2000), the longtime president of the Summer Institute of Linguistics, who helped to train thousands of missionary translators for Wycliffe Bible Translators while also developing a formal theory of language and culture he called "tagmemics" (Pike 1967). An early collaborator with Pike was Eugene A. Nida (1914–2011), who went on to have a distinguished career of his own with the American Bible Society. Nida's theoretical model of "dynamic [or functional] equivalence translation" (discussed in Smalley 1991, esp. 105–52) has proved extremely influential around the world through the work of the United Bible Societies. Translations based on this approach (such as the Good News Bible in English) show less interest in the goal of achieving "formal correspondence" with source texts. The focus instead is on the recipients and their anticipated understanding and experience of the translation. Ideally, in Nida's model, "the relationship between the receptor and message should be substantially the same as that which existed between the original receptors and the message" (Nida 1964, 159).

Bible translating is but one kind of language-related missionary activity. Evangelists and others intending to share the biblical story with non-Christians may employ any number of media in their work and multiple styles of expression (including nonverbal forms of language). For this reason, missiologists have long been concerned to understand the larger universe of communications theory in which Bible translation occupies an important but relatively small place. Eugene Nida (1960, rev. 1990) has provided a comprehensive introduction to the field of communications theory, written from a missiological point of view. His approach to communication takes into account not only the many functions and forms of language that humans employ but also the impact of social structures and psychological attitudes on interpersonal relations. David J. Hesselgrave (1978) offers another substantial treatment of communication for intercultural mission workers. Particularly insightful is his observation that missionaries have to recognize at least three different cultural situations when preparing for intercultural communication on behalf of the gospel: the respondent's culture, the missionary's culture, and the cultures of the Bible. Hesselgrave's "three-culture model of missionary communication" (67–78) builds on the earlier work of Nida (1960, 33–61) with respect to structures of communication. The suggestion of Hesselgrave that missionaries ought to master communications theory in order to "possess" other cultures for Christ (95–105) is strikingly modernist in tone.

Cultural Analysis

Culture is an elusive concept that continues to elicit multiple definitions. Equally plentiful are the many methodologies developed by social scientists over the years for the purpose of studying cultural phenomena. Thus, the results of cultural scholarship are still in process, but the research undertaken as a whole remains critically important to the study of mission. As Louis J. Luzbetak (1988, 133) has put it: more and better knowledge about culture is "anthropology's most significant contribution to missiology," because "the human dimension of mission action" cannot be understood without an adequate sense of the meaning of culture. Luzbetak's comprehensive study, *The Church and Cultures* (1988), shows just how extensive that contribution to missiology has been and continues to be.

Out of a huge mass of anthropological scholarship on culture two approaches may be highlighted to illustrate how this kind of social scientific research has figured in the development of missiology. The first of these revolves around the idea of "worldview." As applied within cultural anthropology a half-century ago (see, for example, Geertz 1957), "worldview" refers to the distinctive outlook of a social group with respect to its most deeply held common values, notions of proper behavior, and shared symbols of meaning. Worldview in this sense is not a personal life philosophy, an ideology, or a psychological state. It is a more or less tacit conceptual framework within which a given society (or dominant majority) articulates its own peculiar identity and attempts to exert indirect control as a collective over the behavior of its individual members. Religious beliefs, practices, and symbols may be featured in some expressions of worldview. A heightened awareness of ethnic identity can be another vital factor. If they are to be sustained, worldviews must be taught from generation to generation. Worldviews are not static, but resistance to a fundamental change in outlook is typically high and the weight of tradition accumulated over time can be great.

"Worldview" has lost much of its currency within cultural anthropology; evidence of this shift is provided by the second edition (2008) of the *International Encyclopedia of the Social Sciences*, which no longer includes an entry for this term. The influence of this approach to cultural analysis has nevertheless persisted within missiology, primarily through the anthropological work of David J. Hesselgrave (1978), Paul G. Hiebert (1983, 2008), and Charles H. Kraft (1996, 2008). In fact, many students of mission have been introduced to anthropology through textbooks written by these three scholars. In each case, the idea of worldview has been employed to demonstrate the importance of anthropology for missiology.

Kraft's argument on behalf of worldview analysis is founded on the conviction that the Christian gospel "is intended to influence and change people at the deepest possible level—the worldview level," where basic assumptions guide one's perception and interpretation of reality (1996, 57). Cross-cultural missionaries, therefore, should strive to become "advocates of change" (398–413), who give witness to "alternative assumptions, values, and allegiances, and commend their acceptance" (442). Hiebert agrees that "transforming worldviews" is the point of mission. While acknowledging that a fully comprehensive "biblical" worldview lies beyond the grasp of limited human beings (2008, 267), Hiebert maintains that "tentative models" of reality drawn from scripture may still be used to critique any and every possible understanding of the world and our place in it that a missionary might adopt or encounter.

Semiotics is a second method of cultural analysis developed within anthropology that some missiologists have found especially useful. In this way of looking at culture, patterns of communication and signification are examined closely in order to discern how particular societies create and express meaning. The whole in each case is an "imaginative universe" of symbols (Geertz 1973, 13) that can be read out of a people's verbal language, gestures, rituals, and artifacts, as the anthropologist observes them performed or used in actual social situations.

Missiologist Robert J. Schreiter sees in semiotics a creative means by which to listen carefully to another culture. He argues (1985, 57–61) that those using this method of cultural analysis can be aided by its focus on the insider's experience of culture, its equal concern for the perspectives of hearers and speakers, and the attention it gives to messages that pass among the general (non-elite) population. Luzbetak (1988, 155) further emphasizes the advantages of the "holistic" approach to culture provided by the semiotic model. Important in this regard is the idea of semiotic domain, defined by Schreiter (1985, 69) as "an assemblage of culture texts relating to one set of activities in culture (economic, political, familiar), which are organized together by a single set of messages and metaphoric signs." These domains (religion is another one) are naturally interlinked with each other. They may be arranged hierarchically and a single one may clearly dominate the rest. All of these elements (and the relationships among them) are susceptible to change. Whether one intends to construct a local theology (the larger topic Schreiter is discussing) or to engage in cross-cultural communication of some kind, a thoroughgoing semiotic analysis of indigenous culture could help to prepare the way.

Religious and Cultural Change

There was a time in the development of anthropology when its most scientific practitioners showed relatively little interest in the topic of cultural change. Especially under the influence of functionalism (strongest in the period between the 1920s and 1970s), many anthropologists were predisposed to view primitive societies as self-contained, almost timeless social worlds. Suddenly inserted into one of these alien environments, their great challenge was to comprehend and describe as completely as possible the totality of native life, including its everyday activities and rhythms, language, social roles, patterns of kinship and marriage, child-rearing practices, rituals, myths, institutions, and taboos. Fieldwork reports composed later rendered a picture of what the anthropologist had seen and heard. It was customary for these to be written in the present tense ("the ethnographic present"), a stylistic nuance that accentuated the photographic quality of the scholarly product. In the brand of functionalism championed by Bronislaw Malinowski (1884–1942) especially, an overriding concern to portray well-balanced non-Western indigenous social orders sympathetically may have led many researchers to ignore or correct for evidence of dysfunction, social tension, and historical development in the life of their subject group (Harris 2001, 559–62; see also Taber 1991, 93–110).

The attention of anthropology having largely been focused elsewhere in the first half of the twentieth century, it was left to other social scientists to consider the interrelated subjects of cultural and religious change. The still developing disciplines of psychology and sociology each had important contributions to make in this regard with implications for the study of mission. The work of William James (1842–1910) on religious experience, for example, provided missionaries and others with a modern, more technical vocabulary to use when talking about what happens to those who commit to the Christian faith with fervor (James 1902, esp. 166–258). Another classic study of conversion by historian Arthur Darby Nock (1902–63) used an analytical framework essentially borrowed from James to answer the question of Christianity's success in the ancient world. How can we account for the beginning of a widespread movement of people into Christianity throughout the Roman Empire by the third century? Not because of Jesus' powerful personality, Nock maintained (1933, 210–11), in opposition to nineteenth-century idealism. Christianity triumphed instead because it met the most basic psychological needs of human beings:

> It satisfied the inquiring turn of mind, the desire for escape from Fate, the desire for security in the hereafter; like Stoicism, it gave a way of life and made man at home in the universe, but unlike Stoicism it did this for the ignorant as well as for the lettered. It satisfied also social needs and it secured men against loneliness.

To what extent such an individualistic (Western) understanding of the human self and the making of life decisions can be applied cross-culturally and over time is a matter now under active discussion in more than one scholarly discipline. Zeba A. Crook (2004, esp. 13–52), for example, cautions against the longstanding tendency of biblical scholars to assume that people in ancient times had the same psychic and emotional needs as those living in modern industrial societies. If it is true that "the mental and emotional experiences of humanity cannot be separated from the cultural context in which they exist" (Crook, 46–47), then Crook is correct to suspect that religious conversion in Western societies and in other cultural settings may not always mean the same thing.

Sociologists have also taken an interest in the complex processes of religious change. As one would expect, these scholars have not typically focused on the individual but more on society-wide trends and movements. Much of this work has been concentrated on the fate of religion in the postindustrial West, but not all of it, as the voluminous writings of Max Weber (1864–1920) on Asian cultures and religions demonstrate. In fact, the ideas of Weber loom large in what I consider two of the most significant contributions of modern-era sociology to the study of mission. The first of these has to do with Weber's basic classification of Christianity, Judaism, Islam, and Buddhism as "world" religions, whose highly "rationalized" systems of belief and practice have enhanced their social power and attractiveness to modern people. These were contrasted in Weber's analysis with "primitive" or traditional religions that have had, on the whole, weaker structures of authority, less intellectual coherence, fewer effective means at hand to control orthodox belief, and narrower or more local fields of vision. Weber's ideas were easily swept up into evolutionary schemes of civilizational development, which many hands were eager to do especially at the beginning of the twentieth century. A more subtle and enduring benefit of his thinking was provided to those social scientists and missiologists who wanted to study what happens when different kinds of religious systems come into contact with each other, especially in the context of modernization. Robin Horton's now classic essays (1971, 1975a, 1975b) on conversion to Christianity and Islam in sub-Saharan Africa show how Weber's analytical categories could be applied to the problem of religious change. Robert W. Hefner (1993) has provided a stimulating survey of the long and consequential discussion sparked by Weber's classification of Christianity as an evangelizing "world" religion.

A second mission-related topic intensely debated by sociologists for over a century is secularization. One understanding of secularization takes it to be that aspect of modernity that works against traditional forms of religion by eroding their explanatory power and perceived relevance to many segments of life (Weber famously called this process "the disenchantment of the world"). Certainly by the late nineteenth century, numerous proponents of mission were prepared to accept the assistance of secularizing forces as these were becoming increasingly manifest in the non-Western world. Indeed, through a vast network of schools established around the world, Christian missions were self-consciously helping to extend the reach of what Presbyterian mission executive Robert E. Speer (1904, 669) called "the tremendous subversive power of our Western movement," which at that time he saw directed primarily against the non-Western religions. As it happened, Speer (1867–1947) would later join with other leaders of the missionary movement gathered in Jerusalem in 1928 to sound the alarm at the possible threat secularization also posed to Western societies. For a growing number of missionaries and their supporters, secularism had begun to mean the dechristianization of the home base and the rise of relativist thinking. Throughout the twentieth century, sociological research on the processes of secularization remained vital to missiology, whether one had in mind the position of the church and its message in the West or the role played by modernizing forces worldwide.

Evidence of increasingly fast-paced cultural change now seems to be everywhere. It is simply a fact that new forms of communication, faster means of transportation, human migration on a larger scale than ever before, and an expanding system of global capitalism are tying together more closely communities of people that had once been quite separate from each other, with the result that cultural isolation and cultural stability have both become more difficult to assert conceptually or to maintain in practice. Modern-era missions have been a part of this globalizing trend and so it is virtually certain that social scientists in a variety of disciplines will continue to feature missionaries in their studies of cultural change.

We can anticipate that a major portion of this burgeoning collection of scholarship will continue to be focused on colonialism and the roles played by Western missionaries in situations of imperial rule. In a few cases, it may be that conversion to Christianity can best be explained as a result of coercion (the influential argument of Beidelman [1982] with respect to an East African mission station). Other researchers have proposed models of religious change that give more recognition to the capacity of indigenous people to make their own religious choices and to initiate innovation within their own culture (an example is Whiteman 1983, esp. 1–28). Especially intriguing are social scientific studies in which movements toward Christianity are documented with respect to locations where foreign missionaries may have once been active but are no longer permitted to operate (as in

China after 1949 or with the Uduk people in postcolonial Sudan after the departure of the Sudan Interior Mission, considered in James 1988, esp. 207–52). There can be no doubt that missiology as a whole has much to gain from the kind of social scientific research cited here and from scholarly projects that succeed in bringing together anthropologists, sociologists, historians, and missiologists for the purpose of studying religious and cultural change (Peggy Brock's edited volume, *Indigenous Peoples and Religious Change* [2005a], is a recent example of this kind of collaboration).

GOSPEL AND CULTURE

This chapter began with the assertion that missiology is a field of research where the concerns of theology regularly engage with issues of culture. In large part, the nature of cross-cultural Christian witness explains the reason for this creative intersection of scholarly interests. Having looked at a selection of material generated from within systematic theology and the social sciences with relevance for missiology, we may now turn to consider some work that quite deliberately participates in both of these arenas at the same time. Our discussion will begin with the particular theological basis on which much of this missiological scholarship rests: the doctrine of the incarnation.

Christology and Mission Theology

We do not find many missionaries through the ages involving themselves in technical arguments over christology. The "how" of the incarnation is not a matter of primary concern, because the truth of the gospel for most missionaries is not thought to hang on precise definitions. It is nevertheless true that some examples can be produced from the history of Christianity in which missionaries dedicated themselves to the propagation of distinctive christological positions. The Nestorians in China quickly spring to mind in this regard. Those evangelizing the Goths in the fourth and fifth centuries likewise communicated their own peculiar (Arian) understanding of christology alongside the gospel, a development deplored by the champions of Nicene orthodoxy. A colorful story survives of christological competition within the sixth-century imperial household of Justinian and Theodora. In this case, the Byzantine emperor and his wife sponsored rival missionary delegations to Nubia that either supported or rejected the results of the Council of Chalcedon (451) with respect to the divine and human natures of Christ.

What these examples prove (again) is that missionaries often reflect the obsessive concerns of the churches that send them out to evangelize and serve. Something more basic and less time-bound than this is indicated by the doctrine of the incarnation. "The Word became flesh and lived among us" (John 1:14; see also Gal. 4:4–5; Phil. 2:5–8; Col. 2:9; 1 Tim. 2:5; Heb. 2:14) is a powerful declaration that not only establishes a scriptural premise for speculation on the natures of

Christ but also says something vital about the manner in which God has chosen to effect salvation. Instead of remaining separate from our reality, God decides to plunge into the midst of human history. Without surrendering the right to act as judge, God commits utterly to the role of advocate. While remaining mysterious, God seeks in a new way to become fully known. Theologies of mission that take seriously the doctrine of the incarnation are challenged to be world-affirming in the same way that God has been. In turn, they demand a missionary commitment to the created order, no matter how many signs of brokenness and alienation from God might be discovered. The doctrine of the incarnation has also been taken as an invitation to think deeply about human culture as the particular sphere within which Christian outreach necessarily takes place.

From Incarnation to Contextualization

The New Testament writings of Paul show the apostle beginning to grapple with the prospect of a multicultural church (for him, both Jewish and Greek). The Acts of the Apostles and the Gospels likewise point ahead to a Christian community that will not be confined within the ethnic and legal boundaries largely maintained by first-century Judaism. The resurrected Jesus sends the disciples with the gospel on their way to "the nations." At Pentecost, a representative gathering of all the world's peoples (Acts 2:5—"every nation under heaven") receives Peter's preached word that "*everyone* who calls on the name of the Lord shall be saved" (Acts 2:21). Even at this very early stage of Christian history, the logic of the gospel appears to be universal. No cultural enclave may be said to stand outside of God's salvific intentions.

The further one moves away from the generation of the apostles, the greater the percentage of Gentiles in the church. At some point, Jewish religious culture lost its normative status within Christianity. Several of the second-century Apologists perceptively grasped the critical theological challenge implied in this demographic shift. How should the church evaluate the cultural heritage of those many and increasingly numerous converts who had not come to Christianity via Judaism? For Justin Martyr (c. 100–165), the doctrine of the incarnation suggested a basis on which to embrace the best parts of Hellenistic culture. Without endorsing idolatry or Greek polytheism, he thought it possible to incorporate the Greek philosophical quest for truth within a Christian understanding of salvation history. The key element in this theological position was the Logos of John 1, which Justin understood to have been active as the "seminal Word" sowing seeds of truth among humanity even before the birth of Christ (*2 Apol* 13; see also *1 Apol* 46 and *2 Apol* 8, 10). The significance of Justin's breakthrough only partially lay in his startling conclusion that certain of the philosophers and pre-Christian prophets had been inspired by the Word. He was also preparing the way for the sources of Christian revelation to be brought into a profound conversation with the very idiom of Hellenistic learning, including its special vocabulary, classic texts, enduring philosophical problems, and authoritative figures from the past.

Origen is the church father who most thoroughly exploited the cross-cultural opportunity created for Christian theology by Justin and his fellow Apologists. So concludes Andrew Walls (1999, 101), who credits Origen (c. 185–253) with the self-confidence needed to plunge into the deep philosophical and literary depths of Hellenism. While Justin showed his willingness to induct a select company of the ancients into the Christian pantheon retroactively, as it were, Origen took on the additional risk of exposing Christian knowledge based on the scriptures to the power of their intellectual arguments. Based on his own experience, Gregory Thaumaturgus (c. 213–70) described the spirit of inquiry cultivated in Origen's classroom (Gregory 1998, 122):

> So to us nothing was beyond words, nor was anything hidden and inaccessible. We were permitted to learn every doctrine, both barbarian and Greek, both the most mystical and the most pragmatic, both divine and human; we pursued the ins and outs of all these more than sufficiently and examined them closely, taking our fill of everything and enjoying the good things of the soul.

Just a few authors remained off-limits for these young scholars: anyone who had "abandoned common human beliefs" by denying the existence of God and Providence altogether (Gregory 1998, 116). Otherwise, Origen's students were encouraged to examine everything in Greek culture with a critical eye in the light of scripture, in order to discern what could be used therein to glorify God. Just as Israel had refashioned the gold and precious items plundered from Egypt (Exod. 11:2) into costly furniture and expensive fabrics for the Holy of Holies, Origen (1998, 190–91) urged his charges to apply the whole of Greek learning to the sacred task of theology. The ultimate result of Origen's program was more than a simple repurposing of philosophy. Christian theology itself was forever transformed by a dynamic encounter with the heritage of Athens. Besides furnishing theology with new materials with which to work and many useful tools for analysis, Walls (1997, 149) observes that "the Greek world posed questions for Christian thought that did not naturally arise in the Jewish world of its origins." At the same time, Neo-Platonism provided the Christian theologian with an entirely new standpoint from which to consider what was already known from scripture about God's revelation in Christ. Thus did the incarnation give rise to the risky but potentially rewarding venture of contextualization.

The Study of Contextualization

For having been the first to put theology into cross-cultural perspective, Walls (1999, 104) suggests that Origen be recognized as the "father of mission studies."

The notion is apt, but many generations would have to pass before the innovator could claim many scholarly descendents. We know, of course, that the processes of contextualization, largely unexamined, continued to work themselves out in countless locations, as missions brought the Christian faith into contact with a growing number of languages and cultural matrices. An intense encounter with Latin culture, influenced in decisive ways by Germanic customs and values (Russell 1994), produced by the early Middle Ages a powerful form of Christianity that would be spread around the world as Roman Catholicism. The history of Bede and the letters of Boniface, among many other sources, show medieval missionaries having to decide whether to accommodate or reject (or attempt to modify) the traditional ways of the peoples with whom they hoped to share the gospel. It is reasonable to assume, even in the absence of extensive documentation, that missionaries in countless other settings also found themselves confronting a host of unanticipated cultural dilemmas with no obvious solutions. Again and again, missionaries attempted to maintain control over the reception of Christianity but achieved only partial success. In many settings, societal Christian norms were worked out over long periods of time with local actors in the end having far more influence over the results of contextualization than the foreign missionaries themselves.

It is only in the modern era that the study of contextualization becomes rigorous and scholarly. Ethnographers and historians led the way. Since a number of these were already discussed in chapter 3 (history of mission), it is not necessary to recount their contributions here. My focus instead will be on the contextualization of theology and the scholarship that has helped the most to explain this process and its significance.

As a technical term within mission theology, "contextualization" first emerged within ecumenical Protestant circles in the early 1970s as an alternative way to describe what had often been called inculturation (Ukpong 1987). The need for new terminology was prompted by the closing of the modern colonial era. Earlier it had been assumed that mission usually occurred as a movement of diffusion spreading out globally from recognized centers. Missionaries took with them already-worked-out theologies, which needed only to be adjusted slightly to fit novel circumstances. Whether one talked about the necessity of indigenization or inculturation, the initiative was thought to remain in the hands of foreign evangelists, who alone were considered qualified to determine how orthodox beliefs and settled practices ought to be expressed in new situations.

The terminology of contextualization indicated a shift of emphasis from the center to what had been considered the periphery and from the missionary to the local church. The task of theologizing now became more dialogical and less a matter of one-way applications. The experience of indigenous communities took on a much greater importance, first by suggesting which problems were most in need of a theological response and then by supplying the idioms and conceptual frameworks within which these conversations would be conducted. The universal pretensions of Western theology were about to be seriously tested.

Initial efforts to do contextual theology tended to reflect the immediate postcolonial moment of world Christianity in the early 1970s. At this point, contextualization stood for the development of non-Western, or third-world, theology. The most pressing issues needing to be addressed first were thought to be political and social, as the impoverished victims of foreign exploitation claimed their independence and voice. It seemed to many that political decolonization ought to have its ecclesiastical counterpart. In several churches outside the West, calls were issued for a moratorium on missions. A global turning point for theology arrived with the publication in English of the groundbreaking work of Gustavo Gutiérrez, *A Theology of Liberation* (1973; first published in Spanish in 1971). Complementary analyses were soon underway in a host of locations and by 1976 an international professional society had been organized in support of these efforts: the Ecumenical Association of Third World Theologians (EATWOT). Missiologists were paying very close attention to these developments in theology. A telltale measure of their interest was provided by William A. Smalley, who surveyed a large collection of dissertations in English on mission completed between 1982 and 1991. According to Smalley (1993, 98), about a third of the 512 theses he reviewed focused on liberation theology, indigenous theologies, or issues of contextualization, compared to less than 3 percent of missiological dissertations devoted to these same topics between 1945 and 1981.

With every passing year, new participants and more contexts are added to the accumulated record of contextual theology. One way to regard this growing corpus of work is to recognize and applaud its rich diversity, well represented in reference tools like the *Dictionary of Third World Theologies*, edited by Virginia Fabella and R. S. Sugirtharajah (2000). Other scholars have been asking questions about the possible relationships that might exist among these disparate theological responses to specific sociohistorical circumstances. Can one do no more than simply put these different analyses side-by-side in ever-larger collections of theological creativity?

In the next stage of work on contextual theology, the contributions of Robert Schreiter have had a large impact both within and beyond missiology. In Schreiter's analysis, the political edge of contextual theology is acknowledged, but an effort is made to understand better the social processes that shape this kind of theology. Contextual theology, according to Schreiter (1985), is a matter of devising "local" theology, which is often a product of community-wide reflection. The manner of its construction can be "mapped," with the assistance of the social sciences (especially semiotics, as discussed above). One may also venture to evaluate specific expressions of contextual theology, with respect to their authenticity or genuineness. Schreiter suggests that this judgment will depend on a given theology's dual relationship to its concrete situation and to a larger Christian tradition that transcends the particularities of geography and history (in a subsequent study of "catholicity" [1997a], Schreiter explores further the universal aspect of Christian identity). Schreiter points out that theology draws on and responds to more than one level of religious experience (both popular and more formal or official). The tangled array of questions Schreiter raises about contextual theology exposes the complexities that surround this apparently simple term, while also exploring the variety of functions that theology can play in the life of a church and its larger community.

A second major contribution from Schreiter has been felt in his suggestion that there are types of contextual theology, which can be separated methodologically from each other. His initial list of three categories is refined and expanded in the work of Stephen B. Bevans (2002). Bevans identifies and describes six different "models" of contextual theology: translation, anthropological, praxis, synthetic, transcendental, and countercultural. A distinguishing mark of Bevans's approach is the emphasis given to social change as a constant factor at work in every cultural context (complementing the notion of more fixed cultural identities that endure over time). Bevans also attempts to clarify the relationship of contextual theology to scripture and tradition, concluding: "contextual theology is done when the experience of the past engages the present context" (2002, xvii). In the end, Bevans (2002, 139–40) refuses to rank his six models, insisting that Christians in different situations may find one or another or a combination of these approaches most suitable to their needs, depending on the context. Bevans and co-author Roger P. Schroeder have also conducted a contextual analysis of mission theology since the beginning of Christianity in their book *Constants in Context* (2004).

The growing realization that every performance of theology is, in some sense, contextual was bound to lead to a reevaluation of Western theology, too. Within missiology, the latest phase of this discussion has largely been conducted around the topic of "missional" theology. While this brand of adjectival theology was coined only recently, the presenting problems that lie behind it may be traced back many decades. In the 1930s, for example, Hendrik Kraemer wrote vividly about a crisis that had suddenly come upon Western theology. Modernization, he warned, not only threatened traditional societies in faraway places and their ancient religious traditions. In the form of strident secularism, relativist thinking, and the totalitarian ideologies then taking root in twentieth-century Europe, modernity also posed severe challenges for the church in the West. The ultimate source of the problem, according to Kraemer (1938, 9), lay in the basic conviction, increasingly embraced in the West, that humanity is "the standard and creator of all truths and norms and values." In this historical context, how does one proclaim the Christian message in what has to be recognized as a truly non-Christian world, even in the West?

Writing some forty years later, after a full missionary career in India and with the benefit of having seen the emergence of many contextual theologies around the world, Lesslie Newbigin reassessed the situation of Western Christianity. What Kraemer had earlier perceived as incipient disestablishment was fast becoming a reality in Europe. The church in the West could no longer operate on the basis of Christendom assumptions. While some church leaders may have found this to be an occasion for mourning, Newbigin applied himself to the missiological task of cross-cultural analysis and theological response. His ideas were widely shared in *Foolishness to the Greeks: The Gospel and Western Culture* (1986). The increasingly pluralist character of Western societies, not yet evident to Kraemer, was further explored in a hugely influential study, *The Gospel in a Pluralist Society* (1989). The point for Newbigin was not just to understand Western society better. His aim was to help the church in the West to prepare for "a genuinely missionary encounter between the gospel and the culture that is shared by the peoples of Europe and North America, their colonial and cultural offshoots, and the growing company of educated leaders in the cities of the world—the culture which those of us who share it usually describe as 'modern'" (1986, 1). In another place, Newbigin succinctly rephrased his essential question in these terms: "Can the West be Converted?" (1987).

Because of Newbigin's advanced age and the size of the task he had described, it was left to others to elaborate and attempt to carry out the program he had begun to outline. The Gospel and Our Culture Network (GOCN), based in North America with affiliates in several other English-speaking countries around the world, has supplied an organizational framework for many of these efforts. This is the point at which the language of "missional" theology makes its appearance (Guder et al. 1998). Besides supplying a distinctive vocabulary for this approach to mission, the network also seeks to foster experiments in evangelization conceived in the light of postmodern Western circumstances (Barrett 2004). For some followers of this trend in theology, Newbigin's ideas about the gospel as public truth (1991) are taken to be the heart of the matter. The GOCN website provides a handy portal through which much of the latest research conducted in support of missional approaches to Christian outreach can be accessed.

Contextual theology does not have to be written. For some missionaries and indigenous Christians, a driving aim has been to contextualize the Christian faith in visual or material terms supplied primarily by local cultures. Naturally, missiologists have been keen to study these efforts, too, which are nonverbal forms of theological discourse. The Jesuits in the sixteenth century were perhaps the first to think systematically about inculturation as both a theological and a social process. Influenced by the Jesuits, the Propaganda Fide issued in 1659 a directive for new vicars apostolic appointed to the Far East, instructing them to ensure that Catholic missionaries under their supervision take care to communicate a basic Christian message to potential converts, while leaving aside the nonessential aspects of their own cultural background (quoted in Ross 1994, 185):

> Do not attempt in any way to persuade these people to change their customs, their habits and their behavior, as long as they are not evidently contrary to religion and morality. What could be more absurd, indeed, than to transport France, Italy or some other European country to the Chinese? Do not bring them our countries but the faith, which does not reject or harm the customs and habits of any people, so long as they are not perverse; but, on the contrary, wishes to see them preserved in their entirety.

Experience gained under the direction of the pope's influential Visitor to the East, Alessandro Valignano (1539–1606), had prepared the way for this extraordinary "Instruction." As the ranking Jesuit missionary in the Far East, Valignano carefully reviewed what had been accomplished up to his time and then worked out a set of principles that not only allowed but encouraged Jesuit missionaries to conduct a variety of inculturation exercises around the world. Roberto de Nobili's adoption of several distinctive Hindu customs pertaining to dress and conduct is one well-known example (Nobili 2000, 53–231). Some missionaries working in colonial Mexico produced art and liturgical resources that drew heavily on the visual imagination of pre-Christian Mesoamerican societies (Lara 2008). Valignano himself directed the Jesuits in Japan to consider carefully the styles of their buildings and to conform to Japanese architectural expectations whenever possible (these instructions are discussed in Schütte 1985, 187–89). He advised, for example, that missionary residences in Japan should include a reception space in which the tea ceremony could be properly conducted, in deference to the Buddhist sensibilities of elite Japanese society. To be sure, most mission architecture in this period and later was unmistakably foreign by design, with just a few local flourishes added here and there, but Valignano's ideas had opened up other possibilities for incarnated Christian witness in stone and decoration. In the eighteenth and nineteenth centuries, Catholic missionaries tended to be less adventurous contextualizers than the early Jesuits. In the century just past, however, the spirit of Valignano was substantially reclaimed.

Protestants, on the whole, were slow to recognize indigenous arts and architectural forms as suitable media for Christian witness. Wary of syncretism and the threat of idolatry (the besetting sins of Catholics, in their view), most Protestant missionaries through the nineteenth century preferred to put their faith in the power of the Word (and words) to communicate a compelling message of salvation. While a few organizations advocated the adoption of native dress by their missionaries (the most famous example being the China Inland Mission), none saw a pressing need before the twentieth century to translate whole visual programs into local idioms. But a change in attitude did finally come. An important figure in this shift was Union Theological Seminary (New York) professor of mission Daniel Johnson Fleming (1877–1969), who began in the late 1930s to publish a series of books on non-European Christian art. *Each with His Own*

Brush: Contemporary Christian Art in Asia and Africa (Fleming 1938; reprinted many times) was a particularly influential volume in this series. Arno Lehmann followed with two substantial studies of Christian art (1957, 1969), which brought the work of many new artists in Asia and Africa especially to the attention of Western audiences. The incarnation, Lehmann suggested (1969, 49), is the "ultimate and real reason" why the church ought to encourage the production of indigenous art everywhere: "the condescension of God permits us to preach in pictures (Gal. 3:1)."

In the studies of Fleming and Lehmann we can see the first steps being taken in the development of what would become world Christian art. Initially, missionary patronage provided crucial support for relatively unknown native artists. Missionaries also helped to create some important institutional structures that nurtured indigenous painters, sculptors, graphic artists, and others, such as the School of Art at Makerere University in Uganda (established in 1937). Organizations completely outside the control of missionaries and their sending bodies now take the lead in promoting non-Western Christian art (for example, the Asian Christian Art Association, founded in 1978), while participating fully in a global exchange of artistic ideas and initiatives.

Intercultural Theology

Since the 1970s, intercultural theology has become an increasingly attractive way for some West European scholars to describe the task of missiology. In a positive sense, this new term expresses a desire for theology to engage the whole of what is now a global Christian community. Thus, intercultural theologians are expected to recognize and facilitate dialogue among the different contextual theologies being generated from within a thoroughly multicultural, worldwide church. At the same time, the "inter-" in intercultural theology indicates a need for this diverse body to be in conversation with all of its neighbors, including those who identify themselves in terms of other faith commitments or no religious faith at all. Both of these objectives are highlighted in a recent position paper prepared for discussion by a group of German academics and the Administrative Board of the German Association for Mission Studies (Mission Studies 2008).

More negatively, intercultural theology represents a defensive response to the ambivalence many Western Christians feel about some past practices and theologies of mission. Werner Ustorf (2008, 229), in fact, has characterized intercultural theology as "an act of theological repentance in the North," made necessary by the hegemonic impulses widely thought to be embedded deep within the modern missionary movement. In this sense, intercultural theology is a mode of missiology especially well suited to destabilize vested theological positions on mission, especially when these appear to be triumphal or overly confident with respect to the truth claims of classical theology. A genuine dialogue of equals, after all, demands that one set aside any presumption of hermeneutical privilege, in exchange for the prospect of mutual understanding.

Intercultural theology also has its practical aspect. In the state-funded university systems that dominate higher education in most European countries, missiologists have to compete with scholars in many other fields for scarce faculty positions and program support. To the extent that the field of mission studies is perceived to be a sectarian enterprise, its case for state patronage may be weakened. As the position paper cited above puts it, albeit obliquely: "In both contemporary public and theological discourse, the term 'mission' often leads to confusion and stereotyping, which is why the traditional subject title 'Mission Studies' is frequently the cause of misunderstandings" (Mission Studies 2008, 103). In this context, intercultural theology seems to offer an approach to the study of mission that could cooperate with and complement secular research on religious subjects, while maintaining its standing within the curricula of European theological faculties.

Volker Küster (2005, 429) sees the "project of an intercultural theology" in competition with such disciplines as theology of religions, global ethics, and comparative theology. In another place, he depicts intercultural theology as a stage of development issuing out of the "plural discipline" of religious studies, missiology, and ecumenics and calls for it to be established as a discipline in its own right within systematic theology (Küster 2009). Some recognition is given to the study of culture in this configuration of missiology, but the particularities of contextualization as a missionary problem tend to be overshadowed by more theoretical concerns. In 1975, three pioneers in the study of intercultural theology—Hans Jochen Margull, Walter Hollenweger and Richard Friedli—launched a new book series: *Studies in the Intercultural History of Christianity*. Over the years, this still-active set of publications has been a major venue (150+ volumes as of 2010) through which much dissertation research and many other high-quality studies have reached missiology.

THEOLOGY, MISSION, CULTURE

Writing about fifteen years ago, Lamin Sanneh perceived that Western theology was just about the last discipline in the modern university to show serious interest in missionary experience. While numerous scholars in the humanities and even a few scientists kept coming back to the missionary archives in support of their research, he observed, his Yale Divinity School colleagues tended to keep their distance (Sanneh 1995). The theologians were quite happy, it appeared, to celebrate the wonderful diversity of a truly global church, but they were doing so, in Sanneh's view, without showing proper respect for the historical processes that had brought world Christianity into being.

Perhaps Sanneh was too pessimistic. One finding of this chapter is that theological reflection and the study of mission have been subtly connected to each other for some time and that a mutually beneficial relationship exists between them. Without a doubt, missiologists are paying attention to the work of the systematic theologians, especially when they write about the topics highlighted here (salvation, conversion, ecclesiology, incarnation, etc.). In turn, missiology poses to theology an implicit cross-cultural challenge that is getting harder and harder to ignore. If consideration of the "other" is indeed a valuable bridge that potentially links the theological and nontheological disciplines of the modern university (Schultze 2004, 326), then missiologists have important contributions to make to these discussions, whether out of personal experience as cultural aliens or as students of religious and cultural difference. One also stands to gain when the hermeneutical questions of theology are examined in the light of what missionaries and missiologists have learned over the course of centuries about cross-cultural communication and the processes of contextualization. In the work of Robert Schreiter already cited, we can see theology and missiology fully engaged with each other. Some other major theologians whose recent writings have shown more than a passing awareness of missiological research are Timothy J. Gorringe (2004), Max Stackhouse (1988, 2005; Pachuau and Stackhouse 2007), and Kevin Vanhoozer (Kirk and Vanhoozer 1999).

Missiology and the social sciences share a long history of interaction, even if relationships between missionaries and some social scientists have not always been cordial. The fact that a leading journal in the field (*Missiology*) was for a time called *Practical Anthropology* says something important about the serious regard many missiologists have given to the study of culture. As noted already, students of mission have made substantial contributions to ethnography. Their work among the world's vernaculars, sometimes grounded in decades of first-hand contact with the people of another culture, continues to inform linguistics research. Other forms of communication routinely fall within the overlapping provinces of missiology and the social sciences, as do the many ways humans organize their social activities in the religious and secular spheres. Not fully appreciated, perhaps, is the way in which sustained research on culture has served to keep missiology closely connected to everyday life, which lessens the risk that its theological concerns will be treated only in the abstract.

5

Christian Mission in a World of Religions

Matters of religion and culture often rise into view bound up together. Where else but in culture can religious conviction find the means needed for its expression? Ritual behaviors, religious institutions, and sacred texts all find their wherewithal in the bailiwick of culture. Even the most abstract notions of belief require language of some sort if they are to transcend the natural limits of personal experience. At the same time, religion has repeatedly demonstrated its sure capacity to embody and transmit cultural values. Ethnic or linguistic groups, for example, may use religious terminology to reinforce the cultural distance they perceive between themselves and others. When widely dispersed and mixed in with social rivals, these same communities may appeal to the categories of religion in order to maintain a common identity and sense of solidarity. Too sharp a division between religion and culture can be artificial and potentially misleading, whether in missiology or in any other discipline that concerns itself with the study of social phenomena.

Without denying a close relationship between religion and culture, some good reasons may nevertheless be submitted in support of the separate but still connected treatments of each to be rendered in this chapter and the one preceding it. For starters, we should acknowledge that cultural pluralism is not the same thing as religious pluralism. While the former raises questions in particular about the nature of the church and the degree to which Christianity can be made at home in any cultural environment, the latter asks about the universality of the Christian message with respect to other assertions of truth. Many missiologists concern themselves with both of these challenges, but typically they do not study them in just the same way. A deep understanding of contextualization will not solve the puzzles of religious pluralism. For that task, one needs expertise in matters having to do with revelation. Coincidently, mission scholars with at least one eye trained on the religions have to consider the problem of proselytization alongside the danger of syncretism. We find, also, that missiologists tend to seek help from a different set of scholarly collaborators outside the field when their emphasis moves from culture to religion. In this case, historical studies of interreligious encounter become increasingly valuable. So does the work of those who specialize in the history of religion. As the profile of history grows within this part of missiology, the influence of the social sciences tends to decrease proportionally.

Mission in the midst of interreligious encounter is the theme of this chapter. An opening section considers how first-century Christians conceptualized other forms of religious devotion (apart from Jewish faith and piety), while exploring the possible influence of these understandings on mission practice. A lengthy review of postapostolic missionary thinking about non-Christian religion then follows in several subsections. It is at the end of this survey that we will find the theology of mission contending with postmodern theories of religious pluralism. In a separate section some additional attention will be given to a few of the special problems attached to the study of Christian mission undertaken among Jews, Muslims, and the followers of African traditional religions. The chapter will conclude by taking up the question of mission in other religious traditions, a comparative subject that is just beginning to secure its place on the research agenda of academic missiology.

OTHER FAITH AND THE APOSTOLIC CHURCH

Within the context of the Roman Empire, an expanding community of early Christians constructed a novel religious identity for themselves that variously puzzled, threatened, and attracted others. The character of their common self-understanding rested partly on the universal scope of Christian faith claims. According to what the New Testament portrays as standard Christian preaching in the first century, the Jesus event (his birth, life, death, and resurrection) represented the decisive turning point in human history. Not only had the coming of Jesus fulfilled Jewish expectations for a Messiah, but the consummation of God's rule at the end of time, which would involve the entire creation, was also thought to depend on him. In such terms the early church put its case for the indispensability (or finality) of Christ and his uniqueness.

The universal significance of Jesus was also reflected in the nature of the church that gathered in his name. Missionary appeals were directed both to Jews and to many different kinds of Gentiles and so led to a high level of ethnic diversity within the body of Christ. New members came from a variety of social and economic backgrounds, which immediately differentiated an emerging church from many other Roman-era religious associations that sought only to draw small slices of elite society together for civic and cultic purposes (Rives 2007, esp. 105–31). Over decades and then centuries, the church developed into an increasingly well integrated group of institutions, with an extensive geographical reach that stood in sharp contrast to what were mostly local forms of pagan religious practice. Far-flung outposts of Christianity built relationships with each other, and sometimes their leaders met together in regional councils in order to strengthen ecumenical bonds and to regulate doctrine. Thus, while the origins of Christianity may be traced back to a specific time and place, the tradition quickly turned into more than a Galilean religious movement or a Jewish offshoot that needed the physical backdrop of Palestine or a central cultic location in order to make sense.

But a narrow staircase led up to the early church's wide-open front door. Which is to say that the church's missionary call, while broadly inclusive, came with a stiff set of demands for those inclined to enroll themselves into the company of faith. This was the other defining aspect of Christian identity at the outset of the movement: its exclusive dimension. If God is one (as the Jews and Christians believed), then the polytheistic logic of the Greek pantheon must be rejected. If Jesus is Lord, then sacrifices to other deities represent a form of idolatry. If Christians are indeed called to be saints, then they ought to strive for purity and trustworthiness, while avoiding debauchery and the pursuit of power for its own sake.

Christianity did not ultimately adopt all the practices that made Judaism seem strange to Roman eyes (especially circumcision), but it did strike many as countercultural and off-beat and so something a right-thinking majority ought to avoid. According to the historian Tacitus, Christians *could* be blamed for setting fire to Rome in the days of Nero because they were generally thought contemptible for their "hatred of the human race" (*Annals* 15.44). Pliny the Younger, a contemporary of Tacitus and the Roman governor of Bithynia-Pontus between 111 and 113 C.E., reported to Emperor Trajan that he saw in Christianity an insidious threat to Roman order, which he thought could be safeguarded by making those accused to be Christians call upon the traditional gods using a formula supplied by the governor, offering incense and wine before an image of the emperor, and cursing the name of Christ (*Ep* 10.96). Not quite Jewish but certainly not pagan, Christians came to be regarded as a "third race" that stood apart from an established framework of accepted religious traditions within the Roman Empire (Harnack 1904, 336–52).

What I have tried to offer in the last few paragraphs is a very brief description of the intellectual setting in which the early Christians formulated their initial ideas about other kinds of religious devotion. This way of proceeding accords with the experience of early Christianity, which commenced with urgent appeals and fervent proclamation, after which came more measured reflection on what had been learned about the religious others met along the way. The observation of Martin Kähler (1835–1912)—that mission is the "mother of theology" (cited in Bosch 1991, 16)—is especially apt with respect to the apostolic church and its different responses to other kinds of piety. At this stage in the development of theology, when the memory of personal encounter with Jesus was still fresh and the Spirit's power visibly palpable, evangelists did not wait for systematicians to work out a program for them to follow. Instead, believers plunged ahead with a saving message for the world and only afterward thought systematically about the alternative belief structures lying behind the various reactions coming back to them. First mission praxis, then theology; this is how the first generations of Christians seem to have worked out their basic approach to the theology of religion.

Of course, the early church already had at hand a familiar set of categories that could have been utilized to assess religious phenomena. By the first century, it had become normative within the Greco-Roman world to evaluate religious practices in terms of civic interests and popular approval. A remarkably broad grouping of cults and traditions fell within the expansive limits of what Roman and provincial opinion was willing to consider acceptable forms of religion (in other words, *religio licita*). An intention to secure the well-being of a city or region by honoring its divinities is the common element that recurs among these different expressions of piety. In addition, the elastic quality of Greek paganism disposed many communities to recognize previously unknown local cults, when these were transplanted to other areas of the empire (including Rome itself). Unacceptable religious customs were most likely to be labeled *superstitio*, a designation that stood generally for bizarre or hopelessly unsophisticated religious behavior meant to manipulate the actions and attitudes of the gods. In a treatise entitled *On Superstitions* (a lost work excerpted in Augustine, *Civ* 6.10), for example, the philosopher Seneca shows particular disgust for acts of self-mutilation he associated with certain religious rites. Then there were those who raised questions about the integrity of believing in the traditional gods of Rome altogether. Such were liable to be called "atheists," especially if their unconventional thinking was perceived to be harmful to society (disrespecting the divine patrons of a city might lead to community disaster). Up to the fourth century, Christians who refused to participate in particular pagan rites could be condemned to death in times of persecution for their perverse "atheism" (Fox 1987, 425–28).

For the apostolic church, the acceptability of any religious practice could not possibly depend on its secular legal standing or aesthetic appeal. As with the Jews and their insistence on the oneness of God and the inadmissibility of divine images, matters of ultimate truth were thought to be at stake. God's revelation in Christ, set within a broader narrative of Jewish salvation history, and the reign of God announced by Jesus became for early Christians the primary interpretive framework through which to evaluate religious attitudes and behavior. Upon close inspection, we find something more subtle than a simple true-false standard being applied to non-Christian religiosity. Even within the New Testament, diverse motivations behind and purposes for religious behavior are recognized. This is the beginning point of Christian reflection in the context of mission on the nature of religion.

Cast into an extremely negative light are those characters in Acts, for example, who appear to be participating in religious culture for selfish reasons. Elymas (or Bar-Jesus) "the magician" (Acts 13:6–12), dismissed by Luke as a "Jewish false prophet," is one such figure. No particular act of wonder-working is attributed to Elymas, but he seems to have been acting as a religious advisor (possibly an astrologer) to Sergius Paulus, a Roman official on Cyprus. In this story of successful evangelization, Elymas is temporarily blinded after failing to keep the proconsul from hearing and believing the message of the gospel. In part, Paul's action appears to be a judgment against Elymas as a religious role-player. The sorcerer is condemned as a shyster ("full of all deceit and villainy") and opponent of righteousness, who serves Satan and thereby impedes the progress of the Word ("will you not stop making crooked the straight paths of the Lord?"). Cursed by Paul, the once-powerful (false) prophet finds himself groping pathetically in the darkness for someone to guide him by the hand.

A similar impression is created with respect to the seven sons of an otherwise unknown Jewish "high priest" named Sceva (Acts 19:11–20), who had formed themselves into a group of itinerant exorcists. Having learned about the miracles of Paul, they are said to have emulated his technique by invoking the name of Jesus in their healing ministry. In this case, an evil spirit and a possessed man become the instruments of their dramatic unmasking. The spirit challenges their right to tap into the source of Paul's power ("Jesus I know, and Paul I know; but who are you?") and then the man drives them out of the house "naked and wounded." That this is a story about the wrong use of religion is made clear at its conclusion, when it is reported that a number of new believers in Ephesus, who had previously engaged in magic, "disclosed their practices" and then publicly burned a valuable collection of secret books.

Explicit reference is made to a profit motive in the story of the fortune-telling slave girl Paul heals at Philippi (Acts 16:16–21). When the "spirit of divination" or "python spirit" empowering her gift is confronted and flees, her owners faced a fiscal crisis. Having lost their livelihood ("their hope of making money was gone"), they lodged a complaint with the authorities alleging that Paul and Silas as Jews threatened the public order of their Roman city. An awareness of religion as business is thus made evident in this story, as it is later in Acts (19:23–41) when the silversmiths of Ephesus are shown instigating opposition to Paul after his activities there appear to threaten the viability of a thriving cult center dedicated to "Artemis of the Ephesians." Given the very small scale of Christianity in the first century, the fears of the craftsmen, who depended on a steady flow of pilgrimage traffic to the renowned shrine, would seem to have been exaggerated. Yet not long after Luke's time, we hear Pliny the Younger telling Trajan about how his decision to intimidate Christian believers had already begun to improve the financial metrics of the religious marketplace operating within his governorate: "There is no doubt that people have begun to throng to the temples which had been almost entirely deserted for a long time; the sacred rites which had been allowed to lapse are being performed again, and flesh of sacrificial victims is on sale everywhere, though up till recently scarcely anyone could be found to buy it" (*Ep* 10.96). In the eyes of his enemies, it would appear, the actions of Jesus in the outer precincts of the Temple (Mark 11:15–18) posed a similar challenge to the economic infrastructure of the Jewish cult in Jerusalem.

What had set the Ephesian silversmiths and their tradesmen allies on edge, according to Luke, was the suggestion of Paul that "gods made with hands are not gods" (Acts 19:26). This is a theological assertion, which is not focused primarily on the alleged self-interest of the parties involved but is more concerned with what their religious customs may be implying about the nature of God. The charge of idolatry, it seems to me, represents a second framing device used by the early Christians to interpret much of the religious behavior taking place around them. Very little needs to be said about this understanding of paganism. It is a familiar line of attack in the Old Testament that the Jews had been using for centuries to delegitimize the nature religions of the ancient Near East. In Acts, an argument against idolatry is employed with some frequency and not only to undermine the foundations of Greek pagan worship (as at 17:24–25, 29 and 14:15, in addition to 19:26). In the long speech of Stephen before his execution, the decision of Solomon himself to build the original Temple is called into question on the grounds that "the Most High does not dwell in houses made with human hands" (Acts 7:48, with a supporting quotation from Isa. 66:1–2).

A third critical assessment of piety to be found in the New Testament addresses the problem of co-religionists who self-identify as followers of Jesus but are judged to have deviated in some important way from the theological or ethical norms of the community. Luke offers up an archetype for this behavior pattern in the figure of Simon Magus (Acts 8:9–24). The whole of Samaria, it is said, acclaimed him as an exceptional magician ("this man is the power of God that is called Great"). Nevertheless, in response to the preaching of Philip, Simon believes and submits to water baptism. Subsequently, a baptism in the Spirit is administered through the agency of Peter and John, sent down to Samaria from Jerusalem. This is the occasion of Simon's grave misjudgment: he offers to buy access to the source of the apostles' power, perhaps in a bid to regain his former status as a sorcerer. Stiffly rebuffed, Simon then appears to see the error of his ways and asks Peter for prayers on his behalf.

Later Christian writers routinely treat the Simon Magus story as a cautionary tale that warns against the practice of selling church offices (hence simony). Some speculate on a possible connection here to second-century Gnosticism. My interest in Simon as an example attaches rather to the possibility portrayed in this narrative that members of the community might find themselves ostracized, despite the fact that their practice of faith in most respects appears to be the equivalent of what others are doing. Simon's essential problem, in the words of Peter, is one of intention not form: "your heart is not right before God" (8:21). Thus, even though he professes to be seeking a worthy end ("give me also this power, so that any one on whom I lay my hands may receive the Holy Spirit") and otherwise conforms to established norms (he seems to acknowledge apostolic authority, for example, and respects the importance of the baptismal rite), Simon has put himself into mortal danger by threatening to corrupt what is holy and good by turning it into a commodity that can be bought and sold. In the memory of the church, Simon is universally regarded as a heretic. The Acts story ends ambiguously, however. Whether or not Simon will be reintegrated into the community is left open.

Luke does offer at least one positive view of pagan religion in Acts. Paul's visit to Athens (17:16–34) and an encounter at Lystra (14:8–18) provide occasions for the apostle to show a measure of respect for a religious tradition other than Judaism and Christianity. To be sure, Paul is shown firmly rejecting the forms of pagan worship he observes in both locations. At Lystra, the crowd's intention to honor Paul and Barnabas as gods come to earth provokes the apostles to rend their garments in dismay and to characterize the sacrifices about to be made on their behalf as homage to "worthless things" (14:15). In Athens, the narrator tells the reader of Paul's distress (even anger) at all the idols he sees in the city (17:16). But these negative evaluations are not the whole story. Beside them Luke provides an alternative, more charitable explanation for some of the pagan religious behavior taking place in the presence of the apostles. He suggests through Paul that the artifacts and practices of Greek paganism he is describing might indicate something positive about a deep human instinct to know God. In this spirit, Paul carefully commends the Athenians for their public expressions of piety: "I see how extremely religious you are in every way" (17:22). He also shows a willingness to understand the inquisitiveness of the philosophers as a kind of earnest reaching for knowledge about God (17:27). His conviction that the seasons and bounty of the earth give continuous witness to an ultimate source of providence (14:17) stands as another reason for Paul in Acts to hope that an impulse to understand the world as it is could prepare one to appreciate its creator.

We are not left on our own to guess at the possible implications for mission practice wrapped up in these different conceptualizations of Greek religiousness. Since each of the stories recounted briefly above is already set in a missionary context, some kind of evangelistic response to the situation encountered naturally follows and often serves to conclude the various narratives. No two stories in Acts portray this dynamic in exactly the same way, but some patterns may be detected. In cases of egregious self-interest (especially when fraud or deception is suspected), the apostles may be expected to act forcefully, sometimes issuing a powerful word of rebuke that has the capacity to effect severe punishment. When the issue is idolatry, forthright proclamation is likely to follow, but these speeches tend to be delivered as entreaties, with an educative function. Somewhat unexpectedly, given his notorious reputation, even Simon Magus is given an opportunity to repent of his wickedness (8:22). At Lystra and Athens, Paul embodies an approach toward other faiths that is remarkably generous, courteous, and culturally sensitive, but he does not hesitate at the same time to assert that pagan religious culture as a whole is founded on a misunderstanding of divine reality.

MISSION AND THE RELIGIONS

Premodern Attitudes and Practices

Constantine's decision to legitimate Christianity immediately put the church and its mission on a new footing. Imperial patronage not only validated but also lent prestige to what had been a socially marginal religious group within the empire. This change in the circumstances of Christianity had implications for paganism, too. Except for a brief period of official reinstatement during the rule of Julian (361–63), the standing of paganism steadily eroded over the course of the fourth century. At first this meant simply a diminishing of government concern for the advancement of pagan interests. By the time of Theodosius (379–95), the apparatus of empire had been put at the disposal of an anti-pagan agenda that included legislation authorizing the destruction of temples and the suppression of certain public rites (MacMullen 1997, 1–73). Pagan religiosity by no means disappeared in this era, persisting especially in rituals and traditions closely connected to family life and the rhythms of agriculture, but the official status of paganism had been substantially degraded.

As the political situation of the church improved within the Roman Empire, new patterns of pagan-Christian relations also emerged. Socially empowered Christians less and less felt the need to engage paganism intellectually. Thus, second-century apologists like Justin Martyr and Clement of Alexandria lacked counterparts of a similar stature in the post-Theodosian church. In that earlier era, at least some Christians had been keen to win the respect of regional neighbors by stressing their commonalities. In the Epistle to Diognetus (second–third centuries), for example, an assertion is made that Christians have no peculiar culture of their own (*Diog* 5). In dress, diet, language, and ordinary conduct, they are more likely than not, it is said, to follow local customs. When Justin and Clement of Alexandria decide to present the claims of the gospel in terms borrowed from Greek philosophy, they imply a common quest for truth that extends beyond the limits of the church in time. Justin goes so far as to suggest that Socrates and Heraclitus, among other pre-Christian wisdom seekers, had lived under the inspiration of the divine Word (*1 Apol* 46; *2 Apol* 8). Bediako (1992, 436) contends that Justin and Clement were approaching their Greek heritage as an alternative "tradition of response" to the reality of the transcendent, a bold interpretive move that allowed them to separate high-minded philosophical activity from the unacceptable excesses of popular religion. Dupuis (1997, 53–83) considers the universal history of the Logos outlined in the early church fathers to be a proper foundation on which to construct a Christian theology of religious pluralism.

One of the last of the great Christian thinkers in antiquity to take paganism seriously is Augustine. In his world, Catholicism was but one of several religious traditions in lively competition with each other. Even if the church's situation within the empire had taken a decisive turn for the better during the lifetime of Augustine

(354–430), its earthly future was hardly secure. Strong advocates of paganism and other ways of faith were still active in all the places Augustine would find himself in the late fourth century (including Carthage, Rome, and Milan) and among these opponents were men of great reputation and power (such as the prefect Symmachus, who had appealed unsuccessfully to the emperor in 384 for the restoration of pagan symbols and rites within the Roman Senate).

In Augustine's writings, we see an eloquent spokesman for Catholic Christianity engaging a variety of people inside and outside the church with respect to doctrinal issues and matters of religious practice. Famous exchanges with adversaries like Faustus are conducted more or less out in the open, as public skirmishes. His letters and sermons (all of which could stand to be examined more carefully from a missiological perspective) show Augustine confronting alternative points of view in the context of his pastoral responsibilities. A full-length argument against the false gods of paganism is mounted in what many consider to be his greatest work, the *City of God.* In that book, Augustine repeats and elaborates on the many warnings in scripture against idolatry. At the same time, he does his utmost to demonstrate the powerlessness of Rome's traditional deities, using the same non-Christian texts to which his opponents could be expected to appeal. Intriguingly, Augustine adds another original layer of analysis that considers the social functions of religion in public life. He is led in this direction by an earlier work of the historian Varro (116–27 B.C.E.), who had discussed religion in terms of its divine and human aspects. Augustine does not accept Varro's argument that "civil theology" or "natural theology" could be disentangled from the "fabulous" or "mythical" theology of the theater (*Civ* 6.5–8), but he does seem to respond to the suggestion that religion involves more than humans showing devotion to one or more deities. In a key passage, Augustine reviews the vocabulary of religion, including the terms commonly used for worship (*latreia*, *servitus*), cult (*cultus*), and piety (*eusebeia*). He concludes: it is wrong to confine the idea of "religion" to the worship of God, since this concept normally refers to "an attitude of respect in relations between a man and his neighbor" (*Civ* 10.1). Augustine suggests further that true "piety" is realized through "acts of compassion," which God not only commands but also prefers "even more than sacrifices."

Coercive measures, applied with increasing comprehensiveness from the time of Theodosius, dramatically reduced the public profile of paganism within the empire and destroyed its institutional infrastructure (temples and schools). Plenty of support for this aggressive policy could be found in Augustine's own writings and in other patristic literature, where far less subtle descriptions of paganism than that offered in the *City of God* ruled the day. Outside the church, it was commonly thought, one ventured into the realm of demons. The proper response to nonorthodox religious behavior was to oppose it outright as an expression of human depravity. Tolerance in the face of what the church considered evil was unthinkable and unfaithful. In this context, the irenic stance of Paul in Athens had difficulty holding its ground when appeals were made to the polemic of Paul in Romans: "For the wrath of God is revealed from heaven against all ungodliness and wickedness of those who by their wickedness suppress the truth. . . . Claiming to be wise, they became fools; and they exchanged the glory of the immortal God for images resembling a mortal human being or birds or four-footed animals or reptiles" (Rom. 1:18, 22–23; on missionary appropriations of this passage, see Walls 1996, 55–67).

In his life of St. Martin of Tours, Sulpicius Severus (c. 363–c. 420) lays down a much-imitated template that countless hagiographers and precritical historians after him will use to interpret the different forms of paganism encountered by the medieval missionaries of Europe. According to his biographer, Martin (c. 316-397) campaigned tirelessly to root out false religion, which he seemed to find everywhere in the lightly evangelized countryside around Tours. Thus, he tears down an altar dedicated to the memory of what the rural population thought was a group of Christian martyrs, after learning through interviews with the oldest members of the community (plus a vision given in answer to prayer) that a robber instead had been buried in that place (*Life of Martin* 11). On many other occasions, Martin is shown destroying pagan shrines, often in the face of fierce local resistance. These confrontations are depicted as contests between the forces of the devil and God's champion, whose solitary strength is augmented by angelic allies and timely divine interventions into the normal processes of the natural world. In one particularly vivid passage, it is said that the devil "thrust his visible presence" onto Martin, using a variety of shapes: "Sometimes he presented himself with features disguised to resemble Jupiter, very frequently Mercury, often even Venus or Minerva" (*Life of Martin* 22). There seems to be no curiosity here about these names, their significance in this part of Gaul, or the specific rites attached to these sacred locations. As Régine Pernoud (2006, 87) has observed, pagan temples "symbolized error" in the narrative of Sulpicius Severus. The will to understand the motives and purposes behind non-Christian piety, so evident in the *City of God*, is nowhere to be found. Apparently, it is enough for the reader to learn that the miraculous triumphs of Martin led many to abandon their traditional practices for Christianity.

When Christianity understands itself to be unique, exclusive, superior, definitive, normative, and absolute (Knitter 1985, 18), its adherents have little incentive to understand or value the religious lives of others. Based on such a self-confident worldview, Christian mission tends to be a matter of displacement and conquest (Bosch 1991, 475). By and large, this was the prevailing attitude of European Christianity through the medieval and early modern periods, which meant that few missionaries or mission theorists in those centuries critically interrogated their own truth claims or sought to engage alternative belief structures at a deep level. But there were some exceptions and this experience is worth recounting briefly, too, not least because many to come later will find in these examples instruction and inspiration for how to imagine a basis for interfaith encounter that does not aspire necessarily to Christian political and social domination.

The Jesuit experiment in the East has already been discussed (see chapter 3). We may recall that Valignano, Ricci, and several generations of missionary colleagues in China did not treat all forms of religious behavior equally. After extended contact with Buddhism, they concluded that irreconcilable differences in theological outlook separated Christianity from that tradition. The decision to stop wearing Buddhist religious dress demonstrated the rejection of what the Jesuits considered to be an unacceptable way of faith. They were similarly negative about many of the "superstitions" observed by ordinary Chinese, but made room in their theory of mission for Confucionist philosophy and "cultural" traditions judged to be free of theological content. Rites associated with the veneration of ancestors eventually became the test case that juridically invalidated the Jesuit position back home in Europe (the so-called "Rites Controversy"). The idea that a non-Western form of philosophy could stand in the place of Aristotle with respect to theology and so offer a pathway by which missionaries could relate to a comprehensive system of meaning and values outside of Christianity has proved more enduring.

Ramon Lull (or Llull) is another premodern figure (c. 1232–1316) who stands out when viewed against the usual background of medieval missionary indifference toward the particulars of other faith communities. Lull dedicated himself to the evangelization of Muslims especially, but he worked for the conversion of Jews and others as well. In the pursuit of his lifelong calling, he studied Arabic, the Qur'an, Muslim theology (*kalam*), and the philosophical traditions of Islam. Lull's many books in Arabic, Latin, and his native Catalan show the deep imprint of these studies on his own thought, with influences felt especially from Sufism (as in his *Book of the Lover and the Beloved*) and the Muslim theological practice of describing God in terms of divine attributes or uncreated virtues (reflected in Lull's *Art*, among other works). In an imagined situation of interreligious dialogue (*The Book of the Gentile and the Three Wise Men*) arguments for Judaism and Islam are presented through fictional spokespersons with remarkable candidness. For more background on Lull and his extensive output of texts, students may want to consult the anthologies edited by Bonner (Llull 1985, 1993). Lull's proposal that monasteries throughout Europe establish programs of language study to equip missionaries for cross-cultural work among Muslims and others was partially realized in his own time but would not be sustained.

Eastern Christians living under Muslim rule provide a third major example of premodern reflection on mission and apologetics in the midst of intense inter-religious encounter. In this case, the political and demographic trends were moving in the opposite direction from what Ramon Lull and his contemporaries were experiencing in the context of Spain's *Reçonquista*. Muslim domination of the Middle East not only diminished the social status of many Eastern

Christians but also transformed their cultural milieu. One by one, the ancient Christian communities of the region adopted Arabic and began to rearticulate their religious identities using the idiom of Islam. The literature produced in this situation is largely defensive in its orientation. Arabophone theologians wrote primarily for their co-religionists, who needed encouragement in the face of decline and arguments with which to defend contested Christian doctrines (especially the Trinity and the Incarnation). Yet the fact that these documents circulated in Arabic created an opportunity for Christian apologists also to speak to Muslim neighbors. We know that Christian intellectuals participated in Muslim debates over the merits of Greek science and philosophy, contributing especially as translators of ancient texts and teachers of philosophy. Sidney Griffith (2008, esp. 106–28) draws attention to an extraordinary "community of discourse" on religion and philosophy that Christians and Muslims assembled together in ninth- and tenth-century Baghdad.

Nineteenth-Century Trends

At the beginning of the modern Protestant missionary movement, cross-cultural evangelists and their sending bodies were confident that most of the world's inhabitants were sure to perish eternally, because they had no means of knowing Christ. Thus, William Carey surveyed the state of humanity in 1792 and concluded that evangelical Protestants had an "obligation" to do something about the situation of the multitudes living unaware in "pagan darkness" (62). Likewise, when the American Board of Commissioners for Foreign Missions ordained its first group of missionaries in 1812, the preacher implored the congregation in attendance to put itself in the condition of the "poor degraded Africans . . . the thousands of children sacrificed in the Ganges . . . the throngs of miserable pilgrims pressing forward to devote themselves to the impure and sanguinary worship of Moloch." If that were not enough to move Christian hearts to "benevolent exertion," one's own family could be interpolated into the picture: "Imagine your children, parents, brothers, sisters this moment in the midst of India, worshippers of the horrid idol of Juggernaut" (Woods 1966, 258–59).

More experience in the field tended to confirm Protestant missionary assumptions of wholesale heathen degradation and lostness, at least through the first half of the nineteenth century. One result of the fact that missionaries were among the few Westerners living for long periods of time in relatively unknown, exotic societies was that they came to be seen back home as experts on those civilizations. Because church members and wider publics learned much of what they knew about the religious traditions of the world through missionary reports, they, too, became accustomed to regard non-Christian religious behavior as evidence of barbarism and futility (the role of missionary periodicals in spreading these views is explored in Oddie 2006, 203–30). Even the most learned missionary writers of the period emphasized the coarsest aspects of what they considered to be false religions. An influential example is William Ward's description of the "history, literature, and religion of the Hindoos," published in many editions from 1811. Another is Alexander Duff's study of the "gigantic system of Hinduism," first compiled in 1839. Ward and Duff agreed that popular religion, in all its lurid idolatrous detail, was the proper level at which to take the measure of a religious tradition, because that is where the effects of belief and doctrine were most widely felt. In good post-Enlightenment style, they insisted that bad religion is a human problem more than it is the work of the devil. (This approach allows Duff also to critique the Roman Catholics for corrupting the pristine apostolic faith handed on to them; cf. Duff 1839, 179.) The modernist sensibilities of Ward and Duff show up especially in the way they make a case for their own interreligious expertise. At a distance, Ward cautions (1817, xcix), "this system of idolatry" may appear to be beautiful, but up-close the fog clears and the deception is exposed. Missionaries with long residence on the subcontinent *know* that Indian religion is perverse, because they have witnessed at first-hand its ill effects. This is an empiricist argument that gives considerable weight to observable "facts" on the ground. In this approach, the basic compatibility of reason and Christian revelation is assumed. Maxwell (2001) explores further how Enlightenment perspectives decisively shaped European Protestant discussions of mission in the late eighteenth–early nineteenth centuries.

The nineteenth-century examples given so far are all drawn from the history of mission in India. Vigorous and consequential debates over Indian religion, which were taking place outside the church, are the reason for this focus. These were an important part of the background against which initial evangelical missionary appeals for public support were issued in this period. Especially crucial at the start of the modern Protestant missionary movement was the matter of Britain's religious policy in India. As Penny Carson (2001) has shown, arguments over what missionaries should be allowed to do in British India touched on many of the era's most explosive religious issues, including Catholic-Protestant relations, the principle of religious toleration, whether or not to export Britain's ecclesiastical establishment, and the civil rights of colonial subjects.

Besides having to negotiate their way through the thickets of imperial politics, the advocates of mission were also obliged to contend with a gathering Orientalist discourse on religion that was inclined to affirm Hinduism as an ancient and venerable wisdom tradition. In Ward's comment above about viewing the religions of India at a distance through fog is a gentle critique of the academics back in Europe who knew Hinduism only through a few of its classic texts. Duff is more direct. He sees in the scholarly attention lavished on Hinduism and Sanskrit in the late eighteenth century an analogue to Gibbon's unbounded admiration for pre-Christian Greece and Rome (1839, 45). What is the reason for the obvious enthusiasm of the European professors (and poets) when they describe the cultural and religious heritage of India that so fascinated them from afar? According to Duff (16–25), Western scholarship could not help itself. It had been swept up into a much broader trend of admiration for the mysterious East that was essentially a romantic impulse. First, the Portuguese fell under the spell of Mogul splendor. Then the generation of the renowned philologist Sir William Jones (1746–94) convinced itself that Sanskrit was the most perfect language in the world and its literature the most sublime. In response, Duff and other missionary apologists will offer what purports to be a more scientific appraisal of Indian religion, with emphasis placed on those aspects of contemporary practice that seem the most out of sync with modernity. According to this line of argument, Hinduism has to be opposed, not only as a form of religious idolatry but also because it impeded the social development of non-European civilizations.

To a large degree, Protestant missions proceeded through much of the nineteenth century on the basis of a theology of religion very close to what had been suggested by Alexander Duff. Not everyone agreed with his recommendations on methods. (Duff emphasized the advantages of mission-sponsored institutions of higher education.) But relatively few would have taken issue with his dim estimate of most non-Christian piety. Representative in this respect is the discussion of religion offered by James Dennis in the context of his 1893 Students' Lectures on Missions at Princeton Theological Seminary. According to Dennis, whose appointment as the inaugural lecturer in this prestigious series stood near the beginning of a marked upsurge of American interest in the academic study of mission, a sharp line of division still separated all false religion from Christianity. The difference between them was not simply one of degree. The "human religions" or "ethnic religions" of the world are held to be "corruptions and perversions of a primitive, monotheistic faith which was directly taught by God to the early progenitors of the race" (Dennis 1893, 250). They are "lapses from the true" (252), which bear only faint traces of an original divine imprint. Whatever greatness may be recognized in the genius of their founders, "their ideals have crumbled, and their followers have lived and moved only amidst the ruins of ideal systems" (257). Indeed, according to Dennis, "the manifest and colossal failure of every human system of religion to satisfy the wants of humanity" (292) has prepared the non-Christian world in a negative way for the optimism and hope finally made available to it in Christian mission. In his most famous publication, *Christian Missions and Social Progress* (1897–1906), Dennis will go on to document those perceived failures in detail, while presenting an upbeat sociological analysis of the Protestant missionary record.

For all his bravado, Dennis gives hints that he sees some serious challenges on the horizon of the modern missionary movement, some of which hail from the realm of the religions. He speaks, for example, of a proposed Muslim mission to America (1893, 281), which would compete with Christianity on its "home" ground. The allusion here may be to the activities of Mohammad Alexander Russell Webb (1846–1916), a Western convert to Islam who founded a Muslim mission in New York City and officially represented his adopted faith tradition at the 1893 World's Parliament of Religions in Chicago (Abd-Allah 2006). Webb's story in some respects parallels that of the better known Swami Vivekananda (1863–1902), who spoke persuasively for Hinduism at the Chicago meeting and then established two organizations in America to carry on his efforts at Hindu outreach to the West, the Ramakrishna Mission and the Vedanta Society.

In retrospect, this cluster of events near the end of the nineteenth century presages an impending transformation of the religious landscape of the United States, with much greater diversity becoming the norm and more American Christians getting an opportunity to hear the adherents of other traditions explain their own beliefs and practices. For many scholars of mission to come in the next century, an awareness of this fundamental shift in the religious demography of the West will cause them to question the very idea of dividing the world conceptually into Christian and non-Christian territorial zones (the notion of Christendom).

The rise of comparative thinking about religion from a secular standpoint is a second challenge to mission theology addressed in the lectures of Dennis. He plainly worries that some in his Princeton Seminary student audience will be swayed by the results of comparativist research, such as that conducted by the renowned philologist Max Müller (1823–1900). A lengthy epigraph (1893, 244) borrowed from Monier Monier-Williams (1819–99) warns against any proposal to regard the Bible as just one of many "sacred books of the East." (Müller edited the monumental fifty-volume series issued under this general title; Monier-Williams was Müller's great rival at Oxford.) A key point for Dennis is whether or not Christianity should be studied alongside other religious traditions, using the same scholarly methods and tools of analysis. The problem, as Dennis sees it, is that "modern" students of religion might lose sight of the fact that the non-Christian religions are false, in their eagerness to discover "naturalistic" explanations for the origin and development of religion (249). James Frazer's influential study of magic and religion (*The Golden Bough*, first published in 1890) may well have been among the scholarly works giving Dennis pause. The theory of Dennis (represented in the quotes above) that all other religions are human corruptions of an original, divinely granted monotheism essentially preserved in Christianity is thus a counterassertion forcefully made in opposition to the findings of much late-nineteenth-century anthropology and the study of religion.

Dennis also rejects the idea of fulfillment theology, reckoning it to be among the illegitimate offspring of comparative religion (278–79). Yet this is precisely the direction that was to be taken by a growing number of mission theorists at the turn of the twentieth century. The best known of these is probably J. N. Farquhar (1861–1929), whose interpretation of Christianity as *The Crown of Hinduism*

(1913) put the fulfillment thesis into one of its most widely read forms. Eric Sharpe's intellectual biography of Farquhar (1965) continues to be an excellent introduction to his thought. Among those who may have influenced the development of Farquhar is T. E. Slater (1840–1912), whose work with highly educated Indian nationals over some forty years induced him to formulate what was a remarkably positive missionary view of Hinduism for its time. Slater appears to be the first Christian missionary in India to suggest in print that Christianity was not the antithesis of Hindu religion but rather its consummation (the publications of Slater are discussed in Sharpe 1965, 94–105; see also Cracknell 1995, 108–19).

Early in his career especially, Slater was very much swimming against the tide of majority nineteenth-century missionary and church opinion in the matter of the non-Christian religions, as illustrated above in the remarks of James Dennis. By the turn of the twentieth century, Farquhar and others would have an easier time of it, not least because many of that generation's leading missionary theologians had come around to the view that the world's "great" religions ought to be treated more sympathetically than in the past. Several powerful factors were influencing this shift in thinking about the non-Christian religions. One was the fact of slow progress nearly everywhere in Asia through the course of the nineteenth century, a time during which antagonistic methods of public dispute and confrontation dominated missionary practice. Did it make sense to continue with the same tactics that had produced so little evangelistic return up until then?

By the late nineteenth century, many thoughtful students of mission also knew that the religious traditions criticized so forthrightly by their forebears had begun to change. The pressure of missionary propaganda and higher levels of education had stimulated internal movements of reform in more than one non-Christian religious tradition. Reformers often took aim at the cruelest social customs still practiced in their time (for example, widow-burning in India or foot-binding in China) and those forms of folk religion most like superstitious magic. To the extent that such practices were abandoned or effectively recharacterized as nonreligious aspects of popular culture (Oddie 2003, 175–77), the old missionary arguments against them could be deflected. As the non-Christian religions modernized in this way, mission theorists had to adopt new apologetic strategies, among which were proposals to treat other kinds of faith in a more positive manner.

A third factor influencing the way many missionaries in the early twentieth century looked at non-Christian religions is the principle of evolution. Darwinist logic, when applied to the matter of religious truth, allowed missionaries to affirm the supremacy of Christianity while also recognizing what they considered to be the partial but still laudable achievements of other faith traditions. Fulfillment theology more precisely asserted that the universal religious aspirations expressed through the non-Christian religions could be fully realized in Christianity (or in Christ). In this way, it becomes possible to speak of the non-Christian faith traditions as providential means by which God prepares their adherents to receive the gospel, with some (the "higher" religions) thought to be doing this more effectively than others (the "lower" or primal religions). A scriptural warrant for something like this approach seems to have been supplied by Jesus himself, who represented his own ministry as a quest to fulfill the law and the prophets, not to destroy them (Matt. 5:17). Paul's irenic apologetic stance at Athens and the Logos language of John 1 are two other biblical resources often invoked in support of fulfillment theology (other passages are discussed in Hedges 2001, 17–21).

The World Missionary Conference of 1910, convened at Edinburgh, is rightly considered a pivotal moment in the history of mission and ecumenism. The two-year study process leading up to the conclave itself, involving hundreds of missionaries and church leaders worldwide, was also a missiological event of the first order. Never before had such a comprehensive and systematic effort been mounted to evaluate the long-term results of modern missions (albeit focused almost exclusively on Protestant activities). The conference also sought to identify the major problems that still lay in the way of further progress and the best methods to recommend for the future. Conference organizers decided to sideline those issues of doctrine and polity that regularly divided missionaries and so impeded their collaboration, including the episcopacy, the details of eschatology, particular schemes for church unity, and the advisability of Protestants evangelizing Catholic and Orthodox Christians. The topic of mission and the religions thus became a leading theoretical concern at the Edinburgh conference, which otherwise tended to concentrate its energies on more practical questions of method and technique. In Brian Stanley's recently published account and expert analysis of the World Missionary Conference, the extensive deliberations and negotiations conducted with respect to the agenda and procedures of the meeting are discussed at length (2009, esp. 18–72).

Commission IV ("The Christian Message in Relation to Non-Christian Religions") was the primary location within the Edinburgh structure at which the problem of the religions was most directly engaged. The Report of Commission IV shows the Protestant missionary movement as a whole seeking after ways to relate constructively to people of other faith, while continuing to affirm the urgency of Christian proclamation and conversion. Just how difficult it was in practice to satisfy these two great aims at the same time is revealed in the detailed answers submitted to the commission in response to its questionnaire (these replies are examined most thoroughly in Stanley 2009, Hedges 2001, Cracknell 1995, and Sharpe 1965). Many of those participating in the survey process indicated their preference for a fulfillment perspective. One sees this, for example, in a number of the replies that came back from missionaries serving in India (including C. F. Andrews, T. E. Slater, Nicol Macnicol, and J. N. Farquhar). Many of these distinguished figures in the global Protestant missionary community were clearly prepared to find in Hinduism aspects of religiosity already in tune with gospel values. One of the questions put to the commission's correspondents in the field may have stimulated some of these data by prompting reflection on "points of contact" with other religions that might be regarded as "preparation" for Christianity (question #6).

The final form of the commission's report was self-consciously constructed using a scale that moved from the "primitive" to "higher" religions (that is, from animism to Hinduism, with the religions of China and Japan, plus Islam, placed in between). As such, the overall structure of the report embodied an evolutionary approach to religious difference that many advocates of fulfillment theology would have considered apologetically useful and theologically appropriate. Sharpe (1965, 288–97) and Stanley (2009, 222–27) have nonetheless drawn attention to language in the "General Conclusions" of the report that qualify its broad acceptance of the fulfillment thesis. They both credit Indian missionary A. G. Hogg with having influenced chairman David Cairns to balance the report's implicit endorsement of fulfillment theology with other statements that stressed the "absoluteness of Christianity" (as at World Missionary Conference 1910 [IV], 268). Hogg was not advocating a return to the antagonistic methods of the early nineteenth century or pushing for a triumphal tone in mission. His driving concern was to respect the integrity of the non-Christian religions by recognizing the human needs they actually met and the particular functions each one played in its own society. Hogg's sophisticated essay on *karma* and Christian redemption (1909) illustrates his method, which emphasized the need to identify the distinctive teachings and moral aims of each religious tradition.

Further evidence of Cairns's apparent ambivalence about fulfillment theology is supplied in a "Concluding Note" added to the report after the meeting (World Missionary Conference 1910 [IV], 275–80). To an unnamed critic, Cairns explained that Hinduism was not to be regarded "as a preparation for Christianity in anything like the same way as the Old Testament is such a preparation" (276). According to Cairns, the commission's intention was rather to suggest that the Hindu tradition stood in relationship to the gospel in much the same way that ancient Hellenism did, with its "noble philosophy" offered up to the apostolic church alongside "its beautiful but poisonous mythology, its corrupt sexual morality, [and] its cruel system of slavery." Cairns indicates that he had solicited further comments from a "friendly critic" who had spoken during the discussion period at the conference and then quotes extensively from the letter submitted to him by C. H. Monahan, a Wesleyan Methodist missionary working in South India. Monahan was prepared to endorse the commission's generous view of the religions, provided that the everyday "cruelty" of the Hindu system be squarely addressed. In his view, the "moral situation" of Indian missions called for a more nuanced handling of the fulfillment thesis than that presented to the conference:

> There is much that must be destroyed before that which is best can be fulfilled. Much rubbish has to be carted away before the foundations of the city of God can be firmly laid in India's life. . . . There are things to be broken down before we can build up. There are chains to be smashed that souls may go free. (277–78)

Cairns declared himself to be in "full agreement" with this statement and welcomed the opportunity to include it as a "supplement" to the report of Commission IV. He went on to suggest that "the completeness of the Christian idea" required two complementary "types" of mission, which he saw exemplified in the approaches taken to the religions of their day by Tertullian and Origen: "the one dwelling most on the evils of those religions and the newness of the Gospel; and the other seeking to show that all that was noblest in the old religions was fulfilled in Christ" (279). Cairns urged precisely the same attitude toward Hindu religion: "No man can really penetrate to the innermost heart of the higher thought of Hinduism unless he antagonizes the manifold evils of its popular religion: and on the other hand, that no man can successfully attack its evils unless he has a true and sympathetic understanding of its nobler thought and life, and so is able to build up as well as destroy." This is the last word from Cairns on fulfillment theology given in the context of the World Missionary Conference.

Edinburgh 1910 subsequently became a touchstone for the theology of religion, but more than one evaluation of the meeting's significance has been offered. Ariarajah (1991, 28–31), for example, sets the work of Commission IV off against the overall aim of the conference, with the latter standing for a desire to conquer the world's religions and the former to understand them. In a similar spirit, Cracknell (1995, 259–60) hails the approach of Commission IV as "an incipient theology of dialogue." Sharpe (1965, 336–37) reminds us, however, that early twentieth-century fulfillment theology generally assumed the eventual replacement of other religious traditions by Christianity as a result of mission. Brian Stanley (2009, 222) sounds a similar note of caution when he observes: "Adherence to fulfillment theology did not imply any diminution in belief in the impending universal triumph of Christianity: it had merely (though radically) reconceived the process which would effect that triumph of displacement." Thus, while it may be true that some missionaries were groping theologically for an entirely new approach to the non-Christian religions, the literature of the conference (including the report of Commission IV), which represented the collective mind of the gathering, had not yet broken with its Protestant missionary past. On the topic of the religions, it would seem, the World Missionary Conference was still a nineteenth-century phenomenon.

Developments since Edinburgh 1910

The Continuation Committee created at the end of the Edinburgh meeting almost immediately decided to launch a scholarly periodical devoted to the science of mission. Begun in 1912, the *International Review of Missions* (*IRM*) soon became an indispensable source of careful reflection on the practice of Christian mission in a world of living religions. Founding editor J. H. Oldham built directly on the extensive research efforts carried out in preparation for the World Missionary Conference at Edinburgh (for details on this point, see Skreslet 2006a, 173–80). At the same time, the direction taken by the journal under Oldham's leadership shows how the study of mission in relation to the non-Christian religions was quickly beginning to expand its scope.

The first thing to notice about the *IRM* is that Oldham solicited articles and other contributions from Catholic missiologists, which signaled an intention to foster an even broader ecumenical approach to mission research than that pursued at Edinburgh. He also pushed to include nontheological materials in the mission bibliography section of the *IRM*, an editorial decision that further expanded the pool of scholarship on the religions to which the journal's audience would be exposed on a regular basis. Within the "Ten-Years' Selected Bibliography" published in volume 11 of the *IRM* (1922), for example, we find a burgeoning collection of research presented under the category of "Christianity and the Non-Christian Religions," encompassing books and articles from many different fields of study, including anthropology, comparative religion, ritual studies, and the history of religion. The importance of this subject to early twentieth-century missiology is indicated by the fact that more space was given to the section on non-Christian religions in this cumulative bibliography than to the topics of mission theory, the methods of mission, missionary training, cooperation and unity, and the social relations of missions—*combined.* Particularly noteworthy is a series of articles published in the *IRM* over its first decade that treated the "vital forces" of Buddhism and Islam.

The Continuation Committee of the World Missionary Conference finally gave way to a more permanent structure in 1921: the International Missionary Council (IMC). Over the next few decades the IMC became a primary sponsor of research on mission and the religions. Much of this scholarship continued to appear in the *IRM*, which had been made the responsibility of the IMC at its formation. Other materials were produced in connection with a series of international missionary conferences convened under the auspices of the IMC. At the Jerusalem conference in 1928 and at Tambaram (India) in 1938, conference participants struggled to clarify further many of the same interfaith issues that had engaged the missionary movement since at least the late nineteenth century, but they had to do their work in quite different historical circumstances than those faced by their predecessors. A disillusioning European conflict, for example, left many advocates of world mission wondering about the true character of Western civilization. The future prospects of European imperialism also had to be reassessed, especially in places such as China, India, and Egypt, where impassioned arguments against colonial rule were often peppered with rhetorical jabs aimed more directly at Western Christian missions as just another kind of unwanted foreign intrusion into the social and religious affairs of one's nation.

Timothy Yates (1994, 94–124) should be consulted for a cogent overview of missionary thinking during the interwar period on the relationship of the Christian faith to other religious traditions and commitments. Werner Ustorf (2000, 83–127) broadens this discussion by focusing on continental European perspectives just before and during the Nazi era. These were years during which the Protestant missionary enterprise as a whole moved away from the language of conquest and occupation expressed so freely at Edinburgh. An expanded definition of religion was also adopted, with secularism put beside the non-Christian traditions as yet another dangerous rival seen to be competing for the ultimate allegiance of modern men and women. The paper of Rufus Jones, "Secular Civilization and the Christian Task," given at Jerusalem in 1928, sharply articulated the profound challenge presented to the church by a rising tide of secularism, evident especially in the Western "home base" of missions. Jones (1928, 273) called on a worldwide Christian community to reconsider its message alongside the devoted followers of other religions, who might be expected for their own reasons to resist the growing influence of materialist philosophies.

The unity of the Protestant missionary movement became more difficult to maintain after the Jerusalem meeting of the IMC. A major issue over which fractious disagreements soon emerged centered on the proper missionary attitude to be struck with respect to the non-Christian religions. One line of thinking continued to stress the idea of continuity among the religions. For some, this meant reasserting the fulfillment thesis in terms not all that different from those used before Edinburgh. Robert Speer's paper on the "value of the religious values of the non-Christian religions," composed soon after the IMC meeting at Jerusalem as a kind of summary of its proceedings (Speer 1928), faithfully reproduces this argument. A few others, some of them finding inspiration in the presentation of Rufus Jones at Jerusalem, began to search for ways to promote collaboration among the adherents of the world's religious traditions as a new form of Christian mission.

It was in the service of this latter vision that the Laymen's Foreign Missions Inquiry was organized in 1930 under the direction of Harvard philosophy professor, William Hocking (1873–1966). For our purposes, the importance of the Laymen's Inquiry is not based solely on its conclusions, but is also attached to the study process carried out in the preparatory phase of the project. With funding provided by John D. Rockefeller Jr., Hocking's select Commission of Appraisal (which included Rufus Jones but no serving missionaries) proposed to evaluate the overall state of Protestant missions worldwide by investigating a few of the places in Asia (China, Burma, India, and Japan) where relatively large numbers of American missionaries and mission-related institutions were then concentrated. After a period of preliminary fact-finding conducted by staff, the commission traveled to Asia and spent the better part of a year interviewing missionaries and national church leaders, in large groups and more personally. They also engaged a number of non-Christian elites, in order to gain Asian perspectives on mission work that were not beholden to any part of the foreign missionary establishment. An impressive seven-volume final report was issued in 1933, after a summary version had already appeared under the title *Re-Thinking Missions* (Hocking et al. 1932). In these publications, recommendations were made to reduce the number of Western missionaries sent abroad while raising their intellectual and professional standards, to devolve responsibility for mission institutions more quickly onto national bodies, and to put the existing mission board structures of the denominations under a central authority in order to realize a more efficient use of resources.

A firestorm of controversy over the Laymen's Inquiry raged through the 1930s. Without a doubt, this extensive study of evangelization pushed advocates and critics alike to question whether the routines of early twentieth-century missions ought to be maintained indefinitely. Even more fundamentally, the Laymen's Inquiry suggested that the aims of Christian mission needed to be reconceptualized. According to the Commission of Appraisal, a long period of "temporary" mission activities was drawing to a close, an era during which it had been appropriate for foreign workers to focus on winning converts, preaching, and church planting. It was now time to take up what the report called the "permanent functions" of mission, which were characterized as a kind of "foreign service" or "ambassadorship" on behalf of Christianity (Hocking et al. 1932, 23–28). At the bottom of this new approach lay a particular view of the non-Christian religions. The finality of Christ, according to historian William Hutchison (1987, 170), was the "do-or-die" issue in this debate over the future of the modern missionary movement. Hocking and his colleagues were arguing for an end to religious competition in favor of a joint quest for "world understanding and unity on a spiritual level" (Hocking et al., 328). To participate fully in this common venture, the next generation of Christian missionaries would have to reimagine themselves as "co-worker[s] with the forces within each . . . religious system which are making for righteousness" (327).

Spinning off in quite another direction after Jerusalem was a view of mission and the non-Christian religions that stressed the uniqueness of the gospel. The impetus for this development within the IMC came particularly from three sources: a developing continental European perspective on the nature of religion influenced heavily by the work of Karl Barth, the experience of most missionaries in Muslim lands, where major differences in theological outlook between Islam and Christianity appeared to be irreconcilable, and the persistent testimony of adult converts to Christianity from other religious traditions. In these quarters, Christian mission made no sense unless it rested on the sure conviction that in Jesus Christ the church had something of utmost value to offer the world that could not be found anywhere else.

Hendrik Kraemer (1888–1965) turned out to be the missiologist of the hour, who put the case for radical discontinuity into its most influential form during the interwar years (1938, esp. 100–141). The Christian revelation, he insisted in concert with Karl Barth, stood in some degree of opposition to religion in all of its expressions, including historical Christianity. Therefore, according to Kraemer, it was beside the point to argue that Christianity is the best religion, in the manner of a fulfillment theologian, or to assert with Hocking that people of goodwill could construct better religious answers to human problems together by using insights selected piecemeal from the world's many faith traditions. Yet Kraemer was still willing to discuss how God might be active outside of Christianity, a move that put some distance between him and Barth. In his view, it was undeniable that the non-Christian religions and even secular culture had within them qualities that gave witness to a genuine sense of God's goodness. Kraemer proposed that it was possible to perceive these glimpses of God's presence in human culture and history, but only with the assistance of the light provided by God in Christ.

Kraemer forcefully presented his argument for discontinuity among the religions in a preparatory volume commissioned by the IMC in advance of its 1938 meeting at Tambaram: *The Christian Message in a Non-Christian World.* Yates (1994, 94) has called this book "the most substantial piece of theological work to emerge from the IMC's life." Even so, many delegates to the conference took issue with Kraemer's approach to the non-Christian religions. Most were puzzled by the term "biblical realism," a shorthand designation he used to stand for the essential core of the Bible's message. Kraemer was never able to explain to the satisfaction of his critics how one could describe the positive content of the Bible ("the Christian revelation") apart from the Christian tradition or the experience of an actual interpretive community. How then could Kraemer (or Barth) or anyone else claim to stand apart from all the religions and so evaluate them by what is supposed to be a completely objective standard? For A. G. Hogg (1939), the fundamental problem with Kraemer's position lay in his treatment of non-Christian faith. While Kraemer concedes the theoretical existence of such faith outside of Christianity, the wholesale judgment leveled against the religions as unfaith (*Unglaube*) appeared to Hogg to render this possibility virtually moot. Kraemer does seem to have convinced many of his readers to regard the non-Christian religions as integrated, independent systems of life and thought (or totalities). When this point is accepted, it becomes more difficult to treat other kinds of religion simply as inferior versions of Christianity.

At Vatican II (1962–65), the Roman Catholic Church thoroughly reexamined its approach to the non-Christian religions. The context of this exercise was a larger project of critical appraisal and renewal (*aggiornamento*) that focused on the church's self-understanding and its mission. Among the sixteen official documents produced by the Council was a "declaration" on the relationship of the Catholic Church to the non-Christian religions (*Nostra Aetate*), plus a "decree" on the church's missionary activity (*Ad Gentes*). A "dogmatic constitution" on the nature of the church (*Lumen Gentium*), issued in advance of these two other pronouncements, anticipated and influenced the final positions to be taken on mission and the religions at the Council. The very interesting story of the lead-up to the conclave, the results achieved there, and the exceedingly complex social processes that surrounded the Council's deliberations are discussed at length in a monumental history of Vatican II (Alberigo and Komonchak, 1995–2006).

Vatican II developed a personality of its own and several of the great themes that marked this singular event in conciliar history also affected the approach taken to the religions at the Council. A crucial example is the pastoral character of Vatican II, which suggested to most participants that the church ought to engage the reality outside of itself in a patient, constructive manner. Accordingly, the Council committed to a more dialogical stance than had been assumed in the past, both with respect to the modern world that had come into being since the Council of Trent in the sixteenth century and to the many contemporary religious traditions existing alongside the Catholic Church in that world (including Orthodox and Protestant communities of Christians). Dialogue in this setting meant a willingness to learn from others and to exchange points of view on matters of ultimate significance. For the first time, the church also gave extended thought to the problem of communicating its message in a global environment increasingly dominated by the mass media. With these and related priorities defining the character of Vatican II, issues of doctrine and discipline became relatively less prominent than they had been in previous general councils of the church.

Without question, the Catholic Church at Vatican II spoke in an exceptionally positive way about the non-Christian religions and their adherents. Eschewing the language of judgment and condemnation, the Council chose instead to name some admirable qualities in several other religious traditions that Catholics were bound to honor, such as Hindu asceticism, the monotheistic impulse in Islam, and the desire for illumination that permeates Buddhism. Coincidentally, by recognizing these differences among the religions, the church was also deciding not to lump all non-Catholic religious observance into an omnibus category of unbelief or idolatry. The Council did not waver in its conviction that the church has a permanent responsibility to evangelize the nations through its missionary activities. Cross-cultural programs of outreach were expected to continue and to include most of the traditional tasks associated with world mission, including preaching and the gathering of converts into newly planted congregations. Nevertheless, the Council encouraged the faithful to cooperate with others on behalf of social, economic, and moral progress. It recognized that some of these potential collaborators would be motivated by deeply held religious beliefs of their own, which Catholic Christians were urged to take seriously.

It is with respect to the non-Christian religions as religions that the Second Vatican Council seemed to break the most new ground. Besides acknowledging that religious behavior of all kinds can indicate a desire on the part of individuals to know God, the Council also taught that the non-Christian religions themselves have a positive value and are, in some sense, related to God. The general principle put forward to guide the church in its relations with the non-Christian religions is this: "The Catholic Church rejects nothing that is true and holy in these religions." The theological basis for this conclusion is also supplied in the Declaration *Nostra Aetate* (2): other "ways" of faith, "comprising teachings, rules of life, and sacred rites," must be respected, because they "often reflect a ray of that Truth which enlightens all [human beings]."

The position taken at Vatican II on the non-Christian religions continues to be vigorously debated even today, nearly fifty years later. Discerning what the Council may have intended to say at the time of its meeting is only a very small part of this involved conversation. Not a few theologians have been prompted by the "spirit" of Vatican II to construct increasingly generous views of the religions, in line with what they see implied but not completely developed in the Council's documents. Paul Knitter may be taken as an influential representative of this interpretive trend. In his critical study of Christian attitudes toward the world religions, Knitter (1985, 120–35) labels Vatican II a "watershed" moment in the history of the church's understanding of non-Christian faith, because it signals to him an intention on the part of the Catholic magisterium to break away from exclusivist thinking. Knitter shows appreciation for Karl Rahner as an architect of Vatican II with respect to this topic, but he does not think Rahner goes far enough with his own proposal to recognize faith expressed through other religious traditions as forms of "anonymous Christianity." Rahner's approach seems to Knitter to be too circumspect. It allows for the non-Christian religions to be considered "lawful" from the standpoint of Catholic dogmatic theology, but only up to the point at which the Christian religion and the church become "historically real" (Rahner 1966, 121) to the adherents of these other traditions, presumably through mission. Thus, even if these religions are seen to possess "supernatural, grace-filled elements" and to have the capacity to function as instruments of salvation in certain circumstances, these attributes and benefits are not considered to be permanent. Knitter will argue, on the contrary, that the non-Christian religions are among the ordinary, enduring means by which God reveals truth and saves humanity. They are "ways of salvation" that do not expire in the presence of Christianity, but in fact complement the efforts of the church to give witness to God.

Within this conceptual framework, Knitter then proceeds to reevaluate the purpose of Christian mission (1985, 220–31). It is, above all, to promote the Reign of God, and to do so in cooperation with others. Mission means also to spread abroad the knowledge of God, but without an assumption that the church already has in its grasp all divine wisdom. In some situations, conversions to Christianity may still be appropriate, but missionaries should be prepared to rejoice with equal fervor whenever Buddhists, Hindus, and others become more devoted to (God's) truth while remaining in their own faith traditions. A global church is now being called to construct a global theology, according to Knitter, which can be accomplished only through the most searching forms of interfaith dialogue. In several subsequent publications, Knitter (1995, 1996) has described in more detail what such a global theology might entail. Hans Küng is another Catholic theologian who has likewise emphasized the ethical responsibilities he believes Christians and other religionists ought to be sharing together (see, for example, Küng 1991).

Official Catholic thinking since Vatican II on mission and the religions has not been entirely uniform. Across the writings and speeches of Pope John Paul II, for example, one can see a persistent resolve expressed to engage the world in a dialogical manner, to show respect for other religious traditions, and to explore carefully what the Holy Spirit may have been doing outside the church. On this last point especially, John Paul II seems to have been keen to develop further, albeit cautiously, what the documents of Vatican II had suggested about the "seeds of the Word" widely sown by the Spirit throughout humanity (*Ad Gentes* 15; *Redemptoris Missio* 28–29, *Dominum et Vivificantem* 53). All of these commitments were in evidence on the occasion of the pope's famous meeting with other religious leaders at Assisi in 1986, at which they prayed for peace.

At the same time, it is not hard to find language in the papal literature that warns against the notion of universal salvation effected through the religions. Indeed, much of what the magisterium has had to say about the official teaching of the church on the religions since Vatican II has been formulated in response to proposals made by venturesome Catholic theologians on this subject, which are thought to be in error or gravely defective because they are liable to be misconstrued as endorsements of theological relativism. *Dominus Iesus* is the quintessential example of this more negative postconciliar official Catholic perspective on the religions. Issued in 2000 as a "declaration" formulated by the Congregation for the Doctrine of the Faith, but "ratified and confirmed" by the pope, the document is dominated by a sharp tone that reinforces its plain-spoken rebuttal of several theological positions considered to be incompatible with Catholic faith. Among the critical points of doctrine addressed in *Dominus Iesus* are these: the sacred writings of other religions may not be considered on a par with the Bible, which alone is held to be inspired scripture (8). To suggest that God's self-revelation in Jesus Christ needs to be supplemented by other sources of revelation, due to its "limited, incomplete, or imperfect" character, is said to be inconsistent with the teaching of the church (6). Any attempt to separate the activity of the Spirit from the work of the incarnate Word is "in profound conflict with the Christian faith" (9–10). Interreligious dialogue is permissible and to be welcomed, but only when situated within a broader program of evangelization (2, 22).

For more on Catholic thinking about the non-Christian religions from Vatican II to *Dominus Iesus*, students may want to consult the concise but quite substantive article of James Fredericks on this subject (2003). Another valuable resource is

Miikka Ruokanen's study of *Nostra Aetate*, which includes in an appendix (1992, 133–56) an exchange of views between Ruokanen and Paul Knitter regarding the teaching of Vatican II on the non-Christian religions. Here I will make just two further remarks by way of a brief conclusion to this section. The first is that the meaning of Vatican II with respect to mission and the religions is not yet settled. We are, in fact, still in the midst of an ongoing struggle between the papacy and the theologians to define the legacy of the Council, as William Burrows (2006, 3) has pointed out in his analysis of John Paul II's mission perspective. To be sure, issues of power have figured during this period, but the larger conceptual challenge imposing itself on the church has been the fact of religious pluralism. Over the last third of the twentieth century, a more conscious awareness of living within a religiously plural world slowly took hold throughout much of Roman Catholicism, such that later interpreters of Vatican II perceived themselves to be living in circumstances of which the Council at the time was only very dimly aware. Increasingly, Catholics have come to understand their situation to be one in which "every religion which exists in the world is . . . a question posed, and a possibility offered, to every person" (this is how Rahner [1966, 117], with extraordinary prescience, put it on the eve of Vatican II).

A second observation is this: contemporary mission theologians outside of Catholicism are also more likely than not to understand themselves to be inhabiting the same intellectual context as postconciliar Catholics with respect to global religious diversity. As a result, we find a broad swath of mission theorists, operating across the theological spectrum within Protestantism and beyond, attempting to grasp what this aspect of postmodern life might mean for the church and its mission. Conservative evangelicals (for example, Pinnock 1992, Ramachandra 1999, Netland 2001, and Tennent 2002) and Pentecostals (Kärkkäinen 2002, 193–239, and Yong 2005), among others, are now participating alongside Protestant mainline theologians such as Lesslie Newbigin (1989) in a sprawling discussion about mission and the religions that at one time had been completely dominated by Protestant liberals in the mold of William Hocking. In a more organized way, groups of evangelical mission theologians have also studied the problem of religious pluralism through the processes of the Lausanne movement (see, for example, Claydon 2005, 1:61–115). Having observed this broad upsurge in research energy since the 1980s, with its intense focus on interreligious issues bearing on mission, Lalsangkima Pachuau (2000, 549–52) concludes that the theology of religions has become the "essential integrating principle" or "hub" of missiology as a discipline.

THREE SPECIAL TOPICS: JUDAISM, ISLAM, AND THE RELIGIONS OF AFRICA

Over the bulk of this chapter, I have chosen to emphasize mission research related especially to the dominant religions of India and East Asia. The relatively high numbers and prominence of (early) modern-era missionaries sent to these locations partially justifies this focus. Another reason to concentrate on these regions is that quite a lot of comparative research on religion, a scientific literature to which some missionary scholars have contributed heavily (a prime example being James Legge, whose role in the development of modern sinology is exhaustively described in Girardot 2002), has tended to give an inordinate degree of attention to the "Eastern" faith traditions. Nonetheless, it has never been the case that the study of mission and the religions has been confined to these parts of the globe. To help fill out the picture sketched thus far and so reflect better the breadth of research conducted in this part of missiology, I propose next to highlight a few materials connected to the study of mission that make special reference to Judaism, Islam, and the primal religious traditions of Africa.

The roots of a Christian mission to the Jews may be traced back all the way to Jesus, who is remembered as having restricted his own efforts at outreach in first-century Palestine to "the lost sheep of the house of Israel" (Matt. 15:24). In Acts, Paul is shown likewise to be in constant contact with Jews, often preferring to begin his visits to new mission centers with a call on the local synagogue. In addition, Paul's reflections on the salvation of the Jewish people (especially Rom. 9–11) continue to be foundational for theologies of mission that seek to address the issue of Jewish evangelization. Students of mission with an interest in apostolic-era initiatives directed toward Jews will want to refer to all the standard exegetical resources at their disposal when examining the relevant New Testament passages. Also valuable, because it ranges well beyond the boundaries of Paul's missionary program, is the lengthy review of Jewish-Christian mission assembled in Schnabel (2004, 729–910). As Schnabel describes the activities of Peter and his closest ministry associates, he examines a huge collection of evidence pertaining to the establishment of Christianity within and beyond the penumbra of diaspora Judaism, whether in Antioch, Rome, Egypt, North Africa, Syria, Mesopotamia, or India. Although it is generally agreed that organized Christian missionary efforts among the Jews dissipated in the early patristic period, the primary cause of this shift is not clearly understood. Did the church simply lose interest in the evangelization of the Jews, perhaps due to a lack of contact as Judaism withered away on its own (so Harnack)? Or was it more a matter of an anti-Jewish attitude (expressed through Justin Martyr and others writing in the *adversus Ioudaeos* apologetic tradition) overwhelming the church's concern for the salvation of the Jews? Missiologists concerned with such questions have to become conversant with the current research in early Christian studies (for example, Becker and Reed 2007), where Jewish-Christian relations in late antiquity have been intensively examined.

The universal horizon of post-Enlightenment Protestantism quite naturally encompassed the Jews. Accordingly, as the modern Protestant missionary movement got under way, agencies specializing in missions to the Jews soon became part of this larger project to evangelize the known world. The London Society for Promoting Christianity amongst the Jews or the London Jews' Society, founded in 1809, would be followed by many more such organizations. Most of these began with a focus on European Jewry or the propagation of Christianity in the Holy Land. Toward the end of the nineteenth century, more intensive efforts to present the gospel to fast-growing Jewish immigrant communities in North America were begun. In 1923, a department of Jewish evangelism was established at the Moody Bible Institute, with the aim of professionalizing this special ministry function. As Yaakov Ariel (2000) has shown, missionary appeals to American Jews up to the 1960s tended to assume that converts would assimilate into Gentile Christian congregations. Over the past fifty years, an alternative view has asserted itself through the rise of messianic Judaism, a social and theological phenomenon described carefully in the work of Carol Harris-Shapiro (1999) and Dan Cohn-Sherbok (2000), among others. Many missiologists would recognize in messianic Judaism an attempt to contextualize the gospel by adopting the institutional forms, ritual gestures, religious symbols, and discursive habits of contemporary American Judaism.

Initial attempts to study Jewish evangelization in a systematic way tended to focus on the practical aspects of the subject. Thus, at Edinburgh in 1910 and within the structure of the mission bibliography section of the *IRM* for several decades afterward, Judaism is treated as a mission "field" and not primarily as one of the religions. In fact, Commission IV at the World Missionary Conference does not discuss Judaism directly. In the aftermath of the Holocaust, issues of strategy and technique have had to accommodate and respond to more strictly theological considerations. In this situation, the most pressing question asks whether or not it is still appropriate to seek the conversion of Jews to Christianity. One can get a sense of this discussion by looking at the most recent study papers generated from within the circles of the Lausanne Consultation on Jewish Evangelism (for example, Claydon 2005, 3:377–433). Gerald Anderson (2003) presents a case for the evangelization of the Jews that likewise takes into account the perspective of messianic Judaism. The extreme sensitivity of this subject for many in the historic Protestant churches is illustrated by the fact that the European academics who edited the volume in which Anderson's essay appeared felt compelled to add a note of disclaimer to his article (no other essay in this *festschrift* to Jan Jongeneel is so treated). Anderson not only argued as a Methodist that a mission to the Jews is the "keystone of the Christian mission," without which a slide into complete theological relativism is inevitable (2003, 126), but that his position fully corresponded to the teaching of Vatican II on this subject. The vehement objections raised to Anderson's argument show that this is another aspect of mission and the religions connected to the Council over which many Roman Catholics now strongly disagree.

Islam is a second faith tradition not easily subsumed under a general discussion of mission and the religions. Established some six centuries *after* the time of Jesus, Islam represents more than just another alternative to Christianity next to the rest of the religions. To the extent that its scripture and teaching embody a self-conscious rejection of the New Testament in its present form, in addition to a number of core church doctrines, Islam is a "reproach" to Christianity (Gairdner 1909). The comparative position developed in the nineteenth century regarding the religions—that they be approached as preparatory foundations for Christian belief—is only with great difficulty applied to Islam, since its explicit claim is to "correct, complete and supersede" the church's witness to God and God's son (Gairdner 1909, 310–12, quoting from an earlier CMS document; discussed in Shelley 1999). The relative paucity of Muslim converts to Christianity over the centuries likewise raises questions about the capacity of Islam to function as a *preparatio evangelica*.

Several kinds of research on Islam relevant to missiology may be identified. One group of studies has focused on the broad history of Muslim-Christian relations, a long story of community encounter all too often defined by mutual hostility and bloody conflict. A sensitive recounting of this history, which takes into account both Muslim and Christian experience, is offered in Goddard (2000). In Goddard's view (4), an honest evaluation of Muslim-Christian engagement in the past has to take place before the current prospects for dialogue and collaboration can be expected to improve. Jane Smith (1999) gives extra attention to the cultural dimensions of Christian-Muslim interaction, while concentrating on the medieval record. Clinton Bennett's more recent treatment of Christian-Muslim relations (2008) complements these other efforts by adding a post-9/11 perspective and an extended discussion of developments in dialogue since the 1970s.

A second set of research has less to do with the geopolitical and intercultural factors influencing Christian-Muslim encounter than it does with Christian perceptions of Islam as a religious tradition. The importance of this work to missiology springs from the fact that every attempt to evangelize Muslims necessarily rests on a particular understanding of Islam. Thus, an early interpreter of Islam, John of Damascus (c. 665–749), considered the religion of the "Ishmaelites" to be a new form of heresy and so a misunderstanding of orthodox Christian doctrine that needed refutation and correction. Many Enlightenment-era commentators (for example, Voltaire) will decide that Islam is a fraudulent religion, invented by Muhammad for his own purposes. Temple Gairdner (1928, 211) was among those who believed that Christian missions progressed so slowly in Muslim lands because they had to contend with an entrenched religion not completely false but full of "half-truths." More generously, Wilfred Cantwell Smith (1981, 124) has suggested that Islam and Christianity be considered "religious sub-communities" of something greater than themselves, in which case the two traditions are really more alike than different. Smith's views reflected his conviction that religious pluralism is a normal aspect of the world's present social condition and his hope that an evolving global theology would eventually transcend all the historical religions. Other committed pluralists (for example, Kimball 2004) have emphasized the common ethical intentions expressed through these two faith traditions, a circumstance that could be expected to stimulate cooperation on behalf of social justice and concern for the poor. In the survey articles of Jane Smith (1998) and David Kerr (2002), one will find helpful discussions of Christian missionary attitudes toward Islam far more detailed than I am able to present here.

The missiological study of Islam also includes reflection on the best ways to approach Muslims with the message of the gospel. This research typically builds on what is known already about the history of Christian-Muslim relations and often takes into account various Christian understandings of Islamic religion but then pushes on to consider the next steps in mission outreach to Muslims. Up to the early decades of the twentieth century, a solid consensus stood behind the strategy of arguing with Muslims over matters of doctrine. Thus, numerous scholar-missionaries sought through their writings to expose weaknesses they perceived in Islam, whether in terms of theological deficiencies or social ills thought to be caused by Muslim culture, in order to prepare the ground for more effective presentations of the Christian message. These materials fall readily into the category of religious polemic.

Other mission researchers have focused on the task of identifying potential bridges to the imaginative world of Muslim believers. Among these efforts have been numerous proposals for how to bypass the roadblock of doctrinal solidarity that seems to be preventing missionary access to the followers of Islam. Thus, we have Paul Hiebert (1989), Rick Love (2000), and Dudley Woodberry (2008) exploring the realm of power encounters and spiritual warfare, where it is thought that missionaries might be able to engage the worldview of "folk" Islam. A subset of this research concerns itself with the phenomenon of dreams and the potential of visionary experiences to draw Muslims to Jesus (Musk 1988). Others (for example, Parshall 1983) have speculated on the possibility that Islamic mysticism (Sufism) might provide a way into popular Islam for Christian missions.

Kenneth Cragg may also be considered a bridge-builder between Islam and Christianity; his prodigious literary output and wide influence within missiology invite a special mention. In his case, it is the conceptual heart of orthodox Islam with which he wants to be in conversation, rather than some experiential corner of Muslim faith and feeling. He has endeavored to make this connection over more than a half-century of scholarly writing by focusing on topics of undoubted interest to both Muslims and Christians, including prophethood, revelation, christology, human freedom, idolatry, and the nature of God. He has been asking, often in the company of Muslims, what God might require from faithful people, while also examining carefully our various expectations of God. As Christopher Lamb (1997, 100–122) has pointed out, the theological goal of Cragg's work has remained quite consistent over his long career—not only to foster mutual understanding across the boundary lines of confession but also to commend the gospel to Muslims using terms made available in the Qur'an and the literary traditions of Islam. Put another way, Cragg's lifelong quest has been to discover "Islamic reasons for being Christian" (Cragg 1981, 166). Uncounted missionaries to Islam since the mid-twentieth century have drawn inspiration from Cragg, although his writings have also attracted not a little criticism and puzzlement.

A final category of research to be mentioned here in connection with Muslim evangelization concerns the planting of new churches in Muslim-majority societies. This is not an easy subject to document, because security fears often prompt authors to adopt a pseudonym or in some other way to obscure the identity of those about whom they are writing. Precision is also impeded by the fact that the later stages of these initiatives tend not to be discussed openly. In other words, new proposals for this kind of church planting are put into print on a regular basis, but published follow-up pieces on the results of such efforts are much harder to come by. Another distinguishing mark of this literature is to be found in the number of specialized terms attached to this topic, including "insider movements," "Jesus mosques," "Christian-Muslims," "MBBs" (Muslim-background believers), and "followers of Isa."

Many of those who have written most fervently in recent decades about the evangelization of Muslims and the goal of gathering converts from Islam into Christian communities of faith have understood their particular challenge to be one of contextualization. From this perspective, the basic problem for evangelists is that conversion often entails extraction from Muslim-majority societies, even when indigenous churches already exist, a situation that tends to short-circuit the development of any large-scale movement out of Islam toward Christianity. Another hindrance to evangelistic progress is the off-putting connection assumed by many Muslims to exist between Christianity and Western culture. A number of experiments have been undertaken to overcome these obstacles to Muslim evangelism. What many of these efforts have in common is an intention to use institutional forms and social practices borrowed directly from Islamic religious cultures. A scale of contextualization in these circumstances has been developed (C1–6; outlined in Travis 1998). C4 believers might call themselves "followers of Isa," for example, while continuing to practice certain aspects of Islam, such as the Ramadan fast. The C5 pattern, resembling in many respects the model of messianic Judaism, allows converts, who may or may not have submitted to some form of baptism, to remain in their communities as Muslims. The C6 grouping designates secret believers in Christ. As might be expected, the wisdom of these approaches has been vigorously debated, with special attention given to the problem of syncretism (for example, in Parshall 2003 and Tennent 2006). A welcome addition to this literature has recently appeared in the published dissertation of Jonas Jørgensen (2008). The distinctive value of this work derives in part from the unusually detailed description he provides for a particular group of Muslim-background Christian believers (the "Jesus Imandars," located in Dhaka, Bangladesh). In Jørgensen's book, the experience and significance of the Jesus Imandars are compared to another example of hybrid Christianity, the Hindu-background "Christ Bhaktas" of Chennai, India (on whom, see also Hoefer 2001 and Tennent 2005).

Missiologists have not always demonstrated a high level of interest in the indigenous religions of Africa, which contrasts sharply with their sustained, intense desire to lay hold of Islam intellectually. In the early modern period, it may be argued that the Catholic missionaries of the era simply lacked the analytical tools needed to comprehend what they were experiencing. Later, most Protestant observers of the African scene assumed that the primal religions of the sub-Saharan regions were doomed to extinction as a consequence of modernity and so did not need to be pondered except as cultural artifacts of a dying age. Many apparently were all too ready to bid them good riddance, if the comments of Indian missionary Nicol Macnicol submitted to the Jerusalem meeting of the IMC do, in fact, represent the majority view at the time: "No one doubts that the religion of the Bantu or of the native of the Congo must go—and the sooner the better—and this is not less the case with the animistic worships that are to be found still alive and powerful in so many regions of India as well" (1928, 3).

The "virtual absence of Africa" (Stanley 2009, 97–102; see also 235–45) at the 1910 World Missionary Conference has been noted on many occasions. For Catholics, a similar dynamic may be observed at Vatican II, where the African religions are not named alongside the monotheistic faiths, Buddhism, and Hinduism, but are more vaguely represented as "a certain perception of that hidden power which hovers over the course of things and over the events of human history" (*Nostra Aetate* 2). As Teresa Okure (2009) has pointed out, the sin of Edinburgh against Africa was not only a matter of demographic imbalances in the distribution of delegates; it was also felt in the way the conference misrepresented the needs, gifts, religious aspirations, and cultural richness of the continent. Yet there were a few signs even then that the Protestant missionary movement was about to reassess its stance toward the religions and cultures of Africa. Stanley Friesen (1996), for example, has called attention to the contributions made to the Edinburgh study process by several experienced African missionaries with anthropological interests. Despite a widespread commitment to evolutionary models of cultural development (with Africans usually placed at the bottom of the ladder) and no discernible desire to challenge the European colonial order, contributing scholar-missionaries such as Henry Callaway (through his writings), Henri Junod, and R. H. Nassau at least showed respect for African religion by treating it as a serious subject, worthy of study. Few conference participants were yet in a position to appreciate how anthropological research could help them relate more effectively to the religions of Africa, but some of these data would soon begin to affect the discussion of and planning for mission activities in Africa going forward.

After Edinburgh, missiology and African studies directly converged when IMC administrator J. H. Oldham, the German Africanist and former missionary Diedrich Westermann, and a collection of mission advocates and scholarly experts joined forces in 1924 to establish the International Institute of African Languages and Cultures (Clements 2004, 178). A few years later, the institute began to publish the academic journal *Africa*. This same coalition, with the participation of some European colonial officials responsible for African education, was also deeply involved in the 1926 Le Zoute conference on mission in Africa. We can see in these institutional developments between the two World Wars a missionary intention not only to "save" and develop Africa but also, increasingly, to understand the cultural and linguistic particulars of the region more completely. An additional figure of considerable importance from this period, whose contributions to the study of African religions undoubtedly influenced both anthropology and missiology, is Edwin Smith (1929).

Toward the end of the colonial era, a more consistently positive reading of the African religions had begun to emerge in missionary circles. This is not to say that dismissive attitudes entirely disappeared. But alongside the many devout evangelists who still viewed the African religious landscape as an undifferentiated wasteland of superstition and futility rose another voice within the missionary ranks that wanted to talk about the meaning and function of traditional spiritualities in local contexts and the potential relationships that might be identified between these ways of being religious and the outlook of Christianity. Andrew Walls gives credit to Geoffrey Parrinder (1954) for putting the study of African religion on a new footing within missiology (and beyond) through the creation of a new conceptual category he denominated "African traditional religion" (ATR). In his tribute article, Walls (2004, 213–15) also lays stress on the importance of Parrinder's basic insight that Christianity and the older religions of Africa had become inseparably linked since the nineteenth century, with each now able to influence the development of the other. Another scholar whose work during this period would later prove to be seminal for African studies and missiology alike is Bengt Sundkler (1909–95). When Sundkler published *Bantu Prophets in South Africa* (1948), he opened up a scholarly pathway into an African religious world up to then barely known to outsiders: the African Independent Churches (AICs).

Decolonization spurred new efforts to understand the still expanding universe of African religion from many perspectives, including missiology. To comprehend all this scholarly activity is not an easy task, but Adrian Hastings (2000) has produced an invaluable guide to a large segment of this sprawling field of inquiry: African Christian studies. David Maxwell (2006) subsequently added some remarks of his own on this same subject, also penned from behind the editor's desk at the *Journal of Religion in Africa*. As Hastings points out, political independence had its academic counterparts. Within the creative context of an emerging postcolonial African environment, full-scale searches were mounted to find evidence of African initiatives in religion that would offset the pronounced scholarly emphasis previously given to foreign missionary activities. An explosion of studies highlighting the African Independent Churches and the so-called New Religious Movements coming to life across Africa was the uneven but happy result of this quest. The work of Harold Turner (1967) on the Church of the Lord (Aladura) and David Barrett's study of new African religious movements, *Schism and Renewal in Africa* (1968), led the way for many others to come after them. A number of African theologians of this same generation, such as Bolaji Idowu and John Mbiti, also contributed original research with broad significance. A major theme up for discussion at the time and ever since then was how to relate the abiding concerns of Christian theology to the traditional religious heritage of Africa. Kwame Bediako's study of modern African theologians shows how a selection of pioneering figures negotiated this conundrum (Bediako 1992, esp. 267–444). As Bediako makes clear, the underlying issue powering much of this research in theology has been the need to construct authentic African Christian identities in all the places on the continent where the church now finds itself. Evaluating the missionary past of one's community is part of this project. The indigenization of theology in this context also means coming to terms with the whole of African religious experience. To the extent that theologians, historians, and sociologists of religion specializing in African Christianity are paying serious attention to these tasks, a once-absent African perspective will be able to play its rightful part in the study of mission and the religions.

COMPARATIVE MISSIOLOGY

Christianity is not the only religious tradition to exhibit a missionary impulse. Certain ideologies and worldviews likewise appear to contain within themselves strong desires to be spread abroad, whether by word or by deed. Despite these obvious facts, relatively few missiologists have applied themselves to the problem of comparative missiology, which I understand to be the study of mission (or some aspect of mission) undertaken with direct reference to its occurrence in more than one religious tradition or ideology.

An introduction to missiology that recognizes the possibility of comparative analysis is the "missiological encyclopedia" of Jan Jongeneel (1995–97). According to the outline of the field presented in Jongeneel's project, a set of comparative topics is proposed within the major division he designates "philosophy of mission" (*Missionsphilosophie*). However, Jongeneel is able to report only a small collection of material, all of which he lists under the subtopic "phenomenology of mission." I consider just one of the studies cited by Jongeneel to be a full-fledged example of comparative missiology. This is the article by religious studies scholar

Frank Whaling, in which an attempt is made to compare the social processes and religious values involved in the "transplanting of the Buddhist, Christian, and Muslim traditions into different cultures" (1981, 319). Whaling identifies a short list of common elements that help to explain the missionary success of these three traditions in the locations studied. Of paramount importance, in his view, is the crucial combination of "external opportunity" for expansion and "inward dynamism." Whaling also thought he detected in the missionary experience of each community evidence of one or more "hermeneutical bridges" over which new religious ideas could pass into second cultures (323, 325–26, 329–30). Of particular interest here is the attention Whaling pays to the methodology of comparison. He does not think a phenomenological approach will be helpful, because superficial similarities are likely to obscure the substantive differences that separate the religions from each other (316–18). Recognition is given to "an incipient comparative theology of mission" (314), but Whaling intends instead to begin working on a nonnormative "comparative religious study of mission" (316). In any case, Whaling understands himself to be operating in largely "unexplored territory" (319), owing to a lack of extant literature on this subject.

Subsequent to the publication of Whaling's article, comparative investigations of mission have not been particularly numerous and, when they appear, tend not to make reference to each other. The result (with one important exception to be noted below) is a scattered, uncoordinated discourse related to comparative missiology, begun from multiple starting points. A few outstanding resources may nevertheless be recommended. The first is a major article, "Missions: Missionary Activity," included in the *Encyclopedia of Religion*. Max Stackhouse authored the original entry, published in 1987, and then updated his work for the second edition of the encyclopedia, which appeared in 2005. Stackhouse looks beyond the usual group of religions considered to be persistently missionary (Christianity, Buddhism, and Islam), in order to carry out "a systematic overview of organized proselytism and the basic ideational, social, and institutional foundations" on which such activities may be said to rest (2005, 6069). Several themes are shown to be pertinent to a variety of religions and their missionary practices, including contextualization, resistance to mission, relativistic thinking about religion, the roles played by informal and more professional agents of mission, plus the relationship of mission to expressions of nationalism and imperialism. Stackhouse also considers how rival missionary programs have affected each other.

A comparativist perspective is also present in the set of essays published together under the title *Mixed Messages* (Scott and Griffiths, 2005). While the first half of this interesting volume centers on the material culture of Christian missions, several of the essays in part 2 offer accounts of mission in a select group of other religious traditions. These chapters are similar to each other in two respects: (1) they concentrate on *contemporary* developments rather than long since passed eras of missionary expansion; and (2) their scope is further limited to the study of Islamic, Buddhist, and Hindu missions *to the West*. One other chapter looks at some of the leading institutions of Western, liberal democracy (such as the World Bank) and concludes that something like a secular missionary discourse of civilizing uplift has developed to explain their global purpose. Although not finally brought into conversation with each other, these different treatments of mission do provide data potentially of great value to comparative missiology. Another essay collection to be mentioned here is Learman (2005). In this case, the primary focus is on cross-cultural Buddhist missions to the West and elsewhere, but many of the essayists make reference to research on Christian mission.

By far, the most developed sector within comparative missiology is that focused on Christian mission and Islamic *da'wa*. Sustained attention has been given to this subject, with earlier work factoring into more recent scholarship. Much of this activity is reviewed in David Kerr (2000). In addition to the materials cited in Kerr's article, there are other studies with which the comparative missiologist will want to become familiar. Robin Horton's several articles (1971, 1975a, 1975b) on conversion to Christianity and Islam in sub-Saharan Africa, cited earlier, is one example. We also now have a preliminary statistical study of cross-cultural missionaries working on behalf of Islam worldwide and for Christianity within the Muslim world (Johnson and Scoggins 2005). Critical research has begun to appear, too, on the missionary schools of Fethullah Gülen, organized on behalf of Turkism and the renewal of Islam especially in Central Asia after the fall of the Soviet Empire (see Balci 2003). Perhaps the most influential and penetrating comparative treatment of mission in Islam and Christianity made available so far is the analysis offered in Lamin Sanneh's *Translating the Message* (1989, esp. 211–38). Sanneh argues that the essential difference between Christian mission and Islamic *da'wa* lies in the principle of "translatability." The Christian community declares its preference for translatability whenever it decides to do theology in a local idiom or renders its scriptures into another of the world's languages, in contrast to the privileging of Arabic within Islam. Andrew Walls (2002a, 121), among many others, has confirmed this judgment, observing with respect to mission practice in Africa (also Sanneh's primary test case): "it is Christianity, not Islam, that has struck its roots into the vernacular past."

One more factor adding depth to this strain of comparative discourse on mission is the fact that Muslims and Christians have both been participating. On occasion, Muslim and Christian scholars have met together in structured dialogue events in order to discuss Christian mission and Islamic *da'wa*. A milestone gathering of this type took place under the auspices of the World Council of Churches in 1976 at Chambésy, Switzerland. The papers presented at that meeting, plus a transcript of the discussions that ensued, were published in the *IRM* later that year. More recently, the South African Missiological Society invited Islamic scholar Farid Esack to share a Muslim perspective on Christian and Muslim forms of mission in the context of the Society's 2006 annual congress (Esack 2006). Also relevant to this part of missiology are discussions of mission conducted by Christians and Muslims in less formal circumstances. Heather Sharkey's work (2004) on Arabic language anti-missionary treatises illuminates one side of this conversation, as it unfolded in the postcolonial half of the twentieth century. Earlier, the Muslim reformer Rashid Rida (1865–1935) had commented more than once on the effects of Christian mission in the Muslim world in the pages of the short-lived but influential periodical he edited (*al-Manar*). A remarkable exchange of views between Rida and the Danish missionary Alfred Nielson on the subject of mission is described in Umar Riyad (2002).

6

The Means of Mission

When Friedrich Schleiermacher (1768–1834) sketched out a "brief outline" for the study of theology, he made a passing reference to mission and suggested that a "theory of missions" might be included among the concerns of "practical theology" (1988, 153). Since Schleiermacher indicates (134, 140) that this part of his curriculum had to do with "church leadership," meaning "church government and service to the congregation," his conception of mission was unnaturally constricted. Outreach was thought to take place ordinarily in the vicinity of congregations already in existence, whose activities non-Christians could observe for themselves (153). Left unexamined were the evangelizing processes by which entirely new communities of faith might come into being.

Nearly a century later, when the field of missiology began to take shape formally, the parochialism of Schleiermacher had been left far behind. By the turn of the twentieth century, the global dimensions of mission were self-evident to all, and most Christians in the West took for granted that Christianity by nature was a vigorously expansive faith tradition. Yet in at least one respect Schleiermacher's perspective on mission lived on. This was his assumption that mission ought to be studied primarily from a practical standpoint, as a technical subject. So thought Gustav Warneck, whose groundbreaking introduction to the study of mission (1892–1903) emphasized the operational challenges to be faced on the mission field. Warneck's counterpart in the world of Catholic missiology, Joseph Schmidlin, took a similar approach, arguing that scholars of mission had two fundamental questions before them (1931, 4). The first asked about the "why" of mission, which required the theorist to furnish an adequate philosophical basis for the mission enterprise (appealing, for example, to dogmatic, biblical, or ethical principles). A second major question concerned the "how" of mission, which invited scholarly discussion of possible mission agencies, personnel policies, funding mechanisms, ways to share information about mission, and the special demands of ministry work abroad, among other topics. At about the same time, at Edinburgh 1910, one can also perceive a heightened concern for the effective management of what had become a rather unwieldy, complex global campaign of religious activity on behalf of Christianity. Here, too, it was hoped that the study of mission might help those leading the modern missionary movement to do their work more efficiently.

With these roots, it comes as no surprise that academic missiology has always included a significant portion of research devoted to practical issues. As a way to organize my analysis of this material, I have chosen to structure this chapter into four parts. An initial section concentrates on large-scale studies of mission strategy, in which the benefits and liabilities of different tactics are contrasted with each other. Next is a discussion of research more narrowly focused on particular mission techniques and modalities. In a third section, my intention is to treat the organizational aspects of evangelization, which means especially to consider how scholars have investigated the institutional means of mission. A final section will center on the subject of mission finances, after which it should be possible in a brief conclusion to say something about the place of methodological studies within missiology as a whole.

TACTICS AND STRATEGIES

No missionary endeavor in history has had access to unlimited human resources. Supplies of time, money, and opportunity also inevitably grow short at some point, in which case hard choices have to be made with respect to priorities and the most workable solutions to missionary problems. We may assume that the leading proponents of Christian mission in every generation have had to think strategically at some level about how best to advance the cause of the gospel. The apostle Paul, for example, may be appreciated for his organizing genius, in addition to his evangelical zeal and theological acumen (on Paul's various roles in mission, see Skreslet 2006b, 193–203). The Jesuits in the early modern period were similarly astute planners of mission, who took care to gather information and experience from around the world and to adjust their practices based on what had been learned. However, the systematic study of these and other attempts to strategize about mission (the focus of this section) is a more recent scholarly development.

Perhaps the first to publish a comprehensive account of missionary methods was Alexander Duff. It may be recalled from the previous chapter that Duff authored an influential description of Hinduism in the late 1830s, in part meant to establish the need for Christian missions in India. In the same book, Duff advocates a specific kind of missionary venture, one featuring Western forms of education presented in English to a student body drawn particularly from the higher castes of Indian society. Duff's home audience, for whom this proposal was initially prepared, contained more than one constituency. Besides a general church public spread out across England and Scotland and the various judicatories responsible for mission in the Church of Scotland, he was also speaking to a colonial establishment that had the power to restrict or to promote missionary activities on the subcontinent.

Duff identified three basic mission methods used up to then in India. He shows awareness of the fact that each mode of mission had its defenders in the church and that rational and scriptural arguments could be made in support of all three. The most pressing Indian mission question to be answered was essentially strategic: "How, or in what way can the Gospel be most speedily and effectually brought to bear on the entire mass of the people?" (1839, 284). In Duff's view, missionary preaching was a noble pursuit founded on the example of the apostles, but the results after decades of effort had been so meager that it made no sense to him to depend on this method to evangelize the vast population of India, so long as the preachers were a relatively few foreign agents. Alternatively, some advocates of mission had proposed that translation and the circulation of the Christian scriptures ought to be the primary task of those sent abroad by the churches. Duff likened this scheme to a plan to distribute healing drugs to the public without providing any guidance for their use (376). A third way to approach mission was to focus on Christian education, which Duff considered to be a form of preaching directed toward the young (286–87). This method, he believed, was the only one that could reasonably be expected to renew India and to Christianize its population. But to be effective, he argued, mission educators had to stop allocating so many of their resources to the elementary grades and to the lowly village school, in favor of more specialized institutions that could influence the children of India's elites, who would one day hold the future of the nation in their powerful hands.

Duff's ideas about methods became the basis of an enduring model of mission, which the Presbyterians in Scotland, by and large, embraced as their own through the nineteenth century (Walls 1993, 571–72; see also Maxwell 2001). According to this theory, the goal of mission was to renovate "heathen" societies wholesale, using the power of modern education to break down outmoded customs and traditional value systems. It was quite possible, however, to study the situation of Protestant missions in Duff's era and to draw quite different conclusions about what evangelizing activities should receive the highest priority. An alternative approach favored by the leaders of the two largest nineteenth-century Protestant missionary organizations, the CMS and the ABCFM, emphasized the importance of preaching and other forms of direct evangelism. Henry Venn and Rufus Anderson were agreed that educational initiatives were appropriate in some circumstances. Like doctors, missionary educators and their schools were sometimes welcomed into resistant societies when preachers were not and so had the capacity to open closed doors. The schools were also unquestionably justified to the extent that they served to train up an educated native clergy. Venn and Anderson were nevertheless keen to keep their missionaries focused on spiritual activities, which meant avoiding civilizing functions not expected to lead anytime soon to widespread movements of conversion or the gathering of new believers into native congregations.

A substantial literature has accumulated around the figures of Venn and Anderson and their shared goal of the "three-self church" (self-supporting, self-governing, and self-propagating). Henry Venn's "strategic vision" is well described in an essay that emphasizes his persistent support of native episcopacy (Williams 2000). Also still relevant is the book-length treatment Peter Williams gives to the "ideal of the self-governing church" (1990). The application of Venn's ideas through the Sierra Leone Native Pastorate is thoughtfully explored in Hanciles (2001). Two of Venn's most important policy documents are reproduced in appendices to Shenk (1983, 118–37). For Anderson, we now have a fine intellectual biography (Harris 1999) that examines his strategic thinking about mission against the backdrop of domestic pressures bearing down on the ABCFM in the decades leading up to the American Civil War and the hopes for social advancement and economic improvement met everywhere on the mission field. Anderson strongly resisted the idea of putting the larger program of mission he directed under any "civilizational" aim, including the abolition of slavery. He also worried that providing too much education would undermine missionary efforts to create a competent native clergy eager to evangelize their own society, above all else. These positions drove Anderson to advocate a "theory of missions to the heathen" (1845) that valued oral preaching and strictly religious activities over all other forms of mission. While this judgment had to be defended on theological grounds, of course, the most impassioned segment of Anderson's argument (indicated by a unique mix of typefaces used for emphasis at this point in the document) touted the element of efficiency: "*holding up* CHRIST AS THE ONLY SAVIOR OF LOST SINNERS" is "the only effectual way of prosecuting missions among the heathen," because

> . . . it requires the fewest men, the least expense, the shortest time. It makes the least demand for learning in the great body of laborers. It involves the least complication in means and measures. (19–20)

Whatever pragmatic benefits might have accrued to this approach, Harris nevertheless concludes (1999, 163) that Anderson's strategy was inherently flawed, because it sought "to foster native agency by suppressing indigenous aspirations" for advanced forms of education.

Toward the end of the nineteenth century, the Venn-Anderson model of mission gradually yielded pride of place to another set of priorities not so focused on the creation of independent national churches. The new fashion in mission was to build up non-Western societies by permeating them with Christian institutions. A variety of factors influenced this shift in approach, including the rise of the social gospel movement in American Christianity (on this connection, see Fishburn 2004). Others have suggested (for example, Robert 1997, 129–30) that the end of the American Civil War left a generation of women ready to mobilize their resources for benevolent activity throughout the world. Protestant women were not only volunteering for missionary work abroad in ever greater numbers, but they also set about creating their own mission organizations at this time, further boosting the variety of service opportunities available to them. Barred from preaching in most circumstances, these new recruits were ready and eager to engage in other forms of missionary labor. A surge of aggressive European imperialism from the 1880s also influenced the course of the modern missionary movement at this point in its history (an explanation for how this happened is offered in Hutchison 1987, 91–124). Colonial governments had their own preferences respecting mission methods, which ran strongly in the direction of education and social services and away from conversionist activities that might incite native resistance to foreign rule.

Missionary efforts to preach the gospel and to establish churches by no means came to an end at the turn of the twentieth century. In fact, some organizations (for example, "faith missions") continued to specialize in precisely these activities, epitomized in the figures of the vernacular street preacher and the itinerant rural evangelist. What began to change was the proportion of missionaries appointed to what many in previous generations would have considered secular occupations, as teachers, physicians, nurses, social workers, administrators, college professors, literacy experts, printing press operators, and industrial educators. The status of these roles within the overall missionary enterprise was also on the rise, at least within those parts of the church that considered them to be suitable means by which God's Reign could be made visible in the modern age. This was not a return to the ideology of Alexander Duff. He had hoped to use education to "explode and tear up" the traditional structures of Hindu society, in order to clear a way for Christianity to be accepted (Smith 1881, 108–9). This was a moment rather to share from the abundance of Western civilization, widely considered at the time to be among the best gifts of God to humanity. The decision of the WCC during the 1960s to embrace "humanization" as the primary goal of Christian ministry (World Council of Churches 1967) gave new life to this longstanding mission impulse.

In the early twentieth century, Roman Catholics, too, had their debates over mission strategy. In this ecclesial context, the key question did not revolve around the value of civilizing activities to mission, as it tended to do in Protestant circles. Instead, Catholic strategists focused on which of the traditional missionary functions ought to be given the highest priority. One school of thought, commonly associated with the theological faculty at Louvain, emphasized the need to extend the visible structures of the institutional church. The aim of mission, according to this way of thinking, was to plant new communities of faith in places where the church did not already exist and to replicate the organizational structures of settled church life as quickly as possible. Pierre Charles (1883–1954) is widely recognized as the leading theoretician of the "school of Louvain." An alternative view, often linked to Joseph Schmidlin and his colleagues at Münster, stressed the importance of gospel proclamation (even to nominal Christians) and the conversion of individuals (Müller 1987, 34–38).

After Vatican II, the differences thought to separate the rival schools of Louvain and Münster soon receded in significance, which helps to explain the relative lack of current research on these topics within missiology. Vastly more important to postconciliar discussions of mission strategy within Catholicism has been the concept of liberation. In this case, the concerns of theology are very closely tied to methodological issues, due to the praxiological edge put on liberation theory right from the start (Gutiérrez 1973; see also Haight 1985).

Reflection on mission methods from a liberation perspective initially focused on problems of injustice, felt especially in the political and economic spheres. For some, this meant identifying and exposing the deep causes of poverty (Romero 1985). Others helped to organize resistance, often by undertaking projects of education that could empower the poor to free themselves from various kinds of exploitation (Freire 1970). Yet others have heard in the mission theme of liberation a call to action to create new social structures that better reflect the Reign of God announced by Jesus (Costas 1982, 21–42). Over time, additional emphases related to liberation have surfaced within the literature of missiology, including concerns for gender justice (Kang 2005), human rights (McCormick 1979), and promoting respect for religious and cultural minorities (Pachuau 2002). An emerging area of research concentrates on the interface of Christian mission and environmentalism (Jenkins 2008). Of course, non-Catholics of various persuasions have been participating fully in all of these discussions. In a remarkable way, the work of missiologist Inus Daneel (2001) on African "earthkeeping" demonstrates the integrative capacity of a liberationist perspective on mission. All, or nearly all, of the different applications of liberation theology mentioned in this paragraph figure in the approach to mission described by Daneel. Different kinds of African Initiated Churches in Zimbabwe are shown leading the way in this story of earth healing, working in concert with like-minded African traditionalists.

Before closing this section, mention must also be made of the strategic analysis offered in the work of Donald McGavran (1897–1990), especially since the church growth methods he advocated have been a magnet for missiological research. McGavran was active as a theorist in the second half of the twentieth century, but his thinking built on the earlier insights of Roland Allen and the Indian mission experience of J. Waskom Pickett (1933). Based on his time in China (1895–1903), Allen faulted the missionary establishment of his day for restraining the power of the Holy Spirit. In his view, they did this by relying on the vitality of their own institutions instead of God's strength (Allen 1927, esp. 131–95). He observed that missionaries as a rule were eager to control the behavior of those converting to Christianity but reluctant to entrust them with any real authority. Missionaries routinely fostered a culture of dependence on the mission field, which ensured that foreign workers would always be needed. Most assumed the universality of Western church forms. A more faithful course of action, Allen proposed (1912), would be to emulate the apostles, who did not spend most of their time constructing and servicing complex social organizations. Theirs was a light and very temporary missionary presence. They concentrated on the initial stages of proclamation and quickly baptized those who responded to their message. As soon as possible, they transferred responsibility to local leaders, who took charge of the new faith communities that had sprung to life. Allen was struck by the spontaneous manner in which the church seemed to expand over its first century. He feared that the modern missionary movement, symbolized in his era by the all-too-stationary mission compound, was in danger of losing its momentum altogether.

Donald McGavran gladly received Allen's critique of modern Protestant missions (1955, 88–89). Alongside Allen, he also advocated a return to apostolic methods, by which means he expected episodes of mass conversion based on "people movements" to multiply. As Newbigin has observed (1995, 130), Allen wanted the missions to stop over-planning, so that God's Spirit could do its work unfettered by human schemes. McGavran, on the other hand, pushed for a new kind of strategizing that incorporated a sociological perspective. He urged mission leaders to concentrate their resources on those initiatives with the greatest promise for numerical success. Where popular movements toward Christianity were already underway, these should be supported to the utmost. When established institutions no longer served to draw new people to the church, the huge sums usually needed for their upkeep should not be allowed to monopolize mission budgets. McGavran counseled the abandonment of an old strategy based on individual conversions and small Christian colonies maintaining stable but separate existences apart from the dominant social groups in their contexts. Significant growth would occur, he believed, only when more missionaries began to understand how communities of people decide to convert together to a new religious point of view. They have to be able to recognize when a clan, tribe, or caste suddenly becomes receptive to the gospel. According to McGavran (1955), these are the surest "bridges of God" over which the greatest number of people have been and will continue to be drawn to Christ.

The ideas of McGavran concerning evangelism have been intensively studied and debated within missiology. One of the most controversial aspects of his theory has been the "homogeneous unit principle," which holds that people are generally more responsive to evangelists from their own culture and want to join churches "without crossing racial, linguistic, or class barriers" (McGavran 1970, 198). While this principle may be sociologically valid (contra McClintock 1988) and usefully warns against (Western) cultural imperialism, many commentators (for example, Padilla 1982) take McGavran to task for appearing to bless the formation of churches based on cultural differences assumed to be more or less permanent. What then to make of the radical unity effected in Christ between Jews and Gentiles in Paul's day? Was this not a template for the future? Similarly, McGavran's argument (1962) that God intends the church to find lost sheep and not merely to seek after them half-heartedly may well be an appropriate challenge to missionary complacency with the religious status quo, but his insistence on numerical growth as the leading indicator of faithfulness in mission has been vigorously disputed (for example, by Newbigin 1995, 121–59).

McGavran (1955, 150–54) recommended that the dynamics of people movements be studied more carefully and that "controlled experiments" using his recommendations be conducted around the world in order to discover the most effective methods to use in connection with this kind of evangelism. His own Institute of Church Growth and the School of World Mission McGavran helped to found at Fuller Theological Seminary sponsored a great deal of this work. Others have concentrated on the preliminary step of identifying and understanding the world's different people groups and their languages (on this research, see Johnstone 2007). Another of McGavran's emphases—the importance of counting for mission strategy—has been developed into the subdiscipline of "missiometrics" (Barrett 1995). Two editions of the *World Christian Encyclopedia* (1982, 2000) stand as the most visible products of this impulse within contemporary mission studies. David Barrett and Todd Johnson (1990, 25–40) have also contributed to missiology the strategic notion of dividing the world's population into three groups, based on their response to the Christian faith: unevangelized, evangelized non-Christian, and Christian, or Worlds A-B-C. A related concept that some have used to focus thinking about the deployment of missionaries worldwide is the "10/40 Window" (discussed in Coote 2000). The current state of statistical research on mission is substantially (and attractively) represented in the *Atlas of Global Christianity* (Johnson and Ross 2009).

METHODS AND MODES OF MISSION

In this section I propose to discuss a selection of research primarily having to do with particular mission methods. No attempt will be made to present a comprehensive roll call of techniques at the disposal of the church and other mission agencies. It should be possible, however, even in just a few pages, to illustrate the wide range of topics I see falling within this part of a larger scholarly discourse on the means of mission. Practices that have already received extended treatment above, such as translation or church growth methodologies, will not be discussed again in this section, in order to leave room for scholarship on methods not yet described in much detail. Four broad areas of research will be highlighted: social transformation, healing, communication strategies, and dialogue.

Social Transformation

Christian missions in the modern era have persistently incorporated or featured commitments to improve the social conditions of those being evangelized. In some cases, these intentions substantially influenced the choice of methods used on the field. A growing body of researchers continues to investigate these ministry initiatives, a few of which stand out as particularly well subscribed missionary projects. From the late eighteenth century, for example, the issue of slavery and the problem of its abolition became inextricably bound to African missions. In part, this was because many of the same personalities advocating an end to British involvement in the slave trade were also behind a missionary push to found the Sierra Leone colony in West Africa. A key figure in this regard is William Wilberforce (1759–1833), whose story has been told many times. An African protagonist from the same era is Olaudah Equiano, whose slave narrative concludes with his unsuccessful application to the bishop of London to return to Africa as a missionary and then an account of his role in outfitting the first Sierra Leonean cohort (1995, 220–36). As Lamin Sanneh (1999) has shown in his study of "abolitionists abroad," many different motives lay behind the Sierra Leone venture, not all of them large-hearted. Beside a desire to evangelize Africa and so affirm the essential oneness of the human race in God's eyes were other interests that hoped even more for commercial profits or saw in the establishment of a distant colonial outpost a political opportunity to offload some of London's least desirable inhabitants (the initial group of settlers included scores of destitute blacks and white prostitutes). If religious purposes were ultimately served in Sierra Leone, it was largely due to the fact that thousands of freed slaves intercepted on their way to the New World by British warships after 1807 were resettled in the colony. This population became the focus of an extraordinary community-wide social experiment, in which the teaching of democratic ideals, Western social habits, and gospel truth commingled in missionary programs.

The Sierra Leonean model could not be replicated elsewhere, dependent as it was on a steady inflow of African "recaptives" to the colony, but the idea of combining abolition, mission, and the promotion of commerce continued to figure in African missions well into the nineteenth century. Missionary support for Western commercial undertakings abroad sometimes rested on the conviction that increased trade would boost the civilizational prospects of "backward" societies, thereby paving the way for eventual Christianization (on this view, see Porter 2004, 91–115). A less complicated argument on behalf of international trade could also be constructed, if the abolition of slavery stood near the center of one's missionary agenda. Perceptive supporters of mission devoted to the cause of abolition recognized that some form of "legitimate trade" had to be substituted for the social and economic advantages provided by the slave system to native elites, Western traders, and other interested parties.

Sanneh (1999, 139–50) shows how recaptives led the way into Nigeria for Christianity and commerce from the 1830s. At about the same time, Thomas Fowell Buxton (1786–1845) was agitating in Parliament as the successor of Wilberforce on behalf of aboriginal rights and further measures to restrict slavery in Africa (his influential study of the African slave trade, published in 1839–40, is discussed in Walls 1994). The leaders of the CMS recognized in Buxton's proposals for new forms of commercial activity to displace the slave trade a means to extend their work in Sierra Leone to other parts of Africa. So they eagerly participated in a government-funded expedition up the Niger River in 1841, the purpose of which was to persuade African rulers to renounce slavery in exchange for favorable trade relations with Britain. The whole venture is examined critically in Temperley (1991). A CMS representative on that expedition was an African recaptive, Samuel Crowther, in whose published journal (Crowther 1970) a missionary perspective on Buxton's grand scheme is articulated. A contemplated CMS Niger Mission was intended to work alongside government and private commercial entities in order to advance an ambitious program of evangelism and social transformation. As a character in his own account, Crowther the missionary was ready and willing to speak not only on behalf of the Christian Deity and the Bible and against the evils of slavery (and the dangers of Islam), but also in favor of agriculture (314), the dignity of legitimate commerce (331), and the benevolent intentions of Britain's monarch (307, 315).

The leading edge of the anti-slavery campaign eventually moved to East Africa. David Livingstone (1858) captured the imagination of his generation with a stirring call to cooperate with Providence by opening the Zambezi basin to the benefits of Protestant Christianity and commerce, at the expense of a regional slave-trading system that thrived on inter-tribal conflict (for a recent description of Livingstone's missionary career, see Ross 2002; the slogan "Commerce and Christianity" is expertly examined in Porter 1985). A Catholic counterpart to Livingstone was the founder of the White Fathers, Cardinal Charles Lavigerie, whose missionary program not only stood in opposition to slavery (Renault 1994, 367–85) but also testified to the virtues of Christian civilization. With the help of colonial power, Lavigerie hoped for nothing less than the transformation of a continent.

Adrian Hastings (1994, 282–93) has written perceptively about how average missionaries were apt to translate the large-scale civilizational objectives expounded by the likes of Livingstone and Lavigerie into daily activities. Theirs was not the realm of geopolitics or complicated financial transactions (stock offerings, mining contracts, etc.). While a few may have instigated high-profile campaigns of protest against social injustice, such as William Sheppard and Samuel Lapsley, who exposed the cruelties of King Leopold's Congo to the world (recounted in Benedetto 1996), most did not operate at that level. In local contexts judged to be in need of social improvement, more modest techniques were often the only ones that could be applied. The missionary decision might be to introduce the plough alongside the gospel or to teach simple industrial skills or to suggest new ways to irrigate and plant. Part of the mission might be to advocate or model a radically different approach to personal hygiene or to suggest new patterns of marriage and child rearing. Of course, every effort made to advance literacy had enormous social implications. Particularly when education was made available to women, previously unthinkable opportunities for work outside the home or new civic involvements suddenly became possible to imagine. Oddly enough, almost all of the great social projects proposed by the most prominent advocates of mission in Africa (and many other places) ended in collapse and failure. The accumulated effects of many small-scale missionary actions, on the other hand, proved to be thoroughly transformative in many circumstances, although not always in the ways the strategists may have intended.

Healing

Even before the advent of modern scientific medicine, doctors had claimed a small but secure place for themselves within missionary ranks. Colleagues on the field, especially those living in less salubrious climates, knew that their survival might one day depend on the quality of medical care available to them and so were eager to have trained physicians stationed nearby. Many missionaries and mission executives were also persuaded that medical doctors could win a hearing for the gospel in some places otherwise closed to Christian outreach, as noted earlier. Of course, the most powerful argument in favor of medical missions was the one based on scripture. Jesus had healed the sick and the apostles followed his example. Even if later generations were not able to work similar miracles, were they not still obliged to respond with compassion to the same kinds of physical, emotional, and psychological distress that had so moved the heart of Jesus? In the modern era, some Western sending agencies have given a high priority to medical service and a few have specialized in this form of mission. In their own way, Pentecostals have also endeavored to blend together ministries of healing and evangelism.

Students of mission with a particular interest in health ministries may now consult Christoffer Grundmann's detailed survey of medical missions (2005). Here one will find an extremely full bibliography covering the literature up through the 1980s and a careful account of how this special form of mission service took shape in the nineteenth century (somewhat updated in Grundmann 2008). The work of the early pioneers is described, with particular attention given to the careers of Karl Gützlaff, Thomas Colledge, and Peter Parker (on Parker, now also see Anderson 2006). Grundmann not only recounts the stories of exceptional individuals. He also treats the institutional aspects of missionary medicine (the founding of medical mission societies, for example) and investigates the theological significance of work done abroad in the name of Christ by nurses, doctors, and other health care professionals. Another basic orientation to medical missions is offered in the introduction to Good's study of the "Steamer Parish" operated by the UMCA on Lake Nyassa between 1885 and 1964 (Good 2004, 1–49; see also Etherington 2005a, 275–84). Jansen (1995) has contributed a valuable set of reflections on what he calls "medical missiology." Additional scholarship on women missionary physicians is available in Singh (2005), Blaufuss (2005), Francis-Dehqani (2002), and Brouwer (2002, 34–95; 2006). A recent study of

Canadian nurses laboring in north China (Grypma 2008) sheds light more generally on the development of missionary nursing. In a still-relevant classic essay, Andrew Walls (1996, 211–20) adroitly situates the figure of the medical missionary within the milieu of nineteenth-century missions. Rennie Schoepflin (2005) takes a further step by examining critically how medical missionaries were portrayed in a selection of juvenile and children's literature prepared for American church school audiences between 1880 and 1980. In what appear at first glance to be simple, winsome stories of missionary service meant to inspire children, Schoepflin finds a complex tangle of social values and implicit messages related to healing, superstition, race, and gender (562). The culture of medical missions is analyzed from another perspective in Nancy Rose Hunt's study of childbirth in the Belgian Congo. Special attention is given in this book (Hunt 1999) to mission-trained midwives, nurses, and teacher-evangelists. John Stanley (2010) considers mission efforts in China to develop nursing into a profession for a new "female medical elite."

In the postcolonial period, many mission hospitals and other church-related public service institutions passed from foreign to national control. Coincidently, some governments outside the West began to restrict the number of new visas issued to missionary physicians and others, often with the intention of promoting the development of their own domestic health professions. In the 1970s, some new organizations dedicated to international health also began to appear, such as Doctors Without Borders (*Médecins Sans Frontières*) and Doctors of the World (*Médecins du Monde*). Among other things, these groups represented an increasingly attractive secular alternative to missionary medicine on the world stage.

As the postcolonial context of evangelization evolved, some new patterns of mission service emerged with respect to health ministries and these topics have also become research subjects within missiology. The short-term medical missionary represents one such trend. These might be individual specialists or teams of health care workers. In many cases, the delivery of care to underserved areas is still the primary objective, but sometimes there is also an intention to provide advanced training to indigenous colleagues. The number of North Americans involved each year in short-term missions is substantial. Wuthnow (2009, 23) and Priest et al. (2006, 432) are convinced that well over a million Protestants now participate annually. Just how many of these volunteers are performing medical tasks cannot be determined with certainty, however. In the research of Dohn and Dohn (2006) and Montgomery (1993, 2007), the efficacy and unintended consequences of short-term medical missions are thoughtfully analyzed.

Increasingly, missionary medicine has been practiced within a global network of humanitarian organizations. This is a second trend reflected in the recent literature. It is simply a fact that the critical problems many churches and denominations hope to address through their international health ministries now tend to be so huge in scale that cooperative arrangements, involving many different kinds of organizations, often represent the only possible way forward. Furthermore, the factor of poverty often adds deep complexity to what might have appeared in the past to be strictly medical problems. As a result, church-sponsored health workers and their sending agencies have had to think more and more in terms of social solutions and not just individuals in need or the technical problems of disease eradication. Gerard Jansen (1999) has described the international health order within which many Christian ministries of healing are now self-consciously operating. The WCC has sponsored several conferences in which an integrative approach to mission, health, and healing has been explored (Matthey 2006). In a remarkably fresh study of mission experience and theological reflection, Agbonkhianmeghe Orobator (2005) explores the ecclesial identity of African Catholicism in the light of that tradition's engagement in Africa with HIV/AIDS, refugees, and poverty.

As Horsfjord observes (2007, 10), the rhetoric of healing became more prominent within the WCC when this part of the ecumenical movement committed itself to serious theological conversation with Pentecostal churches. Pentecostals have not only taken their expectations about divine healing into dialogue situations with other Christians but have also carried these convictions into mission on a regular basis. It could hardly have been otherwise, since the idea of salvation often featured in Pentecostal preaching typically embraces every sphere of human life, including physical well-being. Asamoah-Gyadu (2007b) shows how an intense concern for evangelism might intersect with an equally strong Pentecostal emphasis on the benefits of exorcism and healing. In the West African context he studies (Ghana), confidence in the power of the Spirit to restore the sick to health is sometimes made to stand in opposition to the practice of modern medicine, especially when the primary causes of illness and misfortune are assumed to be demonic. A more complementary relationship is also possible to imagine, in which case Pentecostal church leaders and theologians may explicitly recognize the importance of both spiritual and scientific means of healing (for example, in Onyinah 2006). Another dichotomy often imposed on the study of Pentecostal missions pits social concerns against ministries of deliverance and healing. Allan Anderson (2004, 206–42) suggests that the "full gospel" experience so ardently promoted within Pentecostalism worldwide may be expected to lead to "holistic" concepts of mission that are inherently expansive, not narrow. In the research of Miller and Yamamori (2007), numerous examples are produced to illustrate a global Pentecostal movement in which social engagement and deliverance ministries happily coexist.

Communicating the Word

Just as the church in mission from the beginning has had to think about how to communicate its message effectively, so have many generations of missiologists taken an active interest in the study of the various means used to pursue this objective. Bible translators and their work, discussed earlier, represent one aspect of this topic. At one time, the missionary sermon was a particular focus of scholarly attention (Jongeneel 1997, 267–89), but this seems not to be the case more recently. Throughout the modern period, missionaries have embraced a wide array of communication techniques besides the circulation of Christian literature or formal addresses from the pulpit, and many contemporary researchers have been drawn to study these other forms of missionary discourse. Most recently, advances in technology have created entirely new ways for churches and mission agencies to share the Word of God with those outside the fellowship of Christian faith.

Already in the early modern period Catholic missionaries were experimenting with new strategies of communication. In part, this was a result of the fact that the Age of Discovery was thrusting waves of Catholic evangelists into an expanding universe of societies quite unlike their own. Preliterate groups encountered outside of Europe posed a special challenge to those who hoped to evangelize them. Jaime Lara's study of sixteenth-century Mexico (2008), for example, explores the deep complexity that often marked missionary attempts to communicate their purposes in colonial Mesoamerica. Of particular importance here is the attention paid in this superb work of cultural analysis to missionary creativity, as many different means of expression were employed to overcome the problem of illiteracy (in this case, the Mexica were visually literate but unlettered) by constructing new ways to achieve cross-cultural understanding. In this historical context, missionaries could not depend on the written Word alone to convey their meaning. Their message had to be spoken, depicted, and enacted (Lara 2008, 9), using indigenous media and familiar metaphors. So it was that the sacraments and many other aspects of the church's liturgical life (including architecture, religious art, taught devotional practices, and music) became dynamic instruments of religious encounter, through which the processes of evangelization took hold at a very deep level. In Lara's view (13), Nahua Christians were partners with the friars in this highly imaginative work of cultural translation.

Other scholars have focused on the Jesuits and their particular interest in drama as a means of proclamation. Châtellier (1997), for example, studied Catholic rural missions in France and Italy over the sixteenth and seventeenth centuries and found that some of the best-known evangelists of the era became successful, in part, because they learned how to communicate in theatrical fashion with large audiences in open fields and other public settings. In these circumstances, penitential processions and outdoor performances of the gospel story became teaching events for the rural poor, most of whom had only a superficial grasp of the Catholic faith they may have nominally confessed. The Jesuits' use of "missionary theater" in an urban environment (in this case, seventeenth-century Naples) is examined in Selwyn (2004, 211–42).

Missionary contacts with preliterate societies have continued right up to the present time. In many of these social contexts, modern-age missionaries have decided to emulate the example of their forebears by creating written languages for the benefit of those with whom they might hope to share their message. This has been a useful strategy, with obvious benefits, but researchers who focus exclusively on text-centric missionary communication may be missing a large part of what happens in multilingual, cross-cultural evangelistic encounters. Even in highly literate societies, some people prefer to communicate or to receive new information without primary reference to written texts, perhaps seeing themselves as visual learners. Others are constantly switching back and forth between printed texts and other forms of communication. In any case, literacy is never completely achieved in any society, so there will always be some groups remaining outside the reach of the written Word.

Many recent studies of missionary communication have focused on interactions that occur alongside or apart from written texts. Much of this research touches on the idea of "orality," which has become something of a buzzword within certain mission circles. From a recent issue of *Missiology* (April 2010) constructed around the theme of orality, one can get a good idea about what this concept has come to mean to a number of mission researchers (along with many citations of current research). Scholars who study orality and missions often concern themselves with the social processes associated with storytelling and the use of narrative in various cultures. Jesus the teacher of parables figures in some of this research, for obvious reasons. Others want to explore how stories have been or might be told using nonverbal forms, such as drama, music, art, and dance. The work of Walter Ong (1982) continues to stand as a foundation for much of this research. In his analysis of orality, Ong highlighted the word as event, impermanent but powerful. He describes the special techniques used to convey meaning in oral cultures, such as repetition and formulaic phrasing, while drawing attention to the intersubjectivity of oral communication (in contrast to written texts, which do not need the simultaneous involvement of two human parties). Although Ong himself did not focus directly on missionary matters, his ideas have stimulated many evangelists and their sending organizations (and those who study them) to think again about nonprint forms of gospel communication (Hill 2010).

A final collection of research to be considered in this section has to do with new communication technologies put to use in mission situations over the past two centuries. A number of these innovations have proved to be truly revolutionary, in much the same way that the printing press profoundly influenced the course of the Protestant Reformation. Viggo Søgaard (1993) has provided a still-useful survey of modern communications media and their place in mission and ministry. Included in this introductory text are discussions of television, radio, video, audio cassettes, film, and computers (plus sections on print and the arts). Søgaard is especially concerned to help churches and mission organizations improve their media strategies. To that end, he not only describes a variety of modern media but also lays out a set of basic principles underlying communications theory, before suggesting how religious organizations might evaluate their own use of these available technologies.

A few other studies more narrowly focused than Søgaard may also be mentioned. Several treat the magic lantern, which was the preeminent visual aid carried into mission through the nineteenth century (Simpson 1997 and Martínez 2010). The development of missionary radio broadcasting, pioneered in the 1930s by Clarence Jones in Ecuador, is critically discussed in Stoneman (2007). As Stoneman shows, Jones blazed a trail for international religious broadcasting that eventually reached around the world. Further, Stoneman argues that some of the techniques Jones developed in connection with Station HCJB in Quito ("Voice of the Andes"), including the idea of distributing pretuned radios to the poor (the "Radio Circle") and the concept of broadcasting through "mechanical missionaries" into village settings otherwise inaccessible to missionaries, substantially helped to prepare the way for the phenomenal growth of evangelical Christianity in the global South many decades later. On Protestant Christian radio broadcasting to the Arabic-speaking world, one may consult the comprehensive study of Jos Strengholt (2008). Other forms of media besides radio rose to prominence in the second half of the twentieth century, most notably television, motion pictures, satellite broadcasting (Schmidt 2007), and the Internet (Asamoah-Gyadu 2007a). The *Jesus* film, in particular, has been intensively studied within missiology (for example, Bakker 2004). Communication is an area of research likely to flourish in coming decades, as evangelists around the world avidly embrace new technologies that promise access to remote peoples, especially when these live in societies where Christian missionaries are often viewed with suspicion.

Dialogue

Advocates of interfaith dialogue are largely agreed that this activity should not be employed as a mission tactic. A common argument in support of this position holds that authentic dialogue, intended to achieve mutual understanding and sympathetic relations among the adherents of different religions, is undermined when one or more of the parties involved subordinate these irenic aims to some other more sectarian concern, such as conversion. This judgment about the purpose of dialogue appears to have been embraced within missiology as a whole, based on the principal bibliographic structures that attempt to represent the field (see Skreslet 2006a). Dialogue is not typically classified as a "method" of mission, whether in the cumulative bibliography of the *IRM*, the *Bibliographia Missionaria*, the abstracts section of *Missionalia*, or the *International Mission Bibliography* (Thomas 2003). Across the board within the field, dialogue is considered rather to be a topic that properly falls under the category of "the religions." This makes sense to the extent that interfaith dialogue is a conscious response to the demographic facts of religious pluralism.

If missiologists were also agreed that dialogue stood in simple opposition to mission, there would be no reason at all to discuss this subject in a chapter on methods. But no such consensus exists. While many theologians and commentators who write most fervently in support of dialogue do see it as the antithesis of Christian mission in its most traditional forms (for example, Brockway 1984), self-identified missiologists tend to perceive a more nuanced relationship. In this latter group, dialogue may not be characterized as a "technique" or "instrument" of mission, but it still might be described as a "mode," "aspect," "dimension," or "expression" of the church's missionary impulse. Insofar as discussions about dialogue occur within missiology in response to questions about the "how" of mission, this topic is rightly construed to be part of a broader discourse focused on the "means" of mission.

Sustained reflection on dialogue and its relationship to other kinds of Christian outreach has marked Roman Catholic missiology in particular since Vatican II. Positive descriptions of several non-Christian religious traditions at the Council prepared the way for an entirely new stage in the conduct of that church's approach to interfaith relations. Vatican II may also be said to have initiated a more-than-theoretical move toward the new era by inviting the Catholic faithful "to enter with prudence and charity into discussion and collaboration with members of other religions" (*Nostra Aetate* 2). After the Council, several of the popes themselves engaged in dialogical encounters, while sponsoring theological activity meant to clarify the church's position on evangelism and dialogue. Several official church documents were subsequently produced that have since become major reference points for missiological work respecting dialogue, whether carried out by Roman Catholic scholars or others. Among the most influential of these postconciliar documents are *Dialogue and Mission* (1984), *Redemptoris Missio* (1990), and *Dialogue and Proclamation* (1991). Additionally, issues of dialogue and mission are addressed in *Dominus Iesus* (2000).

A common theme that runs through these official pronouncements of the Roman Catholic Church is that dialogue is a constituent element of a larger task given to the church by Jesus, which is usually referred to as "evangelization." Exactly how this might be so is not consistently stated, however. If dialogue can be set apart from other outreach activities, such as proclamation, one might be led to conclude that evangelization is a matter of aggregation, whereby different discrete means are used in a variety of circumstances by a loose collection of possible missionary agents. A version of this position is articulated in *Dominus Iesus* (22; with a reference back to *Redemptoris Missio* 55), which declares that interreligious dialogue, "as part of [the Church's] evangelizing mission, is just one of the actions of the Church in her mission *ad gentes*." Another line of thinking emphasizes the leavening capacity of dialogue, which may be expected to affect every other aspect of Christian mission it touches. A forthright statement along these lines, often quoted, appears in *Dialogue and Mission* (29):

> Dialogue is . . . the norm and necessary manner of every form of Christian mission, as well as of every aspect of it, whether one speaks of simple presence and witness, service, or direct proclamation. Any sense of mission not permeated by such a dialogical spirit would go against the demands of true humanity and against the teachings of the gospel.

Following Vatican II, Protestants and Orthodox Christians have also engaged in serious reflection on dialogue in the light of the church's missionary mandate. Much of this work has taken place in the context of the World Council of Churches (WCC), which signaled its particular interest in this subject by creating a new program structure on dialogue in 1971 (an office that eventually became known as the Sub-unit on Dialogue with People of Living Faiths and Ideologies). Subsequently, the Dialogue subunit of the WCC has coordinated a series of high-level interfaith events around the world, in which official representatives of many faith communities participated, alongside theologians and other experts in the study of religion. These activities and the various reports they generated are recounted in Selvanayagam (2004). Two documents issued by the WCC deserve special mention because of their wide influence. *Guidelines on Dialogue*, initially adopted by the WCC Central Committee in 1979 and then revised as *Ecumenical Considerations for Dialogue and Relations with People of Other Religions* (2004), sets out a basic conceptual framework for interreligious encounter, along with some practical advice about how to smooth and deepen the social processes of faith-sharing in community. *An Ecumenical Affirmation: Mission and Evangelism* (1982) presents a comprehensive approach to mission that respects the new possibilities for Christian witness offered to the church through dialogue.

Within missiology, interest in dialogue and mission continues to be strong. A few resources may be cited here from among those publications pertaining to dialogue that are persistently referenced by mission scholars operating across the theological spectrum. William Burrows (1993), for example, is widely appreciated for having pulled together an edited volume in which authoritative commentaries are provided alongside the official texts of *Redemptoris Missio* and *Dialogue and Proclamation*. The usefulness of this book is further enhanced by the inclusion of several critical responses to the Vatican documents, gathered from a diverse group of mission practitioners and theologians. Lesslie Newbigin has written many times on the subject of the religions and the purposes of dialogue in the context of mission. A succinct statement of Newbigin's views appears in his now-classic *The Gospel in a Pluralist Society* (1989, esp. 155–83). Similarly influential and equally relevant to the concerns of this section is the comprehensive study of mission theology authored by Stephen Bevans and Roger Schroeder (2004). Bevans and Schroeder suggest that Christian mission be reconceived as "prophetic dialogue," by which means they believe insistent late-twentieth-century calls for proclamation, liberation, and dynamic witness could be synthesized. A compatible proposal has been put forward by the Federation of Asian Bishops' Conferences (FABC), which has endorsed an understanding of mission as dialogue that responds to the situation of the poor in Asia, their cultures, and their religions. Jonathan Tan (2004) characterizes this approach, thoroughly imbued with the spirit of dialogue commended at Vatican II, as *missio inter gentes* ("mission *among* the nations"), which he sees replacing the more traditional locution, *missio ad gentes* ("mission *to* the nations"). For further comments on Bevans and Schroeder and the work of the FABC, one may also refer to Peter Phan (2008).

ORGANIZATIONAL STRUCTURES FOR MISSION

Strategies and programs do not implement themselves. Individuals may be able to supply energy and vision, but organizational structures are also usually needed, if intentions and plans are to be turned into realized ministry objectives. Some mission structures are brought into being with deliberate care. Others, especially in premodern times, may appear to have arisen organically within specific historical circumstances. In either case, it is possible to study these particular means of missionary action, too. In so doing, one quickly discovers that this is an area of missiology in which theological convictions may be observed interacting with powerful social dynamics. As a result, it is not unusual in this part of the field to find the scholarly concerns of historians, sociologists, organizational theorists, and theologians overlapping with each other.

The missionary orders of the Roman Catholic Church are an obvious place to begin. The importance of these complex social instruments to the cause of Christian mission has been noted on a number of occasions (see, for example, Bosch 1991, 230–36, on "the mission of monasticism"). Mission studies focused on the sociological functions of these groups are less common than flattering recitals of their achievements, but they do exist and help to explain how organizational factors can shape evangelistic outcomes. Jo Ann Kay McNamara, for example, has written incisively about monasteries as "frontier outposts" in early medieval Europe (1996, 120–47). The institutional character of these establishments influenced the behavior of the monks and nuns residing in them and the means of mission they were able to employ. These included educational initiatives, the production of religious literature, the provision of hospitality, invalid care, acts of charity, and even the governance of nearby villages. Wealth accumulation, out of the question for the voluntary poor but acceptable when practiced by Christian institutions, made all of these activities possible.

Pope Gregory the Great (c. 540–604) may have been the first strategist to realize that the church's missionary program could be harnessed to the engine of monasticism. When he dispatched Augustine and his comrade monks to England, they left with a plan to create a network of foundations loyal to Rome, which could be related to and draw support from the church's institutional assets already established in Gaul. Bede's narrative vividly portrays the many twists and turns encountered on the way to the fulfillment of Gregory's vision. The pope's devotion to Benedict of Nursia (Markus 1997, 68–71) naturally inclined him to favor that pattern of monastic life and its use as a primary instrument of mission. An appreciative discussion of the early Benedictines in England and their importance to the church's mission there and on the continent is conducted in Rees (1997, 1–64).

A crucial element in the study of premodern and early modern mission organizations, sometimes overlooked because precise data can be difficult to isolate, concerns the formation of local Christian institutions. While it is probably true that foreign church structures were simply transplanted to new locations in some cases, one suspects that the deep reality was often much more complicated than that. Liam Brockey provides a sterling example of a sophisticated analysis of institutional church life emerging from within a missionary context in his study of the Jesuits in China between 1579 and 1724. Half of this substantial book is given over to several aspects of a broad theme he denominates "building the church." Within this section is an extended discussion (Brockey 2007, 328–401) of the local and provincial community associations that helped knit together many widely dispersed but still interconnected groups of believers in China, who could not yet be organized using standard diocesan structures. Brockey examines in particular how the Jesuits experimented with the idea of Catholic lay confraternities, in light of what they were learning about the different kinds of traditional voluntary societies (*hui*) they encountered in China. Brockey (2007, 332) agrees with Standaert (2001, 457–58) that these organizations did not have to be imposed on Chinese Christians, who were already accustomed to participate in community associations drawn together for religious and secular purposes. As it turned out, Christian *hui* sustained the church through times of crisis and involuntary periods of missionary absence, while also providing fertile seedbeds in which indigenous local leadership could be cultivated and trained.

Because Protestants did not accept the institution of monasticism on principle, they denied themselves the use of this tried and true instrument of mission. In compensation, perhaps, they devised another social structure to take the place of the Catholic religious order, which was the private voluntary association or mission society. William Carey is widely recognized as an innovator with respect to this development, although predecessor organizations like the Society for the Propagation of the Gospel in Foreign Parts (founded in 1701) anticipated his approach in some respects (Cox 2008, 22-60). In his 1792 *Enquiry into the Obligations of Christians, to Use Means for the Conversion of the Heathens*, Carey pleaded with Protestants to take up Christ's missionary mandate, founded on the Great Commission (for him, the ultimate basis of their "obligations"). At the end of his appeal, he sketched out a plan for an institutional structure through which a renewed effort to evangelize the world might be carried out. This was the mission society, whose sole purpose was to enable more evangelical Protestants to become effective missionary agents in faraway places. He proposed that it might do this under the authority of an independent governing board, which would take responsibility for fundraising, public relations on behalf of missions, the recruitment and screening of candidates, and the evaluation of their work. The benefits of this organizational concept were well demonstrated over the next two centuries, as hundreds of mission societies were founded along lines very near to those suggested by Carey.

What did this new turn in the history of organized Christian outreach mean conceptually for the church and its mission? Fundamentally, missionary societies represented a rare moment of renewal, according to Andrew Walls (1996, 241–54). Their emergence became an occasion for the "fortunate subversion" of the church. They did this, Walls maintains, by disturbing settled views on church government (247), by opening up new opportunities for lay involvement in mission (249–51), and by internationalizing the scope of interchurch relations (253). Brian Stanley (2003) covers some of this same ground when he discusses the "polarities" involved when particular mission structures are chosen for use. Some of these structures are essentially communitarian, for example, while others are institutionally oriented. Voluntarist organizations, likewise, stand in tension with more established ecclesiastical structures. Three other polarities are defined in these terms: denominational vs. nondenominational, national vs. international, and unidirectional vs. multidirectional. Ultimately, what Stanley provides is an interpretive grid that allows one to analyze a wide variety of mission structures and the institutional values potentially embedded in each of them.

Not a little scholarship within missiology has gathered around the topic of the mission society. Walls (2001), for example, clarifies the significance of Carey's initiative by situating it in the context of an evangelical awakening that began long before his time. Hartmut Lehmann (2008) adds a number of crucial details to this picture, when he describes some late-eighteenth-century developments in Central European Pietism and the seminal role played in that context by the Basel-based *Christentumsgesellschaft* (the "Christianity Society," a forerunner of the Basel Mission Society). As Lehmann points out, the "mobilization of God's pious children" for mission at this time within Britain and German-speaking lands may well have been spurred by a common fear of Revolutionary France. In any case, some powerful connections were made between these two cultural spheres at a very early stage of the modern Protestant missionary movement. Unusual levels of international cooperation among mission institutions (such as what developed between the Basel Mission and the CMS) pointed ahead toward the possibility of even deeper commitments to ecumenical mission unity in the future. Along the way toward this outcome, some mission societies acted to construct additional layers of relations among themselves that expanded beyond bilateral agreement. Several large-scale para-church organizations that developed in the second half of the nineteenth century, such as the YMCA/YWCA, the Student Volunteer Movement, the Student Volunteer Missionary Union, and the World Student Christian Federation, became increasingly important instruments of inter-institutional communication and coordination during this era. By and large, these newer social structures were not themselves mission societies but cooperated closely with them in the cause of world evangelization. Showalter (1998), Parker (1998), and Putney (2001, esp. 127–43), among others, have examined the importance of these organizations to the history of Protestant missions.

Another set of relationships had to be created among the denominations, the mission societies, and the domestic church publics that supported both of these expressions of Protestant Christian identity. Such partnerships were by nature very complex and sometimes fraught with difficulties, as independent institutional actors sought to influence each other while competing for support within overlapping constituencies. Susan Thorne's fine study (1999, esp. 57–72, 124–54) of English Congregationalism, the London Missionary Society, and British imperial culture in the nineteenth century gives insight into the interplay of these evangelical institutions at the height of their influence within British society. A more extensive, transatlantic network of mission societies and their relations with each other through the first half of the nineteenth century is examined in Porter (2004, 116–35).

Special mention must also be made here to research on women's mission organizations, particularly since this continues to be an active topic within contemporary missiology. Patricia Hill (1985) may be said to have initiated a new round of scholarly work on the women's foreign missionary movement, when she published a study of the four mainline Protestant women's mission organizations (Congregational, Methodist, Presbyterian, and Baptist) that together dominated the American church scene between 1870 and 1920. Dana Robert's widely appreciated social history of American women in mission enlarged on Hill's findings, especially with respect to the Woman's Foreign Missionary Society of the Methodist Episcopal Church (1997, 125–88). Robert also treated the emergence and experience of some American Catholic women's missionary orders (317–407). Institutional factors that affected the mission efforts of American Catholic women in the twentieth century are also discussed in Dries (2002) and Guider (2002). Amanda Porterfield's (1997) study of Mount Holyoke and its early relationship to the ABCFM shows further how this new kind of institution, the female seminary, prepared substantial numbers of American women for mission service abroad. Selles (2006) has carefully described how women participated in the formation of the World Student Christian Federation and several other movements and organizations that came earlier.

From within this scholarship on women's mission organizations have come several important findings, which had resisted discovery or emphasis when mission institutions of all kinds were studied together. The first of these insights has to do with the contributions of women to mission theory. As Dana Robert has shown, Protestant women in the last third of the nineteenth century increasingly organized themselves into independent mission societies at precisely the same time that they developed a distinctive theory to explain their approach: "woman's work for woman." These organizational structures and the theory that undergirded them considerably strengthened the position of the single woman missionary, who now had a conceptual place to stand that did not depend on a male sponsor, along with a relatively independent source of funding. A fairly sizable shift in the demographic makeup of the Protestant foreign missionary workforce ensued, as a growing network of women's mission societies moved to appoint ever-greater numbers of (single) women missionaries (Hutchison 1987, 99–102).

How these new missionaries and their sending organizations then related to the male-dominated structures that preceded them in time has also been closely investigated. Rowbotham (2002), for example, looks at the rise of ladies missionary societies in the British context and the various ways they responded to the expectations of the majority regarding the subordination of women to men. Dries (1998b, esp. 262–67) describes the different leadership roles assumed by women and men over the history of American Catholic missions. Hardesty (2003) discusses the wide influence of some mission periodicals produced by women's organizations, drawing attention especially to the publishing efforts of the Central Committee on the United Study of Missions between 1901 and 1938. In terms of gender relations, the decisive issue often came down to money. Male mission executives were more apt to give public praise to energetic and resourceful churchwomen who gathered support for missions, so long as these funds stayed under the firm control of men. The struggle of women's mission organizations to maintain their independence is thoughtfully explored in Yohn (2002), who further observes that the "business of mission" conducted by these institutions provided unprecedented opportunities for women to develop entrepreneurial skills and to gain experience in civil affairs to a degree not yet available to them in any other professional sphere.

Yet one more specialized lens through which some researchers have chosen to examine the mission society is the nongovernmental organization or NGO. The fact that many mission agencies are now accustomed to do their work in concert with a variety of nonreligious NGOs and several kinds of government entities is a basis for some of this research. This is certainly the case within the international health order described by Jansen (1999), already cited. Similar levels of cooperation have been taking place among various religious and secular humanitarian organizations focused on issues of poverty, disaster relief, social justice, and the empowerment of women. Within the realm of faith-based NGOs and development, World Vision International seems to have played a uniquely influential role, whether as a generator of theologically informed theory (for example, Myers

1999) or as an object of research attention (Bornstein 2003). The NGO as a particular kind of mission structure is examined in Skreslet (1997 and 1999) and Brouwer (2011).

Besides Catholic religious orders and Protestant mission societies, missiologists have studied several other kinds of social structures that have figured in the spread of Christianity and the giving of Christian witness. One of these is the "house church," which refers in the first instance to the domestic settings in which many groups of early Christians were accustomed to gather for worship and fellowship. With exegetical thoroughness and sociological awareness, Roger Gehring (2004) has demonstrated the importance of the house church to apostolic Christianity on several levels. In terms of social function, for example, the house church was a means by which to order church life and to organize outreach. The small scale of the house church also reflected the political and economic realities experienced by many early Christians, who had good reasons in times of persecution to avoid the attention of the authorities and, in any case, were not yet in a position to erect grand public buildings. At the same time, this social arrangement acquired a theological meaning, especially in Paul's theology, where the *oikos* became a master metaphor for the church.

In Gehring's last chapter he discusses the house church as a possible model for mission today. In so doing, he relates the results of New Testament scholarship on the institutional structures of the early church to the efforts of many contemporary mission practitioners around the world who understand themselves to be followers of an apostolic pattern of church planting and evangelism. Some other mission researchers who have studied modern house church movements include Xin (2008), Jamison (2007), and Wang (1997). According to Lian Xi (2010) the idea of the house church has surfaced with some regularity in popular Chinese Christianity since at least the beginning of the twentieth century, recurring alongside millenarian theologies of salvation, vigorous expressions of worship, irrepressible urges to evangelize the poor, and anti-foreign sentiments. Chao (2010) recognizes John Nevius (1829–93) as an early missionary advocate of the house church model in China.

Another organizational form intensively studied within contemporary missiology is the base (or basic) ecclesial community. The concept is Latin American in origin and was promoted in that region after Vatican II as an alternative to institutional Catholicism. More generally, it now refers to local church structures in which the poor participate fully in a hermeneutical process of ecclesial discernment that directly addresses their needs and the requirements of God's Reign. All the major mission bibliographies include research on base communities within their schema, but they do not agree on precisely where this topic belongs. Thus, we find base ecclesial communities characterized as a form of mission in the abstracts section of *Missionalia*. This is in contrast to the *IRM* mission bibliography, which treats the base communities as an aspect of ecclesiology, or the *International Mission Bibliography*, which locates them within a larger section having to do with local church renewal. Within official Catholicism, base ecclesial communities tend to be discussed under the rubric of evangelization, in line with the perspective articulated in *Evangelii Nuntiandi*, a 1975 papal document. In some contexts, a more specific linkage to social activism has been established (Adriance 1995). Two older texts that continue to be cited quite frequently within the literature devoted to base ecclesial communities are Boff (1986) and Cook (1985).

On occasion, missionaries have endeavored to settle new Christians together in constructed social environments they intended to keep separate from their converts' birth cultures. The result is the so-called Christian village or reduction, which is one more specialized institutional structure in which missiologists have shown a persistent scholarly interest. The Jesuit reductions in Paraguay are probably the best known examples of this social arrangement, thanks to the popularity of the film *The Mission*. Scholarly treatments of this subject are rendered in Caraman (1976) and Ganson (2003), with Ganson taking care to emphasize the agency of the Guaraní. Catholic missionaries elsewhere also experimented with the idea of creating more or less exclusively Christian settlements, as in China (discussed in Charbonnier 2007, 337–49) or East Africa (Kollman 2005). In this latter case, the village of converts established at Bagamoyo by French Spiritans solved an immediate practical problem they faced, which was what to do with the young captives they were redeeming in the nearby slave markets at Zanzibar. Their ultimate hope was to raise up a cadre of fully-formed native Catholic priests out of this group, who would then lead the way in the evangelization of Africa's interior. In Kollman's expert analysis, it becomes very clear that the Spiritans' choice of this particular organizational means rested on several critical assumptions the missionary group held in common with regard to priestly formation, the importance of indigenous clergy, the theological value of Muslim culture, and proper social relations, including the use of discipline with the young.

For their part, many Protestants were also attracted to the idea of the mission village throughout the modern period, beginning with John Eliot and the establishment of his first "praying town" of Native American Christians at Natick in 1650 (Cogley 1999, esp. 105–71). Some early Protestant missionaries to Africa likewise attempted to use this institutional means to further their evangelistic aims, as at Genadendahl and Bethelsdorp in southern Africa and in Sierra Leone. Nearer to the end of the modern Protestant missionary movement is the example of the mission village established at Chali in southern Sudan by the Sudan Interior Mission in 1951 (considered from an anthropological point of view in James 1988, esp. 207–52). Whether Protestants or Catholics are involved, the mission village often appears to represent in physical form what a given group of missionaries believed at the time to be Christian civilizational norms. Hastings (1994,

197–221) presents a wonderfully nuanced discussion of the mission village as that concept was applied across sub-Saharan Africa through the nineteenth century.

FINANCING MISSION ENDEAVORS

No matter what organizational mission structures might be chosen for use, financial obligations are sure to follow. Even mendicants can incur regular expenses, the more so when their missionary work involves extensive long-distance travel, the founding and maintenance of schools, church construction projects, the employment of native agents, or the provision of charity to sizable groups of needy people. Thus, to remain viable over the long term, every mission institution has to attend to budget realities, which means paying attention to how funds gratefully received are eventually spent. Initially, of course, these monies have to be solicited and gathered, a matter that usually entails the costs of a publication program to inform the mission's most likely supporters and a larger church public about the group's successes and most critical needs. Due to the fact that substantial financial resources were and still are required for most forms of organized Christian outreach, this subtopic clearly belongs to a larger discussion within missiology about the means of mission. In what follows, I will divide the scholarship on this subject into two sections, with research on the practicalities of mission finances leading the way. In a smaller group of studies, we find a focus on the moral issues raised when missionaries and their organizations embrace particular patterns of sponsorship and expenditure.

Some mission initiatives have depended on the financial support of powerful patrons. These might be royal figures, members of the nobility, or private philanthropists. For a variety of reasons, many of Europe's kings and queens over the centuries have been eager to underwrite the expenses of missionary work. Most famously, we have the example of the Portuguese *padroado* and the Spanish *patronato*, which together propelled the institutions of the Catholic Church and its message far beyond the limits of Western Christendom. These two systems of early modern ecclesio-political cooperation are briefly described in Hughes (2010) and Bakewell (2004, 137–47). The French monarchy, especially under the influence of Cardinal Richelieu, committed its support to Catholic missions in New France, in part for reasons of state (Crowley 1996, 2–19). With respect to the Belgian Congo, King Leopold sought to enlist the church in his plans to exploit the natural and human resources of that region by maintaining a firm managerial hand over all mission activities taking place within his colonial realm (Leopold's African regime is vividly described in Hochschild 1998). Administrative policies skewed in the direction of certain mission organizations constituted one method by which Leopold and other European monarchs attempted to control missionary behavior. Subventions and grants to loyal Catholic missionary orders was another.

Countless other wealthy individuals and families below the level of royalty have also chosen to use their financial and social power to promote and secure the cause of Christian mission. Many of these actors were historically important for other reasons, so an extensive biographical trove has built up around them over the years, out of which a few outstanding research projects oriented more toward missiological questions may be highlighted. On the Catholic side, for example, we now have a set of primary documents, transcribed and annotated, along with an introductory essay that describes in very fine detail how Maria Theresia von Fugger-Wellenburg (1690–1762), a noblewoman in southern Bavaria, became deeply committed to the Jesuit missions of Asia and their financial well being (Hsia 2006). What is particularly striking about this research is the light that it sheds on the logistical challenges involved when funds were transferred from Europe to the missions or gifts were exchanged halfway around the world in the early modern period. Hsia's work also gives insight into the practice of piety by upper-class German Catholics of the era and the strong attraction the East Asian missions held for some of the most devout laypersons in that church community.

Protestants also had their aristocratic patrons of mission. This was true, despite the arguments of Dutch Reformed theologian Gisbertus Voetius (1589–1676) against the right of princes and magistrates to send missionaries abroad on behalf of the church (Jongeneel 1991, 58–59). Perhaps the most famous member of the nobility to lend material support to Protestant missions was Selina Hastings, the Countess of Huntingdon (1707–91), who was an extraordinarily active proponent of early Methodism in the time of the Wesleys. While most of her efforts were centered in Britain and so might be classified as attempts to spark church renewal, the countess also involved herself in a few missionary projects undertaken abroad, chiefly through her close association with George Whitefield. Lady Huntingdon's engagement with overseas missions is discussed in Schlenther (1997, 83–95).

Eventually, a new form of aristocracy founded on business success produced another set of wealthy mission philanthropists who sought through their giving to shape the development of the modern missionary movement. From within this group, two figures stand out: Robert Arthington (1823–1900) and John D. Rockefeller Jr. (1874–1960). Arthington gave a number of large donations to a variety of mission projects over many decades during his lifetime and then left most of his million-pound estate to the Baptist Missionary Society and the London Missionary Society (discussed in Stanley 1998). Rockefeller's involvement with the missionary movement of his day was substantial and pervasive, whether through his relationship with John R. Mott and a developing ecumenical movement, his sponsorship of the Laymen's Foreign Missions Inquiry in the early 1930s, or the funding he gave to a number of key medical and educational facilities in East Asia, many of which were mission-related institutions. Rockefeller wanted to use his vast wealth to "modernize" missions, which meant bending them toward progressive liberal values and away from conversionist practices.

Schenkel (1995) has examined Rockefeller's mission philanthropy in the context of a long life dedicated to benevolence in multiple spheres.

No matter how much attention might be paid to elite munificence, modern missions were largely sustained and expanded by thousands upon thousands of small gifts intentionally cultivated from the middle and lower classes. In a remarkable way, Justinian Welz (1621–68) anticipated the potential of more democratic approaches to mission fundraising when he proposed that a new "Missionary (Converting) Society" constituted for the purpose of spreading evangelical faith outside of Germany ought to seek regular support from local pious merchants (Welz 1969, 62–68). According to the plan of Welz, these members of the rising middle class would make annual contributions to a common money chest that would be kept under the watchful eye of a trusted merchant member of the Society. William Carey drove the logic of Welz's fundraising impulse to another level when he suggested that a broad-based campaign carried out among the Baptist faithful in Britain, asking for as little as a penny a week from interested congregations, could build a fiscal foundation strong enough to support the worldwide program of evangelization he was outlining in 1792 (Carey 1934, 84–86).

As in so many other aspects of Protestant mission strategy in the modern era, Carey's ideas about fundraising would prove to be seminal, if not prophetic. Most mission societies and all the denominations eventually concluded that their success in world evangelization would depend on legions of small givers participating faithfully over long periods of time in well-organized programs of support. Much creativity was applied to solving the problem of how to engage broad church publics in the venture of global mission, and many of these efforts have been studied by missiologists. For example, we have the research of Thorne (1999, 126–36) on Sunday School collections taken up in support of mission by nineteenth-century English Congregationalists. More broadly, the complex network of fundraising and interpretation structures put together by the five largest nineteenth-century British mission organizations is examined in Maughan (1996). Dries (1998b, 124–25) has discussed the use of women's circles to raise funds for overseas projects and personnel in American Catholicism between the 1920s and 1960s. An innovation begun at the suggestion of Southern Baptist missionary Lottie Moon in 1888—the special congregational offering on behalf of mission—has long since become a standard feature on the mission funding landscape of most denominations. In several of Catherine Allen's publications regarding the Woman's Missionary Union of the Southern Baptist Convention (for example, Allen 1987, 146–64, and 2002, 117–18), the scale of the Lottie Moon Christmas Offering, its historical origins, and its symbolic importance within Southern Baptist church culture are all discussed. In a pair of articles, Dawson (1990, 1991) has examined the role of selected (or designated) giving for mission within American Presbyterianism. An issue that seems to recur with some frequency within this literature is the struggle for control over mission funds, especially when these are raised locally in campaigns that are coordinated nationally (see Tew 2006).

In order to meet operating expenses and to provide additional wherewithal for expansion, some missionaries and their organizations have turned to various kinds of entrepreneurial activity. The silk trade, for example, became a highly controversial source of income for the early Jesuits in East Asia (discussed in Ross 1994, 54–55 and 91–92). Just as famously, the Basel Mission Trading Company gained an international reputation for high-quality tile work and other manufactured items. Danker (1971, 79–142) gives a sympathetic but detailed account of the Basel Mission and the different commercial activities performed on its behalf, especially in India and West Africa. Besides tile making, the Trading Company and the Mission both eventually came to be identified with high-quality weaving, bookbinding, and the production of cocoa. A portion of the profits generated from these ventures, plus a regular dividend, went straight to the bottom line of the Basel Mission, which was for many decades the single largest shareholder in the Trading Company. Apart from the income the Basel Mission received through trade for its primary work in evangelism, education, and church planting, its supporters also tended to see religious value in the lessons good business practices were able to teach about the importance of industriousness, wise management, thrift, self-support, and generous service to human need. Additionally, some converts shunned by their families and communities found much-needed employment in church-related business ventures. For purposes of comparison, Danker (1971, 16–75) also describes the economic activities of the Moravians through the nineteenth century.

In some circumstances, missionaries have also looked to agriculture as a means by which to sustain themselves on the field. The point in these cases was usually not to produce extra income that could be spent on "religious" activities so much as it was a practical way to make the missions more self-sufficient. On the small scale of the mission station, well-tended gardens did this by producing food for missionary consumption. Larger farms might yield surpluses, which could be traded for other needed items. Founders and heads of mission villages especially had to pay close attention to their balance sheets, because chronic deficits run up abroad were not likely to be covered over the long term by mission committees back home. Several factors often worked in the favor of these enterprises, including access to cheap labor, experience with market economies, and the possession of technological advantages not available to indigenous competitors. On occasion, colonial authorities made huge grants of land to favored mission groups (Hastings 1994, 424–27). As the Comaroffs (1997, 119–65) have sharply observed, missionary agriculture, like trade, was never just a matter of economics. Certain methods of cultivation were thought to have the capacity to teach gospel lessons and bedrock cultural values that exemplified Christian civilization. Similarly, in Kollman's analysis (2005), the Spiritans at Zanzibar understood their mission workshops and the agricultural colony they established at Bagamoyo to be, above all else, contexts for Christian formation. Arguably, no one did more than David Livingstone (1858) to stoke missionary confidence in the evangelizing potential of land, as he imagined for eager audiences in Britain the commercial potential of Africa's rural interior.

Here it might also be appropriate to mention several research projects that have used or suggested unusually comprehensive approaches to the study of mission finances. In one of these (Langer 1995), the immediate object of study appears to be quite narrow: Franciscans working among the Chiriguano Indians of southeastern Bolivia during the republican period. The analytical framework Erick Langer applies to this restricted context, however, is anything but simple. This mission, he insists, was a frontier institution that functioned on several levels at once: as a source of labor, a developer of infrastructure, a place of production, and as a market for goods (51). These factors were not constant but fluctuated over the lifecycle of the institution, such that a descriptive snapshot of the mission taken at any point in time cannot be assumed to represent its exact economic situation either earlier or later than that. Another example of a more comprehensive analysis is offered in Clossey, who examines how a global "Jesuit financial network" began to take shape in the sixteenth century (2008, 162–92), supported by an increasingly sophisticated "information network" (193–215) that linked great numbers of far-flung Jesuits mission outposts to each other and to a central planning body in Rome. Porter's treatment of the slogan "Commerce and Christianity," cited earlier, represents an additional attempt to grapple with mission finances in a systemic way, taking into account shifting attitudes among British missionaries toward commercial involvements over the course of the nineteenth century. As Porter (1985, 621) observes, theological concerns on occasion did raise tough questions about how the church in the world was going about its financial business, but the practices of everyday missionary life tended to be shaped by factors other than theology.

Finally, at the level of the individual missionary, a recent trend toward tentmaking may be observed. At the heart of this concept is the idea of self-support, which can lay claim to biblical sanction through the example of St. Paul and his tentmaker colleagues in Corinth (Acts 18:1–5). This pattern of missionary work has become more prominent since the 1960s for several reasons, in my view. One is the fact that within many of the sending organizations that dominated the modern Protestant missionary movement during the colonial period, the career missionary appointment gradually lost its normative status. At the same time, more and more dedicated laypersons from the West were finding short-term work abroad in an era of jet travel and international development initiatives. Adding to the attraction of bi-vocational service is the experience of many secular workers with sought-after technical skills and an interest in mission who have been able to secure visas and therefore entry into sensitive national contexts when most full-time professional missionaries could not.

J. Christy Wilson's influential survey of tentmaking (1979) initiated a new round of research on this specialized form of mission service. Among those who have reflected on the strategic value of tentmaking are Blair (1983), Yamamori (1987), and Ginter (1998). Most recently, the idea of "business as mission" has been vigorously promoted, for example, by C. Neal Johnson (2009) and a host of contributors to Yamamori and Eldred (2003). In the "business as mission" model, lay missionaries are not content to work for others but seek rather to create jobs and investment opportunities abroad through innovative business strategies. In parallel with domestic "marketplace ministries," these companies are often founded on the hope of bringing Christ into the workplace (Johnson 2009, 129–52).

When material considerations appear to govern evangelistic practice, even strong advocates of Christian mission may become uneasy. In some cases, the worry is that unintentional financial entanglements or some other worldly social factor will eventually overwhelm the mission's spiritual aims, despite every sincere desire to keep this from happening. On occasion, missionaries and their organizations have been suspected of willful collusion with forces and interests at odds with the ethical demands of Christ's gospel. Some groups have sought to keep the corrosive influence of the world and its financial systems at bay by relying on the power of prayer to meet the material needs of their workers (on this aspect of "faith missions," for example, see Svelmoe 2008, 63–75 and 192–202). A wider circle of practitioners and theorists has focused on missionary lifestyles. This is a topic that not only asks about missionary standards of living (including issues of salary, housing, and access to education for missionary children) but also about matters of authority and missionary autonomy with respect to local church structures.

Orlando Costas (1982, 58–70) exemplifies the inside critic who becomes unsettled when mission advocates seem to assume or to push for close ties with capitalist structures and ideologies. Costas warns especially against the encroachment of entrepreneurial language into the domain of mission theology. In his view, "mission as enterprise" and "[free] enterprise as mission" are equally problematic formulations. Either way, if missionary vocations are subordinated to some larger domesticating project (modern forms of colonialism, for example, or neoliberal capitalism), the liberative nature of the gospel is likely to be compromised. From another angle, Jonathan Bonk (1991; rev. 2006) looks at the condition of affluence as a particular Western missionary problem. One emphasis in this work falls on the individual missionary in the modern period, whose lifestyle and all the means of mission put at his or her disposal, in Bonk's view, ought to be carefully evaluated in the light of the message being preached. Bonk also recognizes that personal choices are almost always made in contexts shaped by powerful social forces that dwarf the capacity of individuals to effect large-scale change. His critique of missionary affluence, therefore, extends outward from the self to the family, to the missionary community on the field, the cultures of sending agencies, and the entire network of social structures that stands in support of cross-cultural religious workers.

MISSIOLOGY AND THE PRACTICE OF MISSION

A century ago, missiologists as a group were very keen to study every kind of missionary institution in order to assess and improve their effectiveness. An equal degree of interest was shown in the figure of the individual missionary, whose particular challenges and special needs were considered problems that many thought could and should be addressed through scholarly research. That the practice of mission was an overriding concern of missiology in the early twentieth century is indicated by the way in which this part of the field was treated at and just after the 1910 World Missionary Conference at Edinburgh. At the conference, a majority of the commissions focused on pragmatic issues, including relations with governments, inter-mission cooperation, missionary preparation, and how to maximize the contributions of the church back home to world mission. Even the subject of interfaith relations was largely approached in a practical manner, as delegates struggled to identify more effective ways to present the Christian message to adherents of other faith traditions. Just after Edinburgh, the *IRM* began its life as an academic review of mission studies on much the same basis as the conference. Continued interest in practical topics was demonstrated especially in the missionary bibliography section of the *IRM*, a feature of the journal that was configured along lines suggested by the commission structure of the conference (on this similarity, see Skreslet 2006a, 173–80).

Today, it appears that the means of mission is no longer the dominating subject it once was within missiology. While it is true that questions about missionary methods still attract research attention in some quarters, in such journals as *Missiology*, *Evangelical Missions Quarterly*, and the *International Journal of Frontier Missiology*, for example, there are signs elsewhere that this interest is not as widespread as it may have been in previous decades. In the *IRM* itself, issues of theology and social analysis clearly predominate now and tend to crowd out an earlier emphasis in the same journal on the techniques of mission (on this change, see Skreslet 2006a, 180–87). Brian Stanley makes what I think is a telling but quite defensible decision in this regard, when he chooses not to include much comment on two of the Edinburgh commissions in his otherwise comprehensive treatment of the World Missionary Conference. According to Stanley (2009, xxi), Commissions V and VI could be treated more lightly, in part because they are now "of less interest than the others to scholars of missions and world Christianity." A similar approach was adopted by the Scottish Toward 2010 Council, whose study process leading up to the centenary of Edinburgh 1910 likewise paid relatively little attention to Commissions V and VI (Kerr and Ross 2009). Focused as they were on the topics of "missionary preparation" and the "home base," these two Commissions had very practical concerns at the center of their work.

7

Missionary Vocation

Thus far, most of our attention has been focused on forces and ideas that have persistently shaped missionary contexts. With respect to the history of mission, for example, missiologists have been working alongside scholarly colleagues in many other fields to show how the expansion of the church has been affected by factors such as geography, economics, politics, and technological advance. They have concerned themselves with the study of culture, knowing that Christian witness by nature wants to move across the boundaries of kinship, ethnicity, nationality, language, and class. With imagination and increasing precision, they have explored the processes of religious change as these have occurred within and across cultures. They have also looked carefully at the many means used in Christian mission over the centuries, which has meant examining strategies of evangelization, organizational models, fundraising techniques, and methods of communication, among other subjects. As for ideas, missiologists have been eager to identify themes in Scripture that have powered a variety of mission theologies. Different understandings of incarnation, salvation, reconciliation, liberation, and ecclesial authority have figured prominently in these investigations. Many missiologists have likewise found the concepts of conversion, contextualization, and dialogue to be of enduring interest. Such ideas and scriptural themes have shaped missionary contexts by altering the perceptions and expectations of those involved.

Still left to be considered is the figure of the missionary. This person might be salaried or volunteer, full-time or just occasional, working close to home or abroad, but in every case is acting self-consciously to give witness to Jesus Christ in some way. Among the many aspects of missionary vocation that have been studied over the years I have chosen three to highlight here. The first of these has to do with professional missionaries and the work they do. Sending organizations have sponsored much of this research, hoping to learn more about how to make their chosen representatives more effective on the field. Thus a researcher might ask about the recruitment of promising candidates, the best ways to train and support them, or the most suitable methods by which to evaluate their work. A second area of interest revolves around the subject of missionary spirituality and the call to mission. For this subtopic, the emphasis falls not so much on the physical activities associated with Christian outreach as it does on personal qualities or attitudes that can add a certain tone or texture to missionary service. A third major section in this chapter will survey a range of scholarship connected to the trope of the missionary. Here, we will find ourselves on highly contested ground, because "missionary" has become a problematic designation in some circles even within the church while still being revered in others. In this part of the missiologist's brief, depictions and discourses related to missionary vocation take center stage.

THE PROFESSION OF MISSION

Missionary recruitment and the screening of candidates are organizational functions obviously related to each other. Intuitively, one would think that recruitment is always the prior concern, but screening has been the larger issue through most of mission history. This is because the attraction of mission has been quite strong within the church over the centuries, although not always with the same force. On occasion, waves of volunteers have stepped forward for missionary service, often without much effort at all being made to attract them. The influence of charismatic leaders, such as Francis of Assisi, Ignatius of Loyola, or Hudson Taylor, sometimes helps to explain why legions of potential evangelists suddenly appear ready to devote themselves wholeheartedly to the cause of Christian mission. In early-twentieth-century Pentecostalism, when an uncoordinated surge of believers set out for parts quite unknown, the Holy Spirit was widely held to be leading the way for a burgeoning movement of Christian testimony unfolding around the world. In not a few instances, highly motivated coalitions of mission-minded volunteers have forced ecclesiastical bodies to recognize their call to mission, even when church leaders were reluctant to do so. A prime example of this phenomenon is met in the story of the origins of the ABCFM, when the testimony of a small but earnest group of seminary students deeply affected by what had happened to them at a haystack in a storm near Williams College finally spurred their more cautious elders in the church to found North America's first foreign mission society. In some circumstances, the mere mention of a critical need on the mission field has been enough to prompt a vigorous response. This was the case at Mount Holyoke Female Seminary in the early 1840s, when a visiting speaker reported on the death of Judith Grant in Persia and asked if anyone at the school might be willing to take her place. More difficult than recruiting in this situation was the task of selecting the most qualified candidate out of the forty young women (both students and teachers) who immediately volunteered for service (Robert 1997, 109).

Research on Candidate Screening

While the actual criteria used to screen missionary candidates are not always accessible after the fact, scholars have been able to show how some organizations have gone about evaluating potential workers. The experience of the early Jesuits has been studied extensively in this regard. These investigations have been helped by the fact that a rather large collection of petitions from Jesuit novices to their superiors asking for placement abroad in the missions has been preserved. Selwyn (2004, 95–137), for example, offers an analysis of such letters, now collectively known as the *Indipetae*. She finds the number of letters submitted extraordinary in itself, a sign of the strong appeal exercised by the missions on the imaginations of many young Jesuits back in Europe. According to Selwyn, the letters also show how foreign missions were affecting Jesuit initiatives undertaken closer to home. One effect was conceptual, as laborers in the lightly evangelized context of southern Italy that Selwyn primarily studies began to regard their service as a missionary call to the "Indies down here" (137). As Clossey (2008, 232–33) notes, Jesuit leaders applied the metaphor of the Indies to a number of other locations in Europe, too. More pragmatically, many petitioners wrote about their experience in domestic missions as a credential that demonstrated their untapped potential for effective work in more exotic locations. The superiors to whom these letters were sent sometimes added their own marginal comments on the documents, which give insight into the processes of evaluation taking place. Selwyn concludes that certain personal qualities eventually emerged as key criteria for judging applicants, including "good health, piety, sound judgement and obedience, as well as [an] ability to exploit patronage networks" (98). Brockey (2007, 225–33) has examined a selection of *Indipetae* that relate more specifically to Jesuit mission work in China. One other angle to consider here is the screening process stipulated in the Jesuit *Constitutions* (Loyola 1970, 95–102), a method of testing vocational aptitude ordinarily applied in the early centuries of the organization to anyone hoping to join the Society of Jesus. At the heart of this process was a series of six probationary experiences, several of which implied some kind of missionary activity (service to the sick, for example, or preaching in an unfamiliar setting).

Another good example of research on screening is Rosemary Seton's work on the Ladies Committee of the LMS, which allows us to see how one Protestant group scrutinized its candidates around the turn of the twentieth century. Seton (1996) describes a rigorous selection process, which eventually required not only paperwork and a personal interview, but also a period of training, a medical examination, and a final evaluative exercise before a permanent appointment could be made. Nearly half of those who applied to the Ladies Committee of the LMS between 1875 and 1907 were turned away after the initial interview (56). Seton finds on the basis of her research that the committee was looking in particular for candidates who gave evidence of "education, culture and refinement," in addition to a strong sense of vocation, some domestic mission experience, robust health, and a personal status free of family obligations. Peter Williams (1980) has looked at the evaluative procedures of the LMS as a whole during this period, while also considering similar data pertaining to the CMS, the China Inland Mission, and the Wesleyan Methodist Missionary Society. In his view, these societies in the second half of the nineteenth century were selecting and training candidates for a "clerical" model of missionary identity. Successful candidates showed evidence of "orthodoxy, obedience and strong motivation" (306). High educational attainments were not required, but deference to authority most certainly was, alongside a capacity to learn and a willingness to submit to an extensive process of missionary formation.

With an eye on training as well as the selection of missionary candidates, Stuart Piggin (1984) has focused on a defined geographical area (India) in which thirteen different British mission organizations were working up to the middle of the nineteenth century. Like Seton and Williams, he is attentive to the class backgrounds out of which the bulk of those sent to the subcontinent as evangelical Protestant missionaries were coming, but he pays even more attention to their formation in courses of training organized by the most active British mission societies of the time. A useful complement to the work of Piggin is Alvyn Austin's study of the China Inland Mission, in which an analysis is made with respect to the different patterns of candidature followed in Britain and North America by the same organization (see, for example, Austin 2007, 312–31). Seton, Williams, Piggin, and Austin have shown the way for much more work to be done in the archives on the topic of missionary candidacy.

Beside historical studies, one now also finds a growing collection of literature focused on contemporary applicants for mission service and the problem of how best to evaluate them. Much of this scholarly activity has been pursued within the realm of the social sciences, with special emphasis often given to the discipline of psychology. Many of the scholars contributing to this part of the field specialize in personnel matters and/or work for agencies that provide mental health services to mission-sending organizations. This research tends to be presented initially in short articles published in periodicals such as the *Journal of Psychology and Theology*, the *Evangelical Missions Quarterly*, or the *Journal of Psychology and Christianity*. Several substantial collections of articles and essays related to this area of study have also appeared over the past quarter-century (for example, O'Donnell and O'Donnell 1988, O'Donnell 1992, Taylor 1997, O'Donnell 2002, and Hay et al. 2007). The leading concerns of those most deeply involved in this kind of missiological writing emerge quite clearly in these collaborative volumes.

Missionary effectiveness is the common objective that drives much of this research, which is largely undertaken by scholars personally committed to the task of world evangelization. The advantages of careful prefield assessment are widely acknowledged, since this is an efficient way to avoid having to respond after the fact to cases of extreme team dysfunction or situations of high stress that otherwise must be solved by emergency measures. The capacity of the candidate to adapt to any new culture is one aspect of the evaluation problem to be solved. An ability to learn other languages quickly and to communicate effectively using a variety of idioms is another obvious qualification for mission service that has long been recognized.

In some studies of assessment, particular stress is put on the importance of psychological balance and the need of candidates to be able to adjust to situations of disorientation (culture shock) or rapid social change. Mission organizations are urged in this literature to make greater use of personality inventories and face-to-face interviews, in order to identify those applicants most likely to be well adjusted socially. Schubert (1991), among others, has underlined the potential advantages gained when a testing instrument like the Minnesota Multiphasic Personality Inventory (MMPI) is incorporated into an organization's routine screening process, since applicants with personality disorders are not likely to be effective on the mission field. Diekhoff (1991), with several collaborators, has questioned whether or not an "ideal" personality profile should be assumed in the case of cross-cultural mission work. Even if their comparison between East Asian and "Moslem" contexts is too simplistic, Diekhoff et al. broke new ground with their suggestion that different cultural contexts might call for more than one personality type (in their study, the key factor to be measured was assertiveness). In Schubert (1999), we find a comprehensive approach to candidate screening described. While the importance of psychological evaluation is forthrightly emphasized in this suggested process, the potential financial costs involved in such procedures are also discussed in a realistic manner.

Training, Pastoral Care, and Crisis Intervention

When the gaze of the scholar moves from screening to the missionary at work, one still often finds a concern for effectiveness at the bottom of the research agenda. Several clusters of studies may be identified. The first of these has to do with training, which might be administered before deployment and/or take place on the field. It may be recalled that missionary training has been studied extensively within missiology for more than a century. As noted earlier, the primary topic discussed by Commission V of the 1910 Edinburgh World Missionary Conference was "missionary preparation." In advance of the gathering itself, experts around the world collaborated over a two-year period to find out as much as possible about how best to train cross-cultural missionaries for a lifetime of service abroad. Two particular outcomes from this intensive study project should be noted here. First, the Commission made recommendations for a comprehensive training program modeled on the example of what Harlan Beach had already instituted at Yale (discussed above, in chapter 4). Second, the Commission produced a bibliography of the most important scholarly and practical resources its members had consulted in the course of their work together. Published as a part of the Commission's report, this bibliography essentially defined a whole sector of missiological research ("the training and qualifications of missionaries") to which many additional materials were subsequently added through the "International Missionary Bibliography" feature of the *IRM* (on which, again, see Skreslet 2006a, 171–80).

A recent issue of *Missiology* (January 2008) devoted to the subject of training illustrates well the continuing appeal of this subtopic within mission studies. Of course, many new emphases have arisen since Edinburgh 1910, including a strong interest in the preparation of short-term missionaries (see Koll 2010). Another way in which the character of this research has changed is reflected in the number of studies that no longer assume a North Atlantic home address for the personnel to be trained. The collection of articles presented in Taylor (1997) is exemplary in this respect, as care is taken throughout this volume to include the perspectives of both "new" and "old" sending countries. In the *Missiology* issue cited above, Whiteman (2008) provides a thoughtful analysis of current training practices followed by many North American mission agencies, while making suggestions about how these programs could be made more immediately relevant and effective.

A second cluster of studies focuses on the pastoral care needs of today's mission worker. This professional interest sits in some tension with the dominant ethos of an earlier age, when a willingness to sacrifice oneself in the cause of outreach was widely considered to be the sine qua non of a fully realized Christian life. A rather long and distinguished history of missionary monks, all committed to lifetimes of poverty, likewise stands as a counterpoint to this more recent trend in thinking about missionary vocation. In any case, much research energy has been applied since the 1970s to the problem of missionary care, now often denominated "member care." Among those issues most intensively studied within this area of scholarly inquiry are health care for missionaries stationed abroad (physical and psychological), professional development after deployment, team building on the field, best practices in personal financial planning, how to cope with family adjustment problems and the special needs of "third-culture kids," plus the challenges of reentry at the conclusion of one's final term of appointment. Within this group of studies, attrition is a particular concern that many researchers are attempting to help agencies manage well. It is generally agreed that early repatriations short-circuit some of the most valuable benefits to be gained from long-term service in cross-cultural environments (realized, for example, in greater language fluency, specialized work experience that can be acquired only on the field, and increasing levels of influence within local social networks). Shorter terms of service also tend to multiply the financial costs associated with the selection, training, and outfitting of missionary candidates.

A third group of studies to be noted here has gathered around the problem of crisis intervention. Many Christian missionaries today find themselves working in locations where they must do ministry in the midst of catastrophe, situations of violence (including violence directed at them), or overwhelming human need. In the risk-averse societies from which many missionaries are still coming, these threats to well-being have made it necessary for sending organizations to plan carefully for a variety of contingencies, lest they be held liable for not having protected their personnel from avoidable dangers. In the anthologies already cited, at least two kinds of research connected to this issue may be identified. The first of these has to do with the safety of missionaries and the conditions under which it might be advisable to evacuate families and workers. In a second group of studies, the primary problem to be examined is psychological trauma and the proper way to help those who suffer from its effects long after the immediate moment of crisis has passed. In this regard, several researchers have written about missionaries and their experience of post-traumatic stress disorder (PTSD), including Grant (1995), Jensma (1999), and Bagley (2003).

Recruitment

The subject of recruitment has not yet been addressed directly in this section but it is another critical topic connected to vocation on which many mission scholars have focused. We may suppose that mission organizations have always had to consider issues of recruitment, so long as they hoped to enlist in their company the most able co-workers possible and not just take into their midst anyone who happened to show up with enthusiasm on their doorstep. Especially in the last two centuries, as missionary work became increasingly professionalized around the world, modern strategies of recruitment slowly took hold among many sending organizations and these techniques have been subjected to missiological analysis. I propose to conclude my discussion of research on the profession of mission with some comments about how missionary recruitment has been investigated.

Several target audiences for recruitment into professional mission service have been identified. Special attention has been paid to young adults and students. The reasons behind this emphasis are not difficult to imagine. When one is younger, one's health tends to be better and new languages can be acquired more quickly than at later stages of life. In addition, long periods of service are a possibility for this age group, which means that a significant investment in training might pay dividends over several decades of work. Relevant here, too, is the fact that for some groups of young people programs of formation can be particularly effective, giving organizations an opportunity to construct and apply through their recruitment efforts a consistent and coherent approach to mission theory and practice.

Catholic attempts over many centuries to attract young people into mission-focused religious orders may be considered an early form of missionary recruitment. The practices of the Society of Jesus have been examined carefully in this regard, due to the sophisticated manner in which the order has used its educational infrastructure to support its missionary aims. Through their schools and colleges, the Jesuits put the idea of a call to mission in front of innumerable cadres of youth (both in Europe and around the world), while beginning to prepare the ablest among them for service in a variety of cultural contexts. At the higher levels of the system, some of these students made pledges to become Jesuit missioners and so were recognized as "scholastics" within the institutional framework laid down in the Jesuit *Constitutions*. Jesuit scholastics took simple vows of poverty, chastity, and obedience. A final decision to admit them either to profession or as formed coadjutors was not guaranteed. Liam Brockey's description of the Jesuit educational system and its relationship to the order's religious activities in China is wonderfully detailed with respect to curricular matters, while also capturing the missional spirit of the venture (2007, 207–42). On Jesuit education more generally, one should consult John O'Malley (1993, 200–242). Clossey (2008) reflects carefully on the various reasons why so many early modern Catholics were attracted to the Jesuit order and the means used in Europe to promote the missions.

Protestants were generally slower than Catholics to think systemically about how to involve large numbers of young people in the missionary enterprise. Here again Justinian Welz was a pioneer with respect to theory, although once again he could not in the end find enough support to launch the organizational scheme he had in mind. To his seventeenth-century contemporaries he proposed not only that pious merchants ought to fund the running of his "missionary (converting) society," as mentioned in chapter six, but that unemployed university graduates in theology ought somehow to be drafted into service abroad (Welz 1969, 62–76). Discussing this possibility, Welz speculated on some of the different motives that might impel students into mission, including their desire for travel. As Welz (67) put it, they have "a hankering for going places."

Within continental Pietism and early American evangelicalism, a few Protestant students were drawn into cross-cultural mission ventures as early as the eighteenth century. The names of David Brainerd, Bartholomäus Ziegenbalg, and Heinrich Plütschau immediately come to mind. Large-scale efforts to recruit students into mission could not begin, however, until the second half of the nineteenth century, when a thick network of youth-oriented, mission-minded Christian organizations began to form across the North Atlantic region. Within this broad set of interrelated groups, the Student Volunteer Movement (SVM) stands out with respect to student recruiting. Lautz (2009, esp. 5–8) has reviewed the personal qualities most avidly sought in candidates who presented themselves to the SVM. In Michael Parker's analysis (1998), the spectacular success of the SVM, its methods and institutional structures, and its historical context are all carefully described, alongside the reasons for the organization's rapid decline in the 1920s.

The SVM cooperated with and recruited for a host of other mission organizations, including many denominational boards and the YMCA/YWCA. It was tied into an international fellowship of student groups that largely shared its evangelizing aims, including the Student Christian Movement and the World Student Christian Federation. The literature attached to each of these organizational structures to which the SVM related closely is substantial and can be found easily. Less studied and more difficult to access because of the non-European languages involved are the various national counterparts to the SVM established outside the

West from the beginning of the twentieth century. Yihua Xu (2009) has provided a stimulating example of such an investigation, focused on "The Committed Chinese Student Volunteer Movement for the Ministry." In keeping with the ethos of the SVM, the strategy behind this indigenous effort to mobilize students for mission was to win Chinese converts to Christ by calling young Chinese Christians to join in and add to the evangelizing work already underway across their developing nation. Many more local studies of this kind are required before the full impact of a worldwide SVM movement can be adequately assessed.

After World War II, another major surge in student recruitment took place in North America. The Student Foreign Missions Fellowship prepared the way for this development by organizing a number of small-scale events meant to rouse student interest in evangelistic missions, beginning in the mid-1930s (Norton 1993). Following a merger in 1945 with the InterVarsity Christian Fellowship, leaders from the two organizations planned for what would become a massive triennial recruiting event that eventually came to be known by the name of the Illinois city in which most of the conventions have taken place: Urbana. Attendance at these conferences continues to be robust, with Urbana 09 drawing over fifteen thousand participants (see the *Urbana.org* website for more attendance statistics). Harris (2002) is right to point out that the Urbana phenomenon increasingly sits in the middle of a Web-based recruiting environment for Protestant evangelical missions that does not stop working between conventions. Harris also emphasizes in her article the perceived benefits of short-term missions, not least their potential to function as an "early identification program for the missionary vocation" (46). The *Perspectives* course (Winter and Hawthorne 1981), aimed at laypersons, is now another basic tool of mobilization that continues to spur students and many others to consider missionary service.

Women form another group toward which some mission-sending organizations at certain times in their history have directed a good portion of their recruiting energy. The founding of many women's mission societies in the second half of the nineteenth century helps to explain much of this activity. To be sure, some women were also students and so cannot be separated completely from that population, but efforts to seek after women candidates for specialized, cross-cultural work among women and children is a discernible subtopic on its own within the broad rubric of recruitment. In this regard, several research strategies have already been deployed to good effect. Peter Williams (1993), for example, has studied how some late-nineteenth-century English mission societies attempted to increase the number of women missionaries serving in their ranks, focusing especially on the China Inland Mission under Hudson Taylor. Other investigators have looked into the enlistment of indigenous female workers, such as Biblewomen (Wood 2008). More broadly, Dana Robert (2006) has suggested that world Christianity, which includes the history of modern missions, should be re-analyzed as a women's movement. Proceeding in this way, Robert argues, will enable researchers to recognize many overlooked examples of female religious leadership. According to Robert, women leaders, in a "cycle of female activism" (185), by their actions and community standing drew many other women and girls into the church and the modern Protestant missionary movement, where they, too, found opportunities to develop and exercise their leadership gifts.

Class considerations led to yet one more set of recruiting initiatives that took aim at the higher reaches of Western and other societies. Again, there is overlap here with other efforts at student recruitment, since advanced levels of education tended to be restricted to well-heeled social elites, at least until quite recently. Many Protestant missionaries in the early nineteenth century, including some of the most widely celebrated at the time, came out of relatively humble circumstances (Piggin 1984, 28–54). In this respect, the lower-class backgrounds of William Carey, Robert Moffett, and David Livingstone were emblematic of an age when piety and resourcefulness could count for more than wealth and formal education as credentials for missionary service. Livingstone himself was a catalyst for change, however, as he challenged those attending Britain's great universities near mid-century to put their manifold advantages to good use in the cause of Christian mission.

Andrew Porter (2004, 225–54) provides a nuanced account of what was shifting in terms of mission and British class distinctions between 1860 and 1895. The Universities' Mission to Central Africa, founded in response to Livingstone's plea in 1859, was a crucial first step. The Cambridge Mission to Delhi and the Oxford Mission to Calcutta were established fairly soon thereafter, which meant that Anglo-Catholics could participate in evangelical missions, too, without sacrificing their high church sensibilities. Coincidentally, the CMS was making its own inroads into the upper classes of British society, primarily through the processes of Keswick revivalism, a recruiting pathway they shared with the China Inland Mission, the largest of the faith missions. The recruitment of a famous group of aristocrats into the China Inland Mission, the so-called Cambridge Seven, put the missionary vocation in an attractive new light for church publics on both sides of the Atlantic. Their story of self-sacrifice, which required the abandonment of great social privilege and athletic acclaim for the sake of the gospel and the world's salvation, became for many friends of mission a powerful call narrative worth repeating, especially for the benefit of the sophisticated and the most highly educated. Alvyn Austin (2007, 206–9) assesses the impact of the Cambridge Seven on recruiting for mission among students in North America and Britain.

Finally, we have a growing number of studies related to the crisis in vocations that has overtaken the Catholic Church. As William Burrows (2010, 131) has observed, too few priests and declining numbers of religious relative to population growth since the 1960s make it exceedingly difficult to see how the Roman Catholic Church could possibly carry out its announced aim of a "new evangelization" in the West. Burrows looks to the religious orders to become engines of missional renewal once again, but acknowledges that profound differences of opinion within the church about the nature of vocation have yet to be resolved, especially with respect to priestly celibacy and the ordination of women. The Center for Applied Research on the Apostolate (CARA) at Georgetown University has become an important source of the demographic data on which Burrows and other missiologists are basing their current analyses. CARA's recent assessment of global Catholicism (published in Froehle and Gautier 2003), which includes statistical information on baptisms, seminary enrollments, clergy numbers, and religious memberships, is a benchmark study that not only considers the worldwide circumstances of the church at the beginning of the twenty-first century, but also tracks regional trends. In a follow-up publication from CARA, Bendyna and Gautier (2009) have surveyed some four thousand new members of religious institutes in the United States, in order to determine the particular reasons why these post–Vatican II Catholics have been attracted to the religious life and the various institutes to which they are now attached. Equipped with these data, the authors go on to suggest what the "best practices" of vocation promotion and formation might be, a subtopic that relates directly to all the primary research areas explored in this section: the recruitment, training, and selection of missionary candidates. James Kroeger (1991) has critiqued the unhealthy practice of "vocation piracy" or "vocation skimming," by which some older religious institutes in the West with unfavorable demographic trends at home have recruited in poorer countries where employment and educational prospects for the young are especially grim.

SPIRITUALITY

One of the major findings of the CARA study just cited on recent vocations to religious life is that many new members were attracted to their particular institutes by the ethos or spiritual character of the group they eventually joined. According to the report (Bendyna and Gautier 2009, 9), new members

> . . . were attracted to their particular *religious institute* by its spirituality, community life, and prayer life. Although the ministries of the institute are also important to most new members, they are less important than spirituality, prayer, community, and lifestyle.

Many of the religious institutes surveyed by CARA are missionary orders. In keeping with the history of missionary monasticism, each of these institutes would be expected to have a particular gift or "charism" that defines the group's distinctive purpose and signature style of evangelization. What this recent study of vocation reminds us is that for many members of these orders Christian mission cannot be reduced to a set of tasks or a strategy. Leavening the effort in some way is a quality of life in ministry that the group as a whole claims for its own. This insight would appear not only to apply to American Catholics but also to hold true more generally.

In his comprehensive description of missiology, Jan Jongeneel (1997, 1–47) underscores the importance of spirituality to missionary vocation when he locates "missionary ascetics" at the center of missionary theology (or theology of mission). According to Jongeneel (1997, 17), "every form of mission, and also every form of (missionary) theology, including systematic and practical (missionary) theology, which lacks spirituality, is Spirit-less and is, therefore, doomed to die." Jongeneel is not only laying down a criterion here by which to judge the adequacy of different theologies of mission when he makes such a declaration. In the context of his project, which is the academic study of mission, he is also saying something about spirituality as a particular subject within the broad area of scholarship he labels *Missionstheologie*, understood to be conceptually separate from *Missionsphilosophie* and *Missionswissenschaft*. Within this understanding of the field, "missionary ascetics" is considered to be "foundational" for *Missionstheologie*, in that "all other missionary theological disciplines are grounded upon this one" (Jongeneel 1997, 47; cf. also 373).

Celtic, Franciscan, and Ignatian Spiritualities

The rest of this section is meant to give a sense of what might be included under the topic of mission spirituality. I begin with a selection of historically oriented research, in which various aspects of spirituality have been highlighted, often with the intention of promoting in the present some missionary virtue a scholar sees exemplified in the past. Such a linkage is plainly evident in much that has been written over the past twenty years about the missionary activities of Irish monks. Thomas Cahill's bestselling account of the Irish and how they "saved" Western civilization is a case in point. In this rendering of Irish Christianity, two movements of evangelization are described within a larger story of cultural heroism. The first concerns the conversion of Ireland to a non-Latin form of Christianity in the time of Patrick. On Patrick the missionary and the possibility of Celtic theology, one should consult Thomas O'Loughlin (2000). A second movement has to do with the diffusion of this peculiar amalgam across Western Europe, as Irish monks wandered and reseeded the continent with a new set of Christian monastic institutions. Cahill recognizes in Irish Christianity a world-affirming theological stance that was prepared to live with and learn from the nature religions of a pre-Christian age. He praises the monasteries for the frontier hospitality they so generously shared with near neighbors and travelers in need. In outposts of light scattered across a darkening continent, industrious copyists are credited with having "reconnected barbarized Europe to the traditions of Christian literacy" (Cahill 1995, 171), thereby preserving the cultural legacy of Christian Europe when Rome itself could not.

George Hunter (2000) covers much the same ground as Cahill but in a more self-consciously missiological manner. Building on the work of John Finney (1996), Hunter urges churches in the postmodern West to lay aside more familiar "Roman" and "traditional evangelical" models of conversion in which abrupt either/or decisions are expected to be made for Christ, in order to employ a gradual, interpersonal "Celtic way of evangelism." According to Hunter, Patrick and his successors ought to be admired especially for their openness to local customs (a sign of commitment to the principle of indigenization), their deep dedication to contemplative prayer, and a teamwork approach. An extensive set of primary texts connected to Celtic spirituality is now available in Davies (1999). O'Loughlin (2008) discusses with great insight the chief explanatory uses to which Celtic and other forms of ancient spirituality have been put in recent times.

A second historical tradition of mission spirituality that continues to attract considerable research attention today is connected to the memory of Francis of Assisi. Like the Dominicans, Francis and his followers aspired to an authentic form of the *vita apostolica*. According to Bevans and Schroeder (2004, 158–59), the Franciscans constructed their distinctive expression of mission spirituality by emphasizing the *vita* in *vita apostolica*, which meant "witnessing to and imitating the passion of Christ through austere poverty, with the apostolate or work of mission growing out of the whole *way of life*." Over time, a strict mendicant lifestyle would not hold for all who called themselves Franciscans, but a special concern for the poor persisted and more often than not this emphasis has defined the mission focus of the order. The Franciscan mission impulse to identify with the poor at the margins of society is explored in Dries (1998a). An influential study that works hard to connect St. Francis to liberation theology is Boff (1982). The Franciscans also maintained contact with the notion of itinerancy by means of the ministries they provided to pilgrims in the Holy Land.

To be sure, the Friars Minor have had their critics in the modern era. Especially suspect is the role they played in the establishment of Spanish America, where their evangelization activities were carried out in the context of a brutal colonial order that just a few Franciscans actively opposed (Franciscan enthusiasm for the Inquisition process applied by the Spanish in early-sixteenth-century Mexico is carefully examined in Don 2010). Yet several aspects of their distinctive spirituality have won wide appreciation within and beyond missiological circles. The desire of the Franciscans to promote peace and to avoid religious disputation has been consistently praised. Hoeberichts (2008), for example, argues that the "model of the holy gospel" Francis hoped to follow continues to be relevant today, precisely because it has less to do with antagonistic preaching than with works (*operatio*) demonstrating God's deep desire for peaceful relations in societies rent by violence and division. The Franciscans are also often commended for having created new ways for nonordained believers to participate in mission, whether through tertiary orders or the Poor Ladies (on the role of women in the early

Franciscan missionary movement, see Schroeder 2000). A strong surge of interest in ecotheology has likewise found a powerful source of inspiration in the spiritual legacy of St. Francis and his remarkable concern for God's creation. While sorting through the various contemporary agendas into which this perennially attractive historical figure has been made to fit, Roger Sorrell (1988) explores how Francis innovated by expanding his mission to include the world of nature.

The Jesuits were a third group in mission history whose ideas about spirituality decisively shaped their missionary program. Several qualities stand out among those most vigorously promoted within the organizational culture of the Society of Jesus. An unequivocal commitment to active ministry in the world, for example, propelled the Jesuits full force into the secular realm. Thus oriented, it soon became clear to the founders that their vocational aspirations could not be accommodated within the cloister. Disciplined learning was another habit that defined the ethos of the group and so led to a famously successful, worldwide ministry of education. The Jesuits also emphasized the need to be flexible in the practice of their piety, even as they agreed to submit together to established ecclesiastical authority. The virtue of obedience multiplied the institutional strength of the order. The cultivation of personal initiative and a capacity for discernment prepared its members to adapt successfully to a variety of contexts and ministry demands. And then there was the willingness to be sent anywhere on mission, a global venture that became the primary means by which this group sought to honor God and to seek their own salvation. As Ignatius (Loyola 1970, 170) succinctly put it in the *Constitutions*: "Our vocation is to travel through the world and to live in any part of it whatsoever where there is hope of the greater service to God and of help of souls."

Quite deliberately, Ignatius and his closest collaborators defined a "way of proceeding" that resisted summing up in a list of tasks, a rigid lifestyle mandate, or a distinctive theological position. Their vision for mission was complex and exceedingly durable, in part because it was never reduced to an inflexible set of requirements or a simple formula. Only a small portion of the scholarly literature pertaining to the Jesuits takes up the question of their mission spirituality, but several important studies should be mentioned. An indispensible resource for missiologists with an interest in this topic is John O'Malley's research on the first generation of Jesuits (1993). Also to be highly recommended is Luke Clossey's imaginative treatment of "salvation and globalization" in Jesuit missions through the seventeenth century. While Clossey (2008, 10) deliberately concentrates on a defined set of secular considerations ("geography, history and logistics of trade, movement, transportation, and communication networks"), he nevertheless pays close attention to several crucial aspects of vocation that are not so easily explained in material terms, including early Jesuit motivations for mission. On a smaller scale, Mooney (2009) has written about "Ignatian spirituality" as a wellspring of still-vibrant principles for apostolic mission today.

Pilgrimage

A few other frames of reference for the practice and theology of mission issuing out of spirituality but not so closely identified with a single religious order or ecclesiastical group may also be described. In the examples that follow, I will briefly mention in each case how a basic idea may be rooted in ancient traditions, but the emphasis in my treatment will fall more on recent reflections. In this part of missiology, researchers and the mission theologians or practitioners they study are focused on enduring aspects of spirituality that have been or might be applied to contemporary circumstances. The nature of Christian mission, its ultimate purposes, and the proper basis of a missionary call are all at stake in these discussions.

One way to look at mission is to see it as a form of pilgrimage. Within this frame of reference, travel can become a spiritual discipline by encouraging self-examination in the midst of alien environments. If physical deprivations are also included, even greater personal growth may be experienced. To the extent that one's strengthened faith is then shared with others, a wider significance yet can be realized. Something like this understanding of pilgrimage undergirded the piety of many Irish monks who itinerated across Europe in the early Middle Ages. To be a *peregrinatio pro Christo* in the manner of a Columbanus meant to forsake one's *patria* voluntarily, to leave family behind without any expectation of ever seeing them again, and to endure hardship along the way. Or, as Michael Richter (1999, 44) has put it: "self-imposed, lifelong exile in obedience to commands by God . . . is the essence of the early medieval Irish concept of *peregrinatio*."

Over the centuries, other evangelizers followed the Irish down the pilgrimage path of mission spirituality, albeit with their own emphases and in response to completely different historical circumstances. Medieval mendicants, for example, found not only penitential value in apostolic poverty but also a life-style that freed them up for service and preaching wherever the Spirit seemed to be leading. Likewise, the Jesuits embraced a way of being in mission that assumed nearly unlimited mobility and a willingness to reside abroad for the whole of one's life. Generations of Protestant missionaries began their work with similar expectations. These, too, were committed to lifelong service in faraway and sometimes dangerous settings in response to God's call. Advocates of mission were eager to highlight the sacrifices these workers were making for the sake of the gospel on behalf of those who stayed at home (see, for example, the 1812 ordination sermon of Leonard Woods [1966, esp. 266–68], given just before the first group of ABCFM missionaries departed from Boston). Such appeals for support, often quite impassioned, gave rise to a widespread impression within the church that *foreign* mission workers were ideal disciples of Christ, who embodied within themselves the missionary calling of the whole Christian community.

From the mid-twentieth century, the idea that travel could somehow sanctify Christian service came under fire. Keith Bridston (1965) was among those who sought to demythologize the vocation of mission by questioning the belief that salt-water voyages miraculously transformed ordinary believers into living saints. Bridston suggested that missionary frontiers might still exist, but geography was not the only factor to consider: "The Christian mission, as an expression of God's mission, means not only going *out to* but also *into* the world" (113). In the wake of what proved to be an effective postcolonial critique of foreign missions, some creative attempts have been made to reappropriate the concept of pilgrimage as a basis for mission spirituality. An example is David Bosch (1979) and his "spirituality of the road." More recently, Peter Phan (2003) has written from an Asian perspective on "crossing borders" as an approach to mission spirituality grounded in the incarnation. A kind of "going" is evident, too, in the notion of Orlando Costas (1982) that mission is a movement toward Christ, who has already positioned himself among those who suffer "outside the gate." Similarly, Anthony Gittins interprets the "journey" of mission as an opportunity to experience God's grace, as well as to share God's love. Gittins (1993, 150) urges all Christians, wherever they might find themselves, to move out from behind their "barriers and bulwarks" of "selfishness, ethnocentrism, prejudice, or fear," in order to follow Jesus into mission. In this understanding of spirituality, social margins become the "epicenter" of mission and pilgrimage a means of personal transformation (163). The work of E. Stanley Jones largely anticipated the kind of postcolonial mission spirituality we now find expressed in the writings of Bosch, Costas, Gittins, and many others. In his *Christ of the Indian Road*, Jones (1925, 57–58) depicted Jesus already standing in the East: "He is there, deeply there, before us. We not only take him; we go to him. . . . We take them Christ— we go to him. He is the motive and the end." Here, too, the missionary journey remains but the route has had to be reconceptualized, because a Western identity for Jesus can no longer be assumed.

Spiritual Warfare

Premodern Christians took it for granted that the church and its ministers had to battle demonic forces on behalf of the one true God. Human responsibility for evil actions and immorality necessarily remained, but the interference of other actors was commonly presupposed. In those places where the church did not yet exist or was weak, some observers imagined landscapes almost entirely given over to malevolent impulses at work just beyond the reach of human control. Within this worldview, mission is easily recast as a form of spiritual warfare. In this case, the call to mission may be heard as an invitation to oppose God's nonhuman rivals, to expose the false basis of their power, and so to liberate the unhappy victims of their debilitating influence. Apostolic exorcists and Jesus himself provide a biblical template for such an understanding of mission. The history of ancient and medieval Christianity is rife with examples of missionaries who appear to have operated conceptually from within a spiritual warfare frame of reference. If anything, hagiographic storytelling tends to accentuate this dimension of the missionary vocation. In retrospect, of course, we may be able to identify many other motives and interests (political, social, and economic, among others) that were no doubt shaping premodern missionary programs, but these analyses cannot wipe away the fact that for many of the evangelizers involved their acknowledged, overriding concerns were spiritual in nature.

The possibility that mission could be an arena for spiritual warfare has not disappeared, despite the spread of modernity around the world since the eighteenth century. Parts of the church in the West and a (probable) majority of believers elsewhere still expect and claim to perceive satanic resistance to Christian missionary activity. Especially in those places where traditional religions are still viable, missionaries may well find themselves confronting demonic adversaries whose reality is unquestioned in context. As a result, this topic continues to be studied within missiology and not only from a historical perspective. An invaluable guide to a large portion of this literature is offered in Kraft (2002). The occasion for Kraft's paper was a Lausanne consultation on spiritual warfare ("Deliver Us from Evil"), held at Nairobi in 2000 (other contributions to the same meeting are posted on the *Lausanne.org* website). Kraft writes as a self-described "third-wave" evangelical, but he is also attentive to scholarship focused on the experience of Pentecostal missionaries. Within this literature several specialized subtopics have emerged, including "power evangelism" (advocated in Wimber 1986), "strategic level" or "cosmic-level" spiritual warfare (critiqued in Lowe 1998), and "spiritual mapping" (discussed in Van der Meer 2001). Allan Anderson's introduction to Pentecostalism (2004, esp. 206–42) provides a way into a large collection of global research on a century of mission undertaken within that set of traditions. Pentecostal approaches to mission have typically included some form of deliverance ministry, carried out in opposition to Satan's dark designs. Special mention must also be made of Paul Hiebert's classic essay on the "excluded middle," which is widely cited across this literature, regardless of denominational affiliation. Writing from an anthropological perspective, Hiebert (1982) critiques the mechanistic worldview of most modern Westerners, arguing for an organic, holistic understanding of God's creation in which dynamic encounters are seen taking place involving humans, spirits, and forces of nature. In the three-tiered universe he describes, a middle zone is postulated between the supernatural realm of the divine and the natural order modern people understand through science. According to Hiebert, theologies of mission that do not recognize this "excluded middle" of principalities and powers will lack appeal for most people living outside the secularized West, because such theologies cannot respond adequately to the deepest questions of life, whether related to divine guidance, providence, healing, suffering, misfortune, or death. The broad impact of Hiebert's essay within missiology is discussed in Anane-Asane et al. (2009).

Hospitality

The militaristic language of spiritual warfare does not resonate equally well in every quarter of the church. While most Protestant fundamentalists and many Pentecostals, plus some traditional Catholics, Orthodox believers, and evangelical Protestants, may find this way of imagining mission attractive and even inspiring, liberal Protestants and progressive Catholics as a rule do not. A nearly opposite pattern of reception may be observed across the church in connection with hospitality, an ancient theme in mission spirituality that has reemerged over the past few decades.

Like pilgrimage and the idea of spiritual warfare, the theme of hospitality may also lay claim to biblical roots, portrayed vividly in the story of the Good Samaritan and Jesus' directive to feed the hungry, welcome the stranger, and visit the sick and those who are in prison (Matt. 25:31–46). Relevant, too, are those Old Testament texts that teach Israel how to treat the aliens and sojourners living in their midst (for example, Exod. 22:21; Deut. 10:19; Deut. 24:17–18). Hospitality survived as a dimension of mission in the monastic traditions of the church and not only among the Irish in their frontier redoubts. The Rule of Benedict, for example, includes a chapter (53) on the reception of guests, in which this responsibility is interpreted in terms drawn from Matthew 25. Pilgrims and the poor are to be received graciously, with humility and kindness. The community is instructed to pray with those who visit, to edify their guests with a reading from the divine law, to wash their feet, and to provide them with food. In this embodiment of mission service, we find not only a ready response to physical need but also a desire to show respect for others, including and especially those of little social account: "Great care and concern are to be shown in receiving poor people and pilgrims, because in them more particularly Christ is received; our very awe of the rich guarantees them special respect (Benedict 1981, 259).

Two factors in particular seem to be influencing current discussions of hospitality within missiology. The first of these is migrancy. As streams of refugees and other displaced persons leave their home regions behind for a variety of reasons, many of these people find themselves strangers in strange lands. How should the church relate to these new neighbors? Among those who have written about hospitality as a missionary virtue to be practiced especially with respect to refugees and migrants of different kinds are Pohl (2003), Hanciles (2003), and Escobar (2003). Some additional examples of current research in this area are presented in Spencer (2008).

New perceptions of religious pluralism are also affecting the way many missiologists relate the concept of hospitality to the vocation of mission. Kōsuke Koyama (1993), for example, has put forward the idea of a "stranger-centered" mission theology, which he considers especially well suited to interfaith relations. Gittins (1994), however, has suggested that Koyama's call to "extend hospitality to the stranger" lacks a proper sense of interpersonal mutuality. According to Gittins, it is better for evangelizers to regard *themselves* as strangers and aliens rather than relating to outsiders in this way. By ceding control and sometimes relying on others to take the initiative, missionaries are enabled to receive hospitality as well as extend it in Christ's name (this argument is developed more fully in Gittins 1989, 84–138). From a Pentecostal perspective, Amos Yong has argued further that a theology of hospitality could become the basis of an inclusive, dialogical, and fully pneumatological performance of the gospel that responds appropriately to our postmodern context of religious pluralism. For Yong (2008, 131), "the Christian mission is nothing more or less than our participation in the hospitality of God."

Vulnerability

Mission may also be entered into as a circumstance of vulnerability. In this kind of mission spirituality, uncertainty is the order of the day. One has to be ready to live simply, sometimes alone, and without recourse to many of the social support structures most people would consider necessary for a normal life. Mission as vulnerability overlaps to a degree with the concept of pilgrimage. To be sure, itinerant monks embraced their own experiences of liminality, often defined by extraordinary austerities and commitments to self-abnegation. But the emphasis here is not on the journey or one's growth in faith so much as it is trained on the character of Christian witness given along the way. Suffering on behalf of the gospel is accepted as a possibility. Weakness and insecurity are not only endured as means of discipline, but are woven into the fabric of the message one hopes to communicate. The divine Word that puts aside its heavenly privileges in order to be made incarnate and then to suffer death on behalf of others is the ultimate model for this understanding of mission spirituality. In the idea of mission as vulnerability, the invitation Jesus gave his first disciples— to take up his cross and come after him— echoes down through the ages as a particular call to mission as costly discipleship.

The subject of vulnerability has already been broached in these pages, albeit indirectly. When radical commitments are made to contextualization, for example, missionaries acknowledge their lack of control over the evangelization process and accelerate the moment when they will become completely redundant. Some have seen in the first-evangelization work of Vincent Donovan among the nomadic pastoralist Masai in Tanzania an example of what a total surrender to local cultural norms in the light of the gospel might look like (Donovan 1982). On those occasions when missionaries have had the courage to oppose the colonizers or to stand against the rich and powerful, intense social pressure to cease and desist from such protests or some other form of coercion against those so engaged has often followed. That missionaries who defend the poor can become modern-day martyrs of the church is argued through Jon Sobrino's reflections (2003) on faithful witness given in the midst of political and economic oppression in El Salvador. A number of other violent contexts for mission, both historical and contemporary, are discussed in Eitel (2008).

David Bosch (1992) warns against any attempt to glamorize martyrdom or idealize missionary victims. Caution is also warranted due to persistent entanglements with Christendom, violence, and colonialism over the centuries, which call into question the church's capacity after Constantine to suffer with Christ. Bosch concludes, nevertheless, that mission in weakness is the only genuine spiritual norm on offer to would-be Christian evangelists. It requires that the cross of Christ be placed at the very center of the church's missionary self-understanding (362):

> Only if we turn our backs on false power and false security can there be authentic Christian mission. Of course, this will lead to opposition, perhaps even suffering, persecution and martyrdom. But martyrdom and persecution have always been among the lesser threats to the life and survival of the church.

Jonathan Bonk (2007) reaches a similar conclusion in his study of mission and ministry in contexts of power and violence, arguing that followers of Jesus risk losing their primary identities as citizens of God's kingdom when they participate in worldly pathologies of power.

DEPICTING THE MISSIONARY

The discussion in this chapter has shown so far that the missionary vocation can be studied as a profession, in which case the methods of social science are likely to loom large. Other researchers, more theologically oriented, have focused on mission as an expression of spirituality. I propose now to describe a third set of research that attends to perceptions of the missionary vocation, both inside and outside the church, as these have been shaped by different kinds of literary and visual works. For the sake of efficiency, the scholarship that pertains to these various creative projects will be considered according to the genre used, with particular attention given to historical writing, biography, literature, and films.

In History Writing

In an earlier chapter, we looked at several forms of narrative used to write the history of mission. One objective of that analysis was to show how historians have employed a variety of styles by which to portray mission and missionaries. Thus, it was noted, for example, that ecclesiastical historians tended to focus on metropolitan centers and not on the peripheries, where episcopal power held less sway. In these accounts, the theological orthodoxy of the evangelizers was often a primary concern and close cooperation between missionary bishops and royal figures appears to be normative. A somewhat less regularized picture of mission has been observed in some of the hagiographical materials surveyed earlier, with more room allowed in these narratives for charismatic actors and wonder-workers to operate without direct reference to the usual channels of ecclesiastical and political authority. Additionally, in some forms of critical ethnography, we found missionaries portrayed as (un)witting agents of modernity and colonial dispossession.

To the literature previously cited in the history of mission chapter we may now add the extended discussion of Andrea Sterk (2010b) on the "representation" of mission in late classical and early medieval historical sources. Following Ian Wood (2001) but concentrating more on the expansion of Christianity within Asia and the roles played by women captives in the evangelization of Armenia, Georgia, and Yemen, Sterk explores how a select group of Christian historians "crafted or reshaped accounts of mission with their own particular details and emphases to pass on their own particular perspectives on mission and conversion" (Sterk 2010b, 304). For Sterk, this meant asking about how mission and missionaries are represented within larger schemes of Christianization (275) and "the role of historians as self-conscious agents as well as interpreters of Christianization" (276). Thus, we find the churchman Agathangelos, writing in antiquity about the conversion of Armenia to Christianity, taking care to show his missionary heroes resisting Zoroastrian religion while not rejecting Iranian culture or language altogether because that was the primary cultural world to which many of his own audience still related (280). Or, using an unusual metaphor, Agathangelos depicts the foreign captive Rhipsime and her virgin martyr companions as "cupbearers," who added their own blood to the two vessels of joy and retribution they carried to Armenia as witnesses to the gospel. In this portrayal of the missionary task, according to Sterk (2010b, 286), "serving as a 'cupbearer' to the world was . . . the vocation of all those who had drunk from the cup of life and joy." Such an understanding is far removed from the idea of mission as "a political ploy for unifying the populace, exalting the ruler, or sanctioning the ecclesiastical hierarchy" (286). In this way, as she carefully examines the stories of Rhipsime and other captive women evangelists, Sterk not only adds to our knowledge of mission history in the East but also expands what we know about non-elite forms of evangelization or "mission from below." In this article and an equally substantive companion piece (2010a), Sterk pulls together a wealth of scholarly material pertaining to the depiction of mission in a wide range of ancient historical sources.

Biography

Biography is another way to write about mission history that focuses even more precisely on the figure of the missionary. The attraction of the genre within the modern missionary movement is not difficult to grasp. Close associates of individual missionaries have used biographies to honor their colleagues, friends, and family members. Sending organizations have also been eager to tell exciting stories of outstanding missionaries they have sponsored, since such publicity can further institutional aims, whether in the realm of fundraising or by communicating in personal terms how the church or mission group intends to go about its work. Likewise, for critics of mission, biography can be an effective way to make their objections vivid and compelling. For all these reasons and more, whether arguing for or against Christian mission, biographical studies have had enduring appeal.

Mission biography has long been considered an integral part of missiology. This is evident, for example, in the "International Missionary Bibliography" section of the *IRM*, devised in 1912. In this first English-language "scientific" review of missionary literature, biography was one of the initial categories used to classify the materials surveyed and proved to be an active research area within the bibliography (Skreslet 2006a, 174–87). When the *IRM* bibliography was revised a half-century later, the category of biography was dropped from the structure. The change reflected a new set of priorities within that part of the ecumenical movement that had begun to shy away from the idea of individual missionaries or mission societies taking the initiative in mission in favor of the concept of *missio Dei*. Outside the WCC, proponents of mission continued to produce missionary biographies at a robust pace, with many of the traditional purposes of this literature still in operation: to laud and memorialize missionary heroes, to teach about mission through individual stories, and/or to advance denominational, institutional, or theological agendas. From about the 1970s, we can see another function of biography emerging more distinctly within missiology. This is the capacity of biographical literature to expand the archive of mission studies, especially by giving more direct attention to women and non-Western missionary actors. An ongoing, long-term project that exemplifies this service to the study of mission is the *Dictionary of African Christian Biography*, published online in multiple languages (the project is described in Bonk 2004). Another angle of approach is suggested by the work of Booth (2002) on Arabic-language biographies of foreign women missionary teachers. The materials Booth describes were originally published as magazine articles and were written from an indigenous perspective.

Scholarly biographical treatments of individual missionary figures are plentiful, and many of these have already been cited in connection with other topics. Not yet mentioned is the outstanding "mission legacies" series that continues to run in the *IBMR* (an initial collection of these biographical essays was published in Anderson et al. 1994). Critical studies of missionary biography as a genre are still not numerous but some of what has been attempted in this part of the field may be described. Several scholars have argued for missionary biography to be recognized as a particular form of missiology. Tucker (1999, 430), for example, contends that biographies add the study of "character" to missiology. Neely (1999) agrees that mission biographies, even when presented as hagiographies, have something special to contribute to the study of mission but cautions that questions of fact and fiction must not be ignored. In his article, Neely discusses how to distinguish hagiography from more objective forms of biography. He also examines side-by-side several accounts of the late nineteenth/early twentieth-century Baptist missionary Lottie Moon as a way to show how the biographer's perspective can affect the telling of a missionary life. Rohrer (2006) has reflected on the complex three-way relationships that can emerge when biographers speak to contemporary audiences about the subjects of their research. Rohrer's case study is the life of George Leslie Mackay (1844–1901), a Canadian Presbyterian missionary to Taiwan. In a very pertinent and stimulating line of investigation, Rohrer asks: to whom does the story of Mackay now "belong"— the divine intention of the *missio Dei*, the organization that sent him, the Canadian nation, the Presbyterian Church of Taiwan, or the secular academy? In other words, whose interpretive frame of reference, if any, should be considered primary with respect to this biographical subject?

Another scholarly approach to the study of mission biographies has focused on the effect this literature has had on a variety of audiences. Thus, Sittser (2007) has written about Protestant missionary biographies and how some of these have functioned as "written icons of faith" that edify individual readers by showing how real-life persons were "transfigured" in the course of their mission experience. Other scholars have studied the social impact of particular mission biographies, which in some cases extended across cultures and generations alike. Conforti (1985), for example, considers the enormous appeal exercised through the nineteenth century by the *Life* of David Brainerd (1718–47). According to Conforti, Brainerd's paradigmatic story not only inspired and guided countless missionaries who came after him and strongly influenced the practice of piety more generally in (Protestant) antebellum America, but it also served to mediate the theology of Jonathan Edwards to an evangelical public spread out on both sides of the Atlantic. Edwards, working from the missionary's private diary, was responsible for putting the *Life of Brainerd* into its final form before publication. Walls (2003, 253) sees Brainerd becoming in death "the Protestant icon of the missionary, its ideal type, as a result of the published journal. Every new missionary—typically, a man in his twenties, was taught thereby to see this young man as the pattern for what his own life ought to be."

Later in the nineteenth century, David Livingstone may well have replaced Brainerd as the quintessential missionary of the age, judging by the torrent of popular lives written about him (on Livingstone's mythic status, which clearly transcended his identity as a religious activist, see MacKenzie 1990). Without disputing these judgments, it is necessary to point out that for many nineteenth-century Protestant women their model missionary would not have been either

Brainerd or Livingstone but more likely Ann Hasseltine Judson. Brumberg (1982) has written about the wide influence of Ann Judson's biography on popular American culture.

A few scholars have attempted to relate biographical works on missionaries to larger fields of literary endeavor. So, for example, Terrence Craig (1997) explores how the writing of missionary lives contributed to the formation of Canadian culture and identity. Craig is equally interested in missionaries who came to Canada or left from there to labor abroad, since he considers both directional movements part of the same evangelistic impulse. Craig (132–37) concludes that this set of national missionary biographies, taken as a whole, reflects and possibly shaped the development of Canadian literature more generally, with narrower views of Canadian (and Christian) identity eventually giving way to a more multicultural social vision. Anna Johnston opens up another path of inquiry when she discusses the biographical materials produced by LMS missionaries in the first half of the nineteenth century as one kind of colonial literature. Johnston (2003, 32–37) is particularly keen to show how most missionary writings of the period were governed by informal editing processes that affected both secular and ecclesiastical literature. According to Johnston, whether writing about foreign missionaries or early converts to Christianity, missionary biographers of the time tended to rely on an "endless recirculation of tropes" on mission and native societies within a broad colonial discourse that did not bother to seek or incorporate non-European perspectives (81). The overall effect was to produce a thick web of stories that relentlessly pushed for religious and other interventions in foreign societies by vividly asserting the cruel depths of indigenous depravity. Although Johnston also looks at missionary texts originating in Polynesia and Australia, she has the most to say about biographical literature written in India.

Fiction

Sometimes only a very small step is needed to move from missionary biography to fiction. But not always, and it bears repeating that a measure of imagination on the part of every depicter of mission is required no matter what form of storytelling might be involved. In any case, missionaries have been featured in many works of fiction. Alan Neely (1996) has surveyed a number of these publications, in addition to a selection of feature films. Besides describing these materials in terms of plot and themes, Neely also considers how missionary characters have been portrayed in them with respect to "their fitness, preparation, calling, conflicts, encounters with other cultures, and their individual strengths and weaknesses" (464). Jamie Scott (2008b) expands considerably the list of print resources discussed in Neely and sorts the whole into several useful categories, including narrative works featuring either Catholic or Protestant evangelical missionaries, modern popular novels about mission, and mission fiction published in languages other than English. In addition, Craig (1997, 110–31) has catalogued a large collection of Canadian mission fiction, but he does not find much to admire in these works, many of which appear to him to embody a crude sort of wish fulfillment on the part of their authors and not much else (120).

Some classic works by Western authors in which missionary characters or settings are used in more than an incidental way have been carefully studied with an eye for missiological issues. William Hutchison (1987, 74–77), for example, brings into his description of the early ABCFM mission to Hawaii an analysis of the rather critical perspective on foreign missions put forward by Herman Melville through his South Sea novels *Typee* and *Omoo*. As Hutchison observes, Melville's depiction of mission was contending in the court of public opinion back home with an official picture that put the results of the work in a far more appreciative light.

Other scholars have been drawn to the study of mission in classic Western novels because of the women characters involved. An example is Valentine Cunningham (1993) on *Jane Eyre*, a nineteenth-century novel in which the title character has to decide if she will marry St. John Rivers, a suitor who intends to go to India as a missionary. The key issue behind Jane's decision, according to Cunningham, is whether or not she will accept the subordinate status of missionary wife that will come with the marriage. Cunningham provides context for his discussion of the novel and its portrayal of women in mission by including a sketch of an actual missionary to India (Mrs. Mary Hill) who would have been a contemporary of the fictional Jane Eyre. Scholar Patricia Hill (1985, 8–22) extends the range of the literature under discussion within this subtopic when she considers several popular works of fiction written between 1860 and 1930 that include missionary characters or themes. Hill shows how the novels she examines became discursive spaces in which competing ideas about missionary vocation, feminism, and secular values could interact with each other. Gill (1998) has added a study of missionary heroines he finds depicted in Victorian-era popular fiction and biography.

In contrast to literary critics, missiologists have been somewhat slow to examine the burgeoning trove of fictional works produced outside the West that put missionary encounters at the heart of their storylines. An exception to this general rule is provided by the Japanese novel *Silence*, which is widely cited within the field and often taught in courses on missiology. The seventeenth-century Portuguese priests brought to life by Shusaku Endo in *Silence* represent a profound literary study of the missionary vocation.

Welcome attention has also been paid to a number of African novels that touch on mission, with Chinua Achebe's *Things Fall Apart* (1958) probably receiving the most emphasis. A critical study of Achebe's work that recently appeared in a volume dedicated to "mother tongue theologies" is Merritt and Sterling (2009). In their treatment of what has come to be regarded as a classic postcolonial novel, Merritt and Sterling focus on the contest taking place at mid-century in Nigeria between Christianity and traditional Igbo religion. An alternative view of the struggle over Christianity in Africa at the end of the colonial era is presented in *Obi*, another Nigerian novel with strong religious themes written by Achebe's contemporary, John Munonye. According to Purcell (2004), the most significant religious conflict portrayed in this book was not the one that pitted the religions of West Africa against each other. The question for Munonye was rather about the future of Christianity on the continent, as foreign missionaries and indigenous Christian leaders clashed over who would direct the development of the tradition following the end of colonial rule. With some similar concerns in mind, Kamau-Goro (2010) has analyzed two novels written in the 1960s by Ngûgî wa Thiong'o (*The River Between* and *Weep Not, Child*). In these and other writings that reflect on aspects of East African mission history from a postcolonial perspective, Thiong'o renders a complex judgment on missionary Christianity that is not easily pigeonholed. Kamau-Goro suggests that Thiong'o's point of view is best explained when interpreted as a vernacular appropriation or reconfiguration of Christianity's sacred texts "through the idiom of Gīkūyū traditional gnosis" (2010, 9). Working in a comparative fashion, Okyerefo (2010) considers the idea of African agency and Christianization as these are portrayed in two Ghanaian novels. In *Two Thousand Seasons*, initially published in 1973, author Ayi Kwei Armah roundly condemns the part played by foreign missionaries in Africa's colonial subjugation, in keeping with the critical perspective established earlier by Achebe, Thiong'o, and many others. More surprising, perhaps, is what Okyerefo finds in Benjamin Kwakye's *The Sun by Night*, published in 2006. In this fictional rendering of West African religious history as that unfolded one generation after independence, the missionary vocation has been wrested away from evangelizing Westerners by independent indigenous preachers of the gospel who understand and are eager to respond to the spiritual and material needs most acutely felt by their fellow citizens (Okyerefo 2010, 66).

Film

Some novels are eventually made into films, which may or may not hew closely to the original artistic visions of their authors. Other screenplays are written without reference to an underlying print version. In either case, the figure of the missionary has appeared with some frequency over the past century in a number of motion pictures, some quite well known and others more obscure. A generation ago, Norman Horner produced a "checklist" of fifty motion pictures he considered "useful" for mission studies (1982, 172). Most of the items listed were documentary or educational in nature, and denominational mission boards produced many of them for Christian education purposes. In the article by Neely (1996) cited above, fourteen feature films are described with respect to their basic storylines and the perspectives offered on mission. Neely shows particular concern for the image of mission likely to be communicated in each of these creative projects. By far the most complete listing of motion pictures with missionary themes and characters now available to students of mission is the compilation Jamie Scott (2008a) published in the *IBMR*. Scott's emphasis is on feature films rather than educational materials, although he does mention several Christian organizations that have sponsored or produced films for commercial distribution, plus a group of biographical pictures, documentaries, and videos that likewise reflect an insider's view of Christian mission (118–20). Included in this article is a remarkably detailed discussion of silent movies that feature missionary characters doing their work in domestic or foreign circumstances (115–16). Scott also makes mention of a few films not in English that relate in some way to missions (120). Not mentioned in any of these compendia are two sets of documentary films produced in the 1930s and early 1940s by the American-based Harmon Foundation, parts of which portray missionary activities in Africa. Weber (2001) describes the aims and results of this ambitious project, which the Foundation carried out in cooperation with a number of American mission boards through the Missionary Education Movement of the Federal Council of Churches. In these films, according to Weber, missionaries and other Western experts are seen striving for the social development of Africa and her peoples.

Apart from movie reviews, which I do not intend to survey here, critical studies of the visual resources catalogued in Horner, Neely, and Scott are still relatively few. Missiologists have given serious attention to one film in particular, however: Robert Bolt's story of eighteenth-century Jesuits in the Amazon attempting to evangelize the Guaraní (*The Mission*). Daniel Berrigan (1986), who served as an on-set advisor to members of the cast and director Roland Joffé with regard to Jesuit history and ethos, published his own reading of the film in the form of a personal journal the same year that the movie was released. Subsequently, Hale (1995) has evaluated the film as an expression of liberation theology, while assessing the role of Berrigan in its production. Hale's comments (85–87) on the film's missionary characters are directly relevant to the concerns of those who write more generally about the depiction of mission in film and fiction. Blossom (2003) has analyzed *The Mission* alongside three other films that also consider the fate of various Amerindian groups affected by missionary activity: *Black Robe*, *At Play in the Fields of the Lord*, and *The Mosquito Coast*. Reaching across all four films, according to Blossom (248–49), is a shared conviction that the Christianization of the New World inexorably led to the destruction of stable and harmonious pretechnological societies. Individual missionaries might exhibit some admirable qualities in these movies, he observes, but they are nevertheless judged harshly for having participated in historical processes the filmmakers largely deplore.

Missiology Reconfigured

The deceptively simple definition of missiology adopted at the outset of this project ("the systematic study of all aspects of mission") has decisively shaped the manner in which I have approached my subject. As noted already, such a definition tends to push the limits of the field outward in a number of ways and to encourage one to consider scholarly work on the subject of mission undertaken from multiple starting points. Theological investigations, proposals for norms in the practice of mission, and specialized studies of the church and its sacred vocation continue to form a huge part of the subject matter that makes up missiology. Alongside these materials commonly found in seminary curricula are many other kinds of research on mission, which come from a variety of disciplinary perspectives, each with its own set of preferred methodologies. Among the academic works outside of theology I have attempted to recognize here are contributions made to the study of mission by historians, area specialists, religious studies scholars, anthropologists, sociologists, psychologists, linguists, communication theorists, experts in the study of human organizations, and feminist scholars, among others. My intention has been to present a representative sample of such research, in order to indicate the broad scholarly landscape I believe the field of missiology now encompasses.

My approach has allowed for the inclusion of various, even contradictory viewpoints with respect to the nature and purposes of Christian mission. I have chosen not to provide a normative definition of mission, in view of the fact that many different understandings of mission have informed the work of missionaries over the centuries and also the scholars who study them. If this introduction to the field of missiology had been conceived instead as an introduction to mission theology or a course of preparation for personal involvement in Christian mission, I may well have made another decision on this crucial methodological issue.

As portrayed in this book, missiology is organized around a series of six primary topics that highlight one or another aspect of this inherently interesting field of study. Even within these defined subject areas, scholars may apply more than one disciplinary approach to the study of mission. We saw this, for example, in the chapter on the Bible and mission, where exegetical, theological, and literary critical methodologies were each featured in turn. The element of culture has been ever-present throughout this book but has not always figured in just the same way. Thus, in chapter 4, one of my aims was to show how the work of missiologists draws from and has implications for those who focus more specifically on systematic theology or social scientific studies of culture. Considered from this perspective, missiology is a field in which such investigations may be observed interacting with each other. In the following chapter, I attempted to give serious consideration to research on the history of religion and on religious systems as these are embedded in particular cultural matrices, in order to show how these studies can deepen our understanding of cross-cultural, interreligious encounters that involve missionaries. In chapter 6, where the means of mission stood front and center, special attention was given to aspects of culture impacted by missionary methods aimed especially at social transformation, healing, the communication of religious messages, or the promotion of interfaith dialogue. I hope to have shown also how cultural analysis has become indispensable to the study of mission history.

Does missiology have a central concern? As we have proceeded through these six broad subject areas, I have mentioned several arguments made recently in favor of particular themes or scholarly interests that might be construed to stand at the "heart" of missiology. Usually, these proposals rest on particular definitions of mission or a sense of what the scholar believes to be the most urgent task facing contemporary missionaries in the field. Phan (2003, 8), for example, makes the case that "crossing borders" is the one aspect of the missionary job description that has remained constant over time, even if our ideas about the nature of the boundaries to be traversed have changed dramatically. Pachuau (2000, 549–52) also recognizes the importance of boundary crossing, especially in the context of a religiously plural world, which leads him to suggest that the theology of religions has become the "essential integrating principle" or "hub" of missiology. Langmead (2008) has argued that reconciliation ought to be considered the "central model" or "integrating metaphor" for mission, in light of his perception that increasing levels of conflict and violence are tearing our world apart. Others have promoted verbal proclamation or demonstrations of healing as actions without which authentic Christian mission cannot take place.

My own position is that missiology does not have a center but effective theologies of mission most certainly do. So long as missiology is understood to encompass more than the theology of mission, it seems to me that it does not need to have a central concern apart from the desire to understand mission in all its aspects as completely as possible. Therefore, I do not consider any one of the six areas of mission study described above to be more central to the field than any other. I am not now inclined either to arrange these topics in some kind of hierarchical scheme. Without a doubt, each of these subject areas is related to the rest in a variety of ways that may not always be apparent. Studies of culture, for example, may illuminate problems of interpersonal (mis)understanding that arise when missionary encounters take place across the boundaries of religious difference. Students of missionary methods and the theology of mission likewise have much to learn from each other. In addition, I am convinced that historians of mission risk incompetence if they are not ready to take into account research that ranges across the entire topical framework sketched out in this book.

An intention from the beginning has been to describe the field of missiology as I believe it is practiced today, rather than to advocate an ideal that does not yet exist. As explained in the introduction to this study, my perceptions of the field are based on three primary sources of data. The first is a general sense of what is being published right now in a diverse set of scholarly journals focused on the study of mission. A second collection of information comes out of my own work on a decade of dissertation research on mission published in English between 1992 and 2001 (Skreslet 2003). I have also written previously about several major bibliographic projects that attempt to represent the field (Skreslet 2006a). More than anything else, these classification structures and the huge variety of studies on mission reported through them have suggested to me that only an expansive definition of missiology could do justice to this wide-ranging branch of learning. Readers do need to keep in mind that missiology has developed over the generations and will continue to change, as new knowledge is discovered and additional points of view are brought into conversations already under way about the record of Christian mission, whether focused on its aims, methods, or effects. Consequently, the layout and understanding of academic missiology presented here should not be taken as a representation of something that is entirely fixed or timeless.

Those calling themselves missiologists today belong to a community of practice that has its own scholarly periodicals, professional societies, specialized conferences, and research networks. For this core group, several habits of professional conduct have been established that appear to me to shape this field of study in distinctive ways, including an intense interest in religious change, respect for the vocation of Christian mission, and a desire to integrate knowledge about mission gathered from many sources and viewpoints. With some justification, readers may understand this project to be an expression of the integrative impulse I have attempted to describe. Beside those who self-identify as missiologists are many other contemporary researchers who likewise are contributing to this dynamic field of study. In some sense, these scholars, too, are functioning as missiologists, as were a host of ancient, medieval, and early modern observers of mission who wrote about some dimension of Christian outreach well before the time when Alexander Duff, Gustav Warneck, and others began to put this scholarly field on a proper academic foundation toward the end of the nineteenth century.

Bright prospects lie ahead for those who might want to study Christian mission in all its aspects. Huge gaps in our knowledge still remain. Increasingly sophisticated research techniques are uncovering layers of complexity and hidden social processes not at all evident to earlier generations of scholars. New kinds of data are becoming available, as heretofore unconventional methodologies are applied to existing archival resources and contemporary mission experience. Fuller narratives of evangelization are also emerging, in part due to the fact that we are beginning to understand better the roles played in cross-cultural mission by indigenous actors. Non-Western perspectives on the study of mission are becoming increasingly prominent within the field and will, I believe, become more influential in the decades to come. In many ways, the integrative potential of missiology is yet to be achieved.

Works Cited

Abd-Allah, Umar F. 2006. *A Muslim in Victorian America: The Life of Alexander Russell Webb*. Oxford: Oxford University Press.

Acosta, José de. 2002. *Natural and Moral History of the Indies*. Ed. Jane E. Mangan. Trans. Frances López-Morillas. Durham, N.C.: Duke University Press.

Adriance, Madeleine Cousineau. 1995. *Promised Land: Base Ecclesial Communities and the Struggle for the Amazon*. Albany: State University of New York Press.

Alberigo, Guiseppe, and Joseph A. Komonchak, eds. 1995–2006. *History of Vatican II*. 5 vols. Maryknoll, N.Y.: Orbis.

Allen, Catherine B. 1987. *A Century to Celebrate: History of Woman's Missionary Union*. Birmingham, Ala.: Woman's Missionary Union.

——. 2002. "Shifting Sands for Southern Baptist Women in Mission." In *Gospel Bearers, Gender Barriers: Missionary Women in the Twentieth Century*, ed. Dana L. Robert, 113–26. Maryknoll, N.Y.: Orbis.

Allen, Roland. 1912. *Missionary Methods: St. Paul's or Ours? A Study of the Church in the Four Provinces*. London: R. Scott.

——. 1927. *The Spontaneous Expansion of the Church and the Causes Which Hinder It*. London: World Dominion.

Anane-Asane, Andrew, Timothy L. Eckert, Jason Richard Tan, and Robert J. Priest. 2009. "Paul G. Hiebert's 'The Flaw of the Excluded Middle.'" *Trinity Journal* NS 30, no. 2: 189–97.

Anastasios of Androussa. 1989. "Orthodox Mission: Past, Present and Future." In *Your Will Be Done: Orthodoxy in Mission*, ed. George Lemopoulos, 63–92. Geneva: World Council of Churches.

Anderson, Allan. 2004. *An Introduction to Pentecostalism: Global Charismatic Christianity*. Cambridge, U.K.: Cambridge University Press.

Anderson, Gerald H. 1996. "The State of Missiological Research." In *Missiological Education for the Twenty-first Century: The Book, the Circle, and the Sandals; Essays in Honor of Paul E. Pierson*, ed. J. Dudley Woodberry, Charles E. Van Engen, and Edgar J. Elliston, 23–33. Maryknoll, N.Y.: Orbis.

——, ed. 1998. *Biographical Dictionary of Christian Missions*. New York: Simon & Schuster Macmillan.

——. 2003. "'To the Jew First': An Interreligious Encounter." In *Towards an Intercultural Theology: Essays in Honour of Jan A. B. Jongeneel*, ed. Martha Frederiks, Meindert Dijkstra, and Anton Houtepen, 117–26. Zoetermeer: Boekencentrum.

——. 2006. "Peter Parker and the Introduction of Western Medicine in China." *Mission Studies* 23, no. 2: 203–38.

Anderson, Gerald H., Robert T. Coote, Norman A. Horner, and James M. Phillips, eds. 1994. *Mission Legacies: Biographical Studies of Leaders of the Modern Missionary Movement*. Maryknoll, N.Y.: Orbis.

Anderson, Rufus. 1845. *The Theory of Missions to the Heathen: A Sermon at the Ordination of Mr. Edward Webb*. Boston: Crocker and Brewster.

Ariarajah, Wesley. 1991. *Hindus and Christians: A Century of Protestant Ecumenical Thought*. Grand Rapids: Eerdmans.

Ariel, Yaakov S. 2000. *Evangelizing the Chosen People: Missions to the Jews in America, 1880–2000*. Chapel Hill: University of North Carolina Press.

Asamoah-Gyadu, J. Kwabena. 2007a. "'Get on the Internet!' Says the Lord: Religion, Cyberspace and Christianity in Contemporary Africa." *Studies in World Christianity* 13, no. 3: 225–42.

——. 2007b. "Pulling Down Strongholds: Evangelism, Principalities and Powers and the African Pentecostal Imagination." *IRM* 96 (no. 382–83): 306–17.

Augustine. 1984. *Concerning the City of God against the Pagans*. Trans. Henry Bettenson. London: Penguin.

Austin, Alvyn. 2007. *China's Millions: The China Inland Mission and Late Qing Society, 1832–1905*. Grand Rapids: Eerdmans.

Bagley, Robert W. 2003. "Trauma and Traumatic Stress among Missionaries." *Journal of Psychology and Theology* 31, no. 2: 97–112.

Bakewell, Peter. 2004. *A History of Latin America: c. 1450 to the Present*. 2nd ed. Malden, Mass.: Blackwell.

Bakker, Freek L. 2004. "The Image of Jesus Christ in the Jesus Films Used in Missionary Work." *Exchange* 33, no. 4: 310–33.

Balci, Bayram. 2003. "Fethullah Gülen's Missionary Schools in Central Asia and Their Role in the Spreading of Turkism and Islam." *Religion, State & Society* 31, no. 2: 151–77.

Barrett, David B. 1968. *Schism and Renewal in Africa: An Analysis of Six Thousand Contemporary Religious Movements*. Nairobi: Oxford University Press.

——. 1995. "'Count the Worshipers!' The New Science of Missiometrics." *IBMR* 19, no. 4: 154–60.

Barrett, David B., and Todd M. Johnson. 1990. *Our Globe and How to Reach It: Seeing the World Evangelized by AD 2000 and Beyond*. Birmingham, Ala.: New Hope.

——. 2001. *World Christian Trends: AD 30–AD 2200: Interpreting the Annual Christian Megacensus*. Pasadena, Calif.: William Carey Library.

Barrett, Lois Y., ed. 2004. *Treasure in Clay Jars: Patterns in Missional Faithfulness*. Grand Rapids: Eerdmans.

Barth, Karl. 1948. "The Living Congregation of the Living Lord Jesus Christ." In *The Universal Church in God's Design: An Ecumenical Study Prepared under the Auspices of the World Council of Churches*, 67–76. London: SCM.

——. 1962. *Church Dogmatics*. Vol. IV/3 (second half). Ed. T. F. Torrance. Trans. G. W. Bromiley. Edinburgh: T. & T. Clark.

Becker, Adam H., and Annette Yoshiko Reed, eds. 2007. *The Ways That Never Parted: Jews and Christians in Late Antiquity and the Early Middle Ages*. Minneapolis: Fortress.

Bede. 1990. *Ecclesiastical History of the English People*. Ed. D. H. Farmer. Trans. Leo Sherley-Price; rev. R. E. Latham. New York: Penguin.

Bediako, Kwame. 1992. *Theology and Identity: The Impact of Culture upon Christian Thought in the Second Century and in Modern Africa*. Oxford: Regnum.

——. 1995. *Christianity in Africa: The Renewal of a Non-Western Religion*. Maryknoll, N.Y.: Orbis.

Beidelman, T. O. 1982. *Colonial Evangelism: A Socio-Historical Study of an East African Mission at the Grassroots*. Bloomington: Indiana University Press.

Bendyna, Mary E., and Mary L. Gautier. 2009. *Recent Vocations to Religious Life: A Report for the National Religious Vocations Conference*. Washington, D.C.: Center for Applied Research in the Apostolate.

Benedetto, Robert, ed. 1996. *Presbyterian Reformers in Central Africa: A Documentary Account of the American Presbyterian Congo Mission and the Human Rights Struggle in the Congo, 1890–1918*. Trans. Winifred K. Vass. Leiden: Brill.

Benedict, Abbot of Monte Cassino. 1981. *RB 1980: The Rule of St. Benedict in Latin and English with Notes*. Ed. Timothy Fry et al. Collegeville, Minn.: Liturgical Press.

Bennett, Clinton. 2008. *Understanding Christian-Muslim Relations*. New York: Continuum.

Berg, Johannes van den. 1956. *Constrained by Jesus' Love: An Inquiry into the Motives of the Missionary Awakening in Great Britain in the Period between 1698 and 1815*. Kampen: J. H. Kok.

Berrigan, Daniel. 1986. *The Mission: A Film Journal*. San Francisco: Harper & Row.

Bevans, Stephen B. 2002. *Models of Contextual Theology*. Rev. and exp. ed. Maryknoll, N.Y.: Orbis.

Bevans, Stephen B., and Roger P. Schroeder. 2004. *Constants in Context: A Theology of Mission for Today*. Maryknoll, N.Y.: Orbis.

Blair, C. F. 1983. "Tentmaking: A Contextualized Approach to Islam." *Missiology* 11, no. 2: 219–27.

Blaufuss, Mary Schaller. 2005. "Healing Mission: Indian Women Shape Mission Emphases of the Christian Medical College in Vellore." *Missiology* 33, no. 4: 397–414.

Blossom, Jay S. F. 2003. "Evangelists of Destruction: Missions to Native Americans in Recent Film." In *The Foreign Missionary Enterprise at Home: Explorations in North American Cultural History*, ed. Daniel H. Bays and Grant Wacker, 237–50. Tuscaloosa: University of Alabama Press.

Boff, Leonardo. 1982. *St. Francis: A Model for Human Liberation*. Trans. John W. Diercksmeier. New York: Crossroad.

——. 1986. *Ecclesiogenesis: The Base Communities Reinvent the Church*. Trans. Robert R. Barr. Maryknoll, N.Y.: Orbis.

Bonk, Jonathan J. 1991. *Missions and Money: Affluence as a Missionary Problem*. Maryknoll, N.Y.: Orbis.

——. 2004. "Ecclesiastical Cartography and the Invisible Continent." *IBMR* 28, no. 4: 153–58.

——. 2007. "Following Jesus in Contexts of Power and Violence." *Evangelical Review of Theology* 31, no. 4: 342–57.

Bonsen, Roland, Hans Marks, and Jelle Miedema, eds. 1990. *The Ambiguity of Rapprochement: Reflections of Anthropologists on Their Controversial Relationship with Missionaries*. Nijmegen, Netherlands: Focaal.

Booth, Marilyn. 2002. "'She Herself Was the Ultimate Rule': Arabic Biographies of Missionary Teachers and Their Pupils." *Islam and Christian-Muslim Relations* 13, no. 4: 427–48.

Bornstein, Erica. 2003. *The Spirit of Development: Protestant NGOs, Morality, and Economics in Zimbabwe*. New York: Routledge.

Bosch, David J. 1979. *A Spirituality of the Road*. Scottdale, Pa.: Herald.

——. 1991. *Transforming Mission: Paradigm Shifts in Theology of Mission*. Maryknoll, N.Y.: Orbis.

——. 1992. "The Vulnerability of Mission." *The Baptist Quarterly* NS 34, no. 8: 351–63.

Braaten, Carl E. 1977. *The Flaming Center: A Theology of the Christian Mission*. Philadelphia: Fortress.

Breisach, Ernst. 1983. *Historiography: Ancient, Medieval and Modern*. Chicago: University of Chicago Press.

Bridston, Keith R. 1965. *Mission, Myth and Reality*. New York: Friendship.

Brock, Peggy, ed. 2005a. *Indigenous Peoples and Religious Change*. Leiden: Brill.

——. 2005b. "New Christians as Evangelists." In *Missions and Empire*, ed. Norman Etherington, 132–52. Oxford: Oxford University Press.

Brockey, Liam Matthew. 2007. *Journey to the East: The Jesuit Mission to China, 1579–1724*. Cambridge, Mass.: Belknap Press of Harvard University Press.

Brockway, Allan R. 1984. "Vancouver and the Future of Interfaith Dialogue in the Programme of the World Council of Churches." *Current Dialogue* 6 (Spring): 4–7.

Brouwer, Ruth Compton. 2002. *Modern Women Modernizing Men: The Changing Missions of Three Professional Women in Asia and Africa, 1902–69*. Vancouver: UBC Press.

——. 2006. "The Legacy of Hilda Lazarus." *IBMR* 30 no. 4: 202–6.

——. 2011. "When Missions Became Development: Ironies of 'NGOisation' in Mainstream Canadian Churches in the 1960s." In *Protestant Missions and Local Encounters in the Nineteenth and Twentieth Centuries: Unto the Ends of the World*, ed. Hilde Nielssen, Inger Marie Okkenhaug, and Karina Hestad Skeie, 259–91. Leiden: Brill.

Brumberg, Joan Jacobs. 1982. "The Case of Ann Hasseltine Judson: Missionary Hagiography and Female Popular Culture, 1815–1850." In *Women in New Worlds: Historical Perspectives on the Wesleyan Tradition*, ed. Rosemary Skinner Keller, Louise L. Queen, and Hilah F. Thomas. Vol 2: 234–48. Nashville: Abingdon.

Burgaleta, Claudio M. 1999. *José de Acosta, S.J., 1540–1600: His Life and Thought*. Chicago: Jesuit Way.

Burrows, William R., ed. 1993. *Redemption and Dialogue: Reading* Redemptoris Missio *and* Dialogue and Proclamation. Maryknoll, N.Y.: Orbis.

——. 2006. "Mission and Missiology in the Pontificate of John Paul II." *IBMR* 30 no. 1: 3–8.

——. 2010. "Catholics, Carey's Means, and Twenty-first-Century Mission." *IBMR* 34 no. 3: 131–38.

Cahill, Thomas. 1995. *How the Irish Saved Civilization: The Untold Story of Ireland's Heroic Role from the Fall of Rome to the Rise of Medieval Europe*. New York: Nan A. Talese, Doubleday.

Capen, Edward Warren, and Lewis Hodous. 1936. *The Kennedy School of Missions: A Sketch of Twenty-Five Years of Service*. Hartford, Conn.: Hartford Seminary Foundation.

Caraman, Philip. 1976. *The Lost Paradise: The Jesuit Republic in South America*. New York: Seabury.

Carey, William. 1934 [1792]. *An Enquiry into the Obligations of Christians to Use Means for the Conversion of the Heathens*. Facsimile ed. London: Henderson and Spalding.

Carson, Penny. 2001. "The British Raj and the Awakening of the Evangelical Conscience: The Ambiguities of Religious Establishment and Toleration, 1698–1833." In *Christian Missions and the Enlightenment*, ed. Brian Stanley, 45–70. Grand Rapids: Eerdmans.

Chao, Samuel H. 2010. "Conversion Methods: Theory and Practice." In *Handbook of Christianity in China,* Vol. 2: 1800 to the Present, ed. R. G. Tiedemann, 417–27. Leiden: Brill.

Charbonnier, Jean-Pierre. 2007. *Christians in China: A.D. 600 to 2000*. Trans. M. N. L. Couve de Murville. San Francisco: Ignatius.

Châtellier, Louis. 1997. *The Religion of the Poor: Rural Missions in Europe and the Formation of Modern Catholicism, c.1500–c.1800*. Trans. Brian Pearce. Cambridge, U.K.: Cambridge University Press.

Claydon, David, ed. 2005. *A New Vision, A New Heart, A Renewed Call*. 3 vols. Lausanne Occasional Papers from the 2004 Forum for World Evangelization (Pattaya, Thailand). Pasadena, Calif.: William Carey Library.

Clements, Keith. 2004. "'Friend of Africa: J. H. Oldham (1874–1969), Missions and British Colonial Policy in the 1920s." In *European Traditions in the Study of Religion in Africa*, ed. Frieder Ludwig and Afe Adogame in cooperation with Ulrich Berner and Christoph Bochinger, 175–86. Wiesbaden: Harrassowitz.

Clossey, Luke. 2008. *Salvation and Globalization in the Early Jesuit Missions*. New York: Cambridge University Press.

Cogley, Richard W. 1999. *John Eliot's Mission to the Indians before King Philip's War*. Cambridge, Mass.: Harvard University Press.

Cohn-Sherbok, Dan. 2000. *Messianic Judaism*. New York: Continuum.

Comaroff, Jean, and John L. Comaroff. 1991. *Of Revelation and Revolution*. Vol. 1: *Christianity, Colonialism and Consciousness in South Africa*. Chicago: University of Chicago Press.

——. 1992. *Ethnography and the Historical Imagination*. Boulder, Colo.: Westview.

——. 1997. *Of Revelation and Revolution*. Vol. 2: *The Dialectics of Modernity on a South African Frontier*. Chicago: University of Chicago Press.

Conforti, Joseph. 1985. "Jonathan Edwards's Most Popular Work: 'The Life of David Brainerd' and Nineteenth-Century Evangelical Culture." *Church History* 54, no. 2: 188–201.

Cook, Guillermo. 1985. *The Expectation of the Poor: Latin American Base Ecclesial Communities in Protestant Perspective*. Maryknoll, N.Y.: Orbis.

Coote, Robert T. 1995. "Good News, Bad News: North American Protestant Overseas Personnel Statistics in Twenty-Five-Year Perspective." *IBMR* 19, no. 1: 6–13.

——. 2000. "'AD 2000' and the '10/40 Window': A Preliminary Assessment." *IBMR* 24, no. 4: 160–66.

Costas, Orlando E. 1982. *Christ Outside the Gate: Mission Beyond Christendom*. Maryknoll, N.Y.: Orbis.

Cox, Jeffrey. 2008. *The British Missionary Enterprise since 1700*. New York: Routledge.

Cracknell, Kenneth. 1995. *Justice, Courtesy and Love: Theologians and Missionaries Encountering World Religions, 1846–1914*. London: Epworth.

Cragg, Kenneth. 1981. "Temple Gairdner's Legacy." *IBMR* 5, no. 4: 164–67.

Craig, Terrence L. 1997. *The Missionary Lives: A Study in Canadian Missionary Biography and Autobiography*. Leiden: Brill.

Crook, Zeba A. 2004. *Reconceptualising Conversion: Patronage, Loyalty, and Conversion in the Religions of the Ancient Mediterranean*. BZNW 130. Berlin: Walter de Gruyter.

Crowley, Terry. 1996. "The French Regime to 1760." In *A Concise History of Christianity in Canada*, ed. Terrence Murphy and Roberto Perin, 1–55. Oxford: Oxford University Press.

Crowther, Samuel. 1970. "Journal of Mr. S. Crowther." In *Journals of the Rev. James Frederick Schön and Mr. Samuel Crowther Who, with the Sanction of Her Majesty's*

Government, Accompanied the Expedition up the Niger in 1841 on Behalf of the Church Missionary Society, 263–344. Reprint of 1842 ed. London: Frank Cass.

Cunningham, Valentine. 1993. "'God and Nature Intended You for a Missionary's Wife': Mary Hill, Jane Eyre and Other Missionary Women in the 1840s." In *Women and Missions, Past and Present: Anthropological and Historical Perceptions*, ed. Fiona Bowie, Deborah Kirkwood, and Shirley Ardener, 85–105. Providence, R.I.: Berg.

Dahling-Sander, Christoph, et al., eds. 2003. *Leitfaden Ökumenische Missionstheologie*. Gütersloh, Germany: Chr. Kaiser/Gütersloher Verlagshaus.

Daneel, Marthinus L. 2001. *African Earthkeepers: Wholistic Interfaith Mission*. Maryknoll, N.Y.: Orbis.

Danker, William J. 1971. *Profit for the Lord: Economic Activities in Moravian Missions and the Basel Mission Trading Company*. Grand Rapids: Eerdmans.

Davies, Oliver, trans. 1999. *Celtic Spirituality*. With the collaboration of Thomas O'Loughlin. The Classics of Western Spirituality. New York: Paulist.

Dawson, David. 1990. "Mission Philanthropy, Selected Giving and Presbyterians." *American Presbyterians* 68, no. 2: 121–32.

——. 1991. "Mission Philanthropy, Selected Giving and Presbyterians." *American Presbyterians* 69, no. 3: 203–25.

Dennis, James S. 1893. *Foreign Missions after a Century*. New York: Fleming H. Revell.

——. 1897–1906. *Christian Missions and Social Progress: A Sociological Study of Foreign Missions*. 3 vols. New York: Fleming H. Revell.

Dickson, John P. 2003. *Mission-Commitment in Ancient Judaism and in the Pauline Community: The Shape, Extent and Background of Early Christian Mission*. WUNT 2/159. Tübingen: J. C. B. Mohr (Paul Siebeck).

Diekhoff, George M., et al. 1991. "The Ideal Overseas Missionary: A Cross-Cultural Comparison." *Journal of Psychology and Theology* 19, no. 2: 178–85.

Dohn, Michael N., and Anita L. Dohn. 2006. "Short-Term Medical Teams: What They Do Well . . . and Not So Well." *Evangelical Missions Quarterly* 42, no. 2: 216–24.

Don, Patricia Lopes. 2010. *Bonfires of Culture: Franciscans, Indigenous Leaders, and the Inquisition in Early Mexico, 1524–1540*. Norman: University of Oklahoma Press.

Donovan, Vincent J. 1982. *Christianity Rediscovered*. 2nd ed. Maryknoll, N.Y.: Orbis.

Dries, Angelyn. 1998a. "Mission and Marginalization: The Franciscan Heritage." *Missiology* 26, no. 1: 3–13.

——. 1998b. *The Missionary Movement in American Catholic History*. Maryknoll, N.Y.: Orbis.

——. 2002. "American Catholic 'Woman's Work for Woman' in the Twentieth Century." In *Gospel Bearers, Gender Barriers: Missionary Women in the Twentieth Century*, ed. Dana L. Robert, 127–42. Maryknoll, N.Y.: Orbis.

Dube, Musa W. 1999. "Consuming a Colonial Cultural Bomb: Translating *Badimo* into 'Demons' in the Setswana Bible (Matthew 8:28–34, 15:22, 10:8)." *Journal for the Study of the New Testament* 73: 33–59.

——. 2001. "'What I Have Written, I Have Written' (John 19:22)?" In *Interpreting the New Testament in Africa*, ed. Mary Getui, Tinyiko Maluleke, and Justin Ukpong, 145–63. Nairobi: Acton.

Duff, Alexander. 1839. *India, and India Missions: Including Sketches of the Gigantic System of Hinduism, Both in Theory and Practice*. Edinburgh: John Johnstone.

Dunn, James D. G. 2009. *Christianity in the Making*. Vol. 2: *Beginning from Jerusalem*. Grand Rapids: Eerdmans.

Dupuis, Jacques. 1997. *Toward a Christian Theology of Religious Pluralism*. Maryknoll, N.Y.: Orbis.

Eitel, Keith E., ed. 2008. *Missions in Contexts of Violence*. Pasadena, Calif.: William Carey Library.

Ellenbogen, Maximilian. 1962. *Foreign Words in the Old Testament: Their Origin and Etymology*. London: Luzac.

Equiano, Olaudah. 1995. *The Interesting Narrative of the Life of Olaudah Equiano, or Gustavus Vassa, the African. Written by Himself.* Ed. Vincent Carretta. New York: Penguin.

Esack, Farid. 2006. "Islamic *Da'wah* and Christian Mission: A Muslim Perspective." *Missionalia* 34, no. 1: 22–30.

Escobar, Samuel. 2003. "Migration: Avenue and Challenge to Mission." *Missiology* 31, no. 1: 17–28.

Etherington, Norman. 2005a. "Education and Medicine." In *Missions and Empire*, ed. Norman Etherington, 261–84. Oxford: Oxford University Press.

——, ed. 2005b. *Missions and Empire*. Oxford History of the British Empire: Companion Series. Oxford: Oxford University Press.

Eusebius. 1926–1932. *The Ecclesiastical History*. Trans. Kirsopp Lake (vol. 1) and J. E. L. Oulton (vol. 2). Loeb Classical Library 153 and 265. Cambridge, Mass.: Harvard University Press.

Fabella, Virginia, and R. S. Sugirtharajah, eds. 2000. *Dictionary of Third World Theologies*. Maryknoll, N.Y.: Orbis.

Fairbank, John K. 1969. "Assignment for the '70's." *American Historical Review* 74, no. 3: 861–79.

Farquhar, J. N. 1913. *The Crown of Hinduism*. London: H. Milford.

Finney, John. 1996. *Recovering the Past: Celtic and Roman Mission*. London: Darton, Longman and Todd.

Fishburn, Janet F. 2004. "The Social Gospel as a Missionary Ideology." In *North American Foreign Missions, 1810–1914: Theology, Theory, and Policy*, ed. Wilbert R. Shenk, 218–42. Grand Rapids: Eerdmans.

Fitzmyer, Joseph A. 1979. "The Languages of Palestine in the First Century A.D." In *A Wandering Aramean: Collected Aramaic Essays*, 29–56. Missoula, Mont.: Scholars.

——. 1998. *The Acts of the Apostles*. New York: Doubleday.

Fleming, Daniel Johnson. 1938. *Each with His Own Brush: Contemporary Christian Art in Asia and Africa*. New York: Friendship.

Flett, John G. 2010. *The Witness of God: The Trinity,* Missio Dei, *Karl Barth, and the Nature of Christian Community*. Grand Rapids: Eerdmans.

Fox, Robin Lane. 1987. *Pagans and Christians*. New York: Alfred A. Knopf.

Francis-Dehqani, Guli. 2002. "Medical Missions and the History of Feminism: Emmeline Stuart of the CMS Persia Mission." In *Women, Religion and Feminism in Britain, 1750–1900*, ed. Sue Morgan, 197–211. New York: Palgrave Macmillan.

Fredericks, James L. 2003. "The Catholic Church and the Other Religious Paths: Rejecting Nothing That Is True and Holy." *Theological Studies* 64, no. 2: 225–54.

Freire, Paulo. 1970. *Pedagogy of the Oppressed.* Trans. Myra Bergman Ramos. New York: Herder and Herder.

Frend, W. H. C. 2001. "Church Historians of the Early Twentieth Century: Adolf von Harnack (1851–1930)." *Journal of Ecclesiastical History* 52, no. 1: 83–102.

Friesen, J. Stanley. 1996. *Missionary Responses to Tribal Religions at Edinburgh, 1910*. New York: Peter Lang.

Froehle, Bryan T., and Mary L. Gautier. 2003. *Global Catholicism: Portrait of a World Church.* Center for Applied Research in the Apostolate, Georgetown University. Maryknoll, N.Y.: Orbis.

Gairdner, W. H. T. 1909. *The Reproach of Islam.* London: Young People's Missionary Movement.

——. 1928. "Christianity and Islam." In *The Christian Life and Message in Relation to Non-Christian Systems of Thought and Life.* With the cooperation of W. A. Eddy. Jerusalem meeting of the International Missionary Council. Vol. 1: 191–229. New York: International Missionary Council.

Ganson, Barbara. 2003. *The Guaraní under Spanish Rule in the Río de la Plata.* Stanford, Calif.: Stanford University Press.

Geertz, Clifford. 1957. "Ethos, World-View and the Analysis of Sacred Symbols." *Antioch Review* 17, no. 4: 421–37. Reprinted in Geertz, *The Interpretation of Cultures*, 126–41.

——. 1973. "Thick Description: Toward an Interpretive Theory of Culture." In *The Interpretation of Cultures*, 3–30. New York: Basic Books.

Gehring, Roger W. 2004. *House Church and Mission: The Importance of Household Structures in Early Christianity.* Peabody, Mass.: Hendrickson.

Gibbon, Edward. 1896–1900. *The History of the Decline and Fall of the Roman Empire.* Ed. J. B. Bury. 7 vols. London: Methuen.

——. 1966. *Memoirs of My Life.* Ed. Georges A. Bonnard. London: Nelson.

Gill, Sean. 1998. "Heroines of Missionary Adventure: The Portrayal of Victorian Women Missionaries in Popular Fiction and Biography." In *Women of Faith in Victorian Culture: Reassessing the Angel in the House*, ed. Anne Hogan and Andrew Bradstock, 172–85. New York: St. Martin's.

Ginter, Gary. 1998. "Overcoming Resistance through Tentmaking." In *Reaching the Resistant: Barriers and Bridges for Mission*, ed. J. Dudley Woodberry, 209–18. Pasadena, Calif.: William Carey Library.

Girardot, Norman J. 2002. *The Victorian Translation of China: James Legge's Oriental Pilgrimage.* Berkeley: University of California Press.

Gittins, Anthony J. 1989. *Gifts and Strangers: Meeting the Challenge of Inculturation.* New York: Paulist.

——. 1993. *Bread for the Journey: The Mission of Transformation and the Transformation of Mission.* Maryknoll, N.Y.: Orbis.

——. 1994. "Beyond Hospitality? The Missionary Status and Role Revisited." *Currents in Theology and Mission* 21, no. 3: 164–82.

Goddard, Hugh. 2000. *A History of Christian-Muslim Relations.* Chicago: New Amsterdam.

Good, Charles M., Jr. 2004. *The Steamer Parish: The Rise and Fall of Missionary Medicine on an African Frontier.* Chicago: University of Chicago Press.

Goodman, Martin. 1994. *Mission and Conversion: Proselytizing in the Religious History of the Roman Empire.* Oxford: Clarendon Press.

Gorringe, Timothy J. 2004. *Furthering Humanity: A Theology of Culture.* Aldershot, Hants, England: Ashgate.

Grant, Robert. 1995. "Trauma in Missionary Life." *Missiology* 23, no. 1: 71–83.

Greer, Allan, ed. 2000. *The Jesuit Relations: Natives and Missionaries in Seventeenth-Century North America.* Boston: St. Martin's.

Gregory Thaumaturgus. 1998. "Address of Thanksgiving." In *St. Gregory Thaumaturgus: Life and Works*, trans. Michael Slusser, 91–126. Fathers of the Church 98. Washington, D.C.: Catholic University of America Press.

Griffith, Sidney H. 2008. *The Church in the Shadow of the Mosque: Christians and Muslims in the World of Islam*. Princeton, N.J.: Princeton University Press.

Grimshaw, Patricia, and Peter Sherlock. 2005. "Women and Culture Exchanges." In *Missions and Empire*, ed. Norman Etherington, 173–93. Oxford: Oxford University Press.

Grundmann, Christoffer H. 2005. *Sent to Heal! Emergence and Development of Medical Missions*. Lanham, Md.: University Press of America.

——. 2008. "Mission and Healing in Historical Perspective." *IBMR* 32, no. 4: 185–88.

Grypma, Sonya. 2008. *Healing Henan: Canadian Nurses at the North China Mission, 1888–1947*. Vancouver: UBC Press.

Guder, Darrell L. 2003. "From Mission and Theology to Missional Theology." *Princeton Seminary Bulletin* 24, no. 1: 36–54.

Guder, Darrell L., et al. 1998. *Missional Church: A Vision for the Sending of the Church in North America*. Grand Rapids: Eerdmans.

Guider, Margaret Eletta. 2002. " 'On Planting Dates': The Consequences of Missionary Activity on U.S.-Based Franciscan Sisterhoods (1960–2000)." In *Gospel Bearers, Gender Barriers: Missionary Women in the Twentieth Century*, ed. Dana L. Robert, 157–70. Maryknoll, N.Y.: Orbis.

Gutiérrez, Gustavo. 1973. *A Theology of Liberation: History, Politics, and Salvation*. Trans. and ed. Caridad Inda and John Eagleson. Maryknoll, N.Y.: Orbis.

Haight, Roger. 1985. *An Alternative Vision: An Interpretation of Liberation Theology*. New York: Paulist.

Hale, Frederick. 1995. " 'The Mission' as the Cinema of Liberation Theology." *Missionalia* 23, no. 1: 72–91.

Hanciles, Jehu J. 2001. "Anatomy of an Experiment: The Sierra Leone Native Pastorate." *Missiology* 29, no. 1: 63–82.

——. 2003. "Migration and Mission: Some Implications for the Twenty-first-Century Church." *IBMR* 27, no. 4: 146–53.

Hardesty, Nancy A. 2003. "The Scientific Study of Missions: Textbooks of the Central Committee on the United Study of Foreign Missions." In *The Foreign Missionary Enterprise at Home: Explorations in North American Cultural History*, ed. Daniel H. Bays and Grant Wacker, 106–22. Tuscaloosa: University of Alabama Press.

Harnack, Adolf (von). 1904–1905. *The Expansion of Christianity in the First Three Centuries*. Trans. and ed. James Moffatt. 2 vols. London: Williams & Norgate.

——. 1957. *What Is Christianity?* Trans. Thomas Bailey Saunders. New York: Harper & Brothers.

——. 1989. *Adolf von Harnack: Liberal Theology at Its Height*. Ed. Martin Rumscheidt. New York: Harper & Row.

Harris, Marvin. 2001. *The Rise of Anthropological Theory: A History of Theories of Culture*. Updated ed. Walnut Creek, Calif.: AltaMira.

Harris, Paul William. 1999. *Nothing but Christ: Rufus Anderson and the Ideology of Protestant Foreign Missions*. New York: Oxford University Press.

Harris, Paula. 2002. "Calling Young People to Missionary Vocations in a 'Yahoo' World." *Missiology* 30, no. 1: 33–50.

Harris-Shapiro, Carol. 1999. *Messianic Judaism: A Rabbi's Journey through Religious Change in America*. Boston: Beacon.

Harvey, Susan Ashbrook. 2008. "Martyr Passions and Hagiography." In *The Oxford Handbook of Early Christian Studies*, ed. Susan Ashbrook Harvey and David G. Hunter, 603–27. Oxford: Oxford University Press.

Hastings, Adrian. 1994. *The Church in Africa, 1450–1950*. New York: Oxford University Press.
——. 2000. "African Christian Studies, 1967–1999: Reflections of an Editor." *Journal of Religion in Africa* 30, no. 1: 30–44.
Hay, Rob, et al. 2007. *Worth Keeping: Global Perspectives on Best Practices in Missionary Retention*. Pasadena, Calif.: William Carey Library.
Hedges, Paul. 2001. *Preparation and Fulfilment: A History and Study of Fulfilment Theology in Modern British Thought in the Indian Context*. Bern: Peter Lang.
Hefner, Robert W. 1993. "World Building and the Rationality of Conversion." In *Conversion to Christianity: Historical and Anthropological Perspectives on a Great Transformation*, 3–44. Berkeley: University of California Press.
Hengel, Martin. 1980. *Acts and the History of Earliest Christianity*. Trans. John Bowden. Philadelphia: Fortress.
Hesselgrave, David J. 1978. *Communicating Christ Cross-Culturally*. Grand Rapids: Zondervan.
Hiebert, Paul G. 1982. "The Flaw of the Excluded Middle." *Missiology* 10, no. 1: 35–47.
——. 1983. *Cultural Anthropology*. 2nd ed. Grand Rapids: Baker.
——. 1989. "Power Encounter and Folk Islam." In *Muslims and Christians on the Emmaus Road*, ed. J. Dudley Woodberry, 45–61. Monrovia, Calif.: MARC.
——. 2008. *Transforming Worldviews: An Anthropological Understanding of How People Change*. Grand Rapids: Baker Academic.
Hill, Harriet. 2010. "Conversations about Orality." *Missiology* 38, no. 2: 215–17.
Hill, Patricia. 1985. *The World Their Household: The American Woman's Foreign Mission Movement and Cultural Transformation, 1870–1920*. Ann Arbor: University of Michigan Press.
Hochschild, Adam. 1998. *King Leopold's Ghost: A Story of Greed, Terror, and Heroism in Colonial Africa*. Boston: Houghton Mifflin.
Hocking, William Ernest, et al. 1932. *Re-Thinking Missions: A Laymen's Inquiry after One Hundred Years*. New York: Harper and Brothers.
Hoeberichts, Jan. 2008. "Francis' Understanding of Mission: Living the Gospel, Going through the World, Bringing Peace." *Zeitschrift für Missionswissenschaft und Religionswissenschaft* 92, no. 3–4: 280–97.
Hoefer, Herbert E. 2001. *Churchless Christianity*. Expanded ed. Pasadena, Calif.: William Carey Library.
Hoekendijk, J. C. 1950. "The Call to Evangelism." *IRM* 39, no. 154: 162–75.
——. 1952. "The Church in Missionary Thinking." *IRM* 41, no. 163: 324–36.
Hofmeyr, Isabel. 2004. *The Portable Bunyan: A Transnational History of The Pilgrim's Progress*. Princeton, N.J.: Princeton University Press.
Hogg, A. G. 1909. *Karma and Redemption: An Essay toward the Interpretation of Hinduism and the Re-statement of Christianity*. London: Christian Literature Society.
——. 1939. "The Christian Attitude to Non-Christian Faith." In *The Authority of the Faith*. Tambaram Series, vol. 1: 102–25. London: Humphrey Milford (for International Missionary Council by Oxford University Press).
Horner, Norman A. 1982. "Checklist of Fifty Selected Films for Mission Studies." *IBMR* 6, no. 4: 172–76.
Horsfjord, Vebjørn. 2007. "Healing and Salvation in Late Modernity: The Use and Implication of Such Terms in the Ecumenical Movement." *IRM* 96, no. 380–81: 5–21.
Horton, Robin. 1971. "African Conversion." *Africa* 41, no. 2: 85–108.

——. 1975a. "On the Rationality of Conversion: Part One." *Africa* 45, no. 3: 219–35.

——. 1975b. "On the Rationality of Conversion: Part Two." *Africa* 45, no. 4: 373–99.

Hsia, R. Po-chia, ed. 2006. *Noble Patronage and Jesuit Missions: Maria Theresia von Fugger-Wellenburg (1690–1762) and Jesuit Missionaries in China and Vietnam*. Rome: Institutum Historicum Societatis Iesu.

Hughes, Jennifer S. 2010. "Patronato, Padroado." *Cambridge Dictionary of Christianity*. New York: Cambridge University Press.

Hunt, Nancy Rose. 1999. *A Colonial Lexicon of Birth Ritual, Medicalization, and Mobility in the Congo*. Durham, N.C.: Duke University Press.

Hunter, George G., III. 2000. *The Celtic Way of Evangelism: How Christianity Can Reach the West . . . Again*. Nashville: Abingdon.

Hutchison, William R. 1987. *Errand to the World: American Protestant Thought and Foreign Missions*. Chicago: University of Chicago Press.

Jaffarian, E. Michael. 2004. "Are There More Non-Western Missionaries Than Western Missionaries?" *IBMR* 28, no. 3: 131–32.

James, Wendy. 1988. *The Listening Ebony: Moral Knowledge, Religion, and Power among the Uduk of Sudan*. Oxford: Clarendon Press.

James, William. 1902. *The Varieties of Religious Experience: A Study in Human Nature*. London: Longmans, Green, and Co.

Jamison, Todd [pseudonym]. 2007. "House Churches in Central Asia: An Evaluation." *Evangelical Missions Quarterly* 43, no. 2: 188–96.

Jansen, Gerard. 1995. "Medical Missiology: An Undeveloped Discipline without Disciples; A Retrospective View." *Exchange* 24, no. 3: 222–46.

——. 1999. "The Tradition of Medical Missions in the Maelstrom of the International Health Arena." *Missiology* 27, no. 3: 377–92.

Jenkins, Willis. 2008. "Missiology in Environmental Context: Tasks for an Ecology of Mission." *IBMR* 32, no. 4: 176–84.

Jensma, Jeanne L. 1999. "Critical Incident Intervention with Missionaries: A Comprehensive Approach." *Journal of Psychology and Theology* 27, no. 2: 130–38.

Johnson, C. Neal. 2009. *Business as Mission: A Comprehensive Guide to Theory and Practice*. Downer's Grove, Ill.: IVP Academic.

Johnson, Todd M., and Kenneth R. Ross. 2009. *Atlas of Global Christianity, 1910–2010*. Edinburgh: Edinburgh University Press.

Johnson, Todd M., and David R. Scoggins. 2005. "Christian Missions and Islamic *Da'wah*: A Preliminary Quantitative Assessment." *IBMR* 29, no. 1: 8–11.

Johnston, Anna. 2003. *Missionary Writing and Empire, 1800–1860*. Cambridge, U.K.: Cambridge University Press.

Johnstone, Patrick. 2007. "Affinity Blocs and People Clusters: An Approach Toward Strategic Insight and Mission Partnership." *Mission Frontiers* 29, no. 2: 8–15.

Jones, E. Stanley. 1925. *The Christ of the Indian Road*. New York: Abingdon.

Jones, Rufus M. 1928. "Secular Civilization and the Christian Task." In *The Christian Life and Message in Relation to Non-Christian Systems of Thought and Life*. Jerusalem meeting of the International Missionary Council. Vol. 1: 230–73. New York: International Missionary Council.

Jongeneel, Jan A. B. 1991. "The Missiology of Gisbertus Voetius: The First Comprehensive Protestant Theology of Missions." Trans. John Bolt. *Calvin Theological Journal* 26, no. 1: 47–79.

——. 1995–1997. *Philosophy, Science, and Theology of Mission in the 19th and 20th Centuries: A Missiological Encyclopedia*. 2 vols. New York: Peter Lang.

——. 1998. "Is Missiology an Academic Discipline?" *Transformation* 15, no. 3: 27–32.

Jørgensen, Jonas Adelin. 2008. *Jesus Imandars and Christ Bhaktas: Two Case Studies of Interreligious Hermeneutics and Identity in Global Christianity*. Frankfurt am Main: Peter Lang.

Justin Martyr. 1997. *The First and Second Apologies*. Trans. Leslie William Barnard. Ancient Christian Writers, no. 56. New York: Paulist.

Kamau-Goro, Nicholas. 2010. "African Culture and the Language of Nationalist Imagination: The Reconfiguration of Christianity in Ngûgî wa Thiong'o's *The River Between* and *Weep Not, Child*." *Studies in World Christianity* 16, no. 1: 6–26.

Kang, Namsoon. 2005. "The Centrality of Gender Justice in Prophetic Christianity and the Mission of the Church Reconsidered." *IRM* 94, no. 373: 278–89.

Kärkkäinen, Veli-Matti. 2002. *Toward a Pneumatological Theology: Pentecostal and Ecumenical Perspectives on Ecclesiology, Soteriology, and Theology of Mission*. Ed. Amos Yong. Lanham, Md.: University Press of America.

Karotemprel, S., chief ed., et al. 1996. *Following Christ in Mission: A Foundational Course in Missiology*. Boston: Pauline Books and Media.

Kent, Eliza F. 2005. "Books and Bodices: Material Culture and Protestant Missions in Colonial South India." In *Mixed Messages: Materiality, Textuality, Missions*, ed. Jamie S. Scott and Gareth Griffiths, 67–87. Oxford: Oxford University Press.

Kerr, David A. 2000. "Islamic *Da'wa* and Christian Mission: Towards a Comparative Analysis." *IRM* 89, no. 353: 150–71.

——. 2002. "Christian Mission and Islamic Studies: Beyond Antithesis." *IBMR* 26, no. 1: 8–15.

Kerr, David A., and Kenneth R. Ross, eds. 2009. *Edinburgh 2010: Mission Then and Now*. Oxford: Regnum.

Kimball, Charles. 2004. "Toward a More Hopeful Future: Obstacles and Opportunities in Christian-Muslim Relations." *The Muslim World* 94, no. 3: 377–85.

Kirk, J. Andrew, and Kevin Vanhoozer, eds. 1999. *To Stake a Claim: Mission and the Western Crisis of Knowledge*. Maryknoll, N.Y.: Orbis.

Knitter, Paul F. 1985. *No Other Name? A Critical Survey of Christian Attitudes toward the World Religions*. Maryknoll, N.Y.: Orbis.

——. 1995. *One Earth, Many Religions: Multifaith Dialogue and Global Responsibility*. Maryknoll, N.Y.: Orbis.

——. 1996. *Jesus and the Other Names: Christian Mission and Global Responsibility*. Maryknoll, N.Y.: Orbis.

Koll, Karla Ann. 2010. "Taking Wolves Among Lambs: Some Thoughts on Training for Short-Term Mission Facilitation." *IBMR* 34, no. 2: 93–96.

Kollman, Paul V. 2005. *The Evangelization of Slaves and Catholic Origins in Eastern Africa*. Maryknoll, N.Y.: Orbis.

Koyama, Kōsuke. 1993. "'Extend Hospitality to Strangers': A Missiology of Theologia Crucis." *Currents in Theology and Mission* 20, no. 3: 165–76.

Kraemer, Hendrik. 1938. *The Christian Message in a Non-Christian World.* New York: Harper & Brothers (for International Missionary Council).

Kraft, Charles H. 1996. *Anthropology for Christian Witness*. Maryknoll, N.Y.: Orbis.

——. 2002. "Contemporary Trends in the Treatment of Spiritual Conflict." In *Deliver Us from Evil: An Uneasy Frontier in Christian Mission*, ed. A. Scott Moreau, Tokunboh

Adeyemo, David G. Burnett, Bryant L. Myers, and Hwa Yung, 177–202. Monrovia, Calif.: World Vision International.
——. 2008. *Worldview for Christian Witness*. Pasadena, Calif.: William Carey Library.
Kroeger, James H. 1991. "Guiding Vocation Recruitment in Mission." *African Ecclesial Review* 33, no. 5: 249–56.
Kuhn, Thomas S. 1970. *The Structure of Scientific Revolutions*. 2nd ed., enlarged. Chicago: University of Chicago Press.
Küng, Hans. 1991. *Global Responsibility: In Search of a New World Ethic*. Trans. John Bowden. New York: Crossroad.
Küng, Hans, and David Tracy, eds. 1989. *Paradigm Change in Theology: A Symposium for the Future*. Trans. Margaret Köhl. New York: Crossroad.
Küster, Volker. 2005. "The Project of an Intercultural Theology." *Svensk Missionstidskrift* 93, no. 3: 417–32.
——. 2009. "Intercultural Theology." *RPP* 6: 526–28.
Kuznetsova, Anna. 2000. "Signs of Conversion in *Vitae sanctorum*." In *Christianizing Peoples and Converting Individuals*, ed. Guyda Armstrong and Ian Wood, 125–32. Turnhout : Brepols.
Lamb, Christopher. 1997. *The Call to Retrieval: Kenneth Cragg's Christian Vocation to Islam*. London: Grey Seal.
Langer, Erick. 1995. "Missions and the Frontier Economy: The Case of the Franciscan Missions among the Chiriguanos, 1845–1930." In *The New Latin American Mission History*, ed. Erick Langer and Robert H. Jackson, 49–76. Lincoln: University of Nebraska Press.
Langmead, Ross. 2002. "Ecomissiology." *Missiology* 30, no. 4: 505–18.
——. 2008. "Transformed Relationships: Reconciliation as the Central Model for Mission." *Mission Studies* 25, no. 1: 5–20.
Lara, Jaime. 2008. *Christian Texts for Aztecs: Art and Liturgy in Colonial Mexico*. Notre Dame, Ind.: University of Notre Dame Press.
Las Casas, Bartolomé de. 1992. *Witness: Writings of Bartolomé de Las Casas*. Ed. and trans. George Sanderlin. Maryknoll, N.Y.: Orbis.
Latourette, Kenneth Scott. 1937–1945. *A History of the Expansion of Christianity*. 7 vols. New York: Harper & Brothers.
——. 1949. "The Christian Understanding of History." *American Historical Review* 54, no. 2: 259–76.
Lautz, Terrill E. 2009. "'The Call': The Student Volunteer Movement for Foreign Missions." In *China's Christian Colleges: Cross-Cultural Connections, 1900–1950*, ed. Daniel H. Bays and Ellen Widmer, 3–21. Stanford, Calif.: Stanford University Press.
Learman, Linda, ed. 2005. *Buddhist Missionaries in the Era of Globalization*. Honolulu: University of Hawai'i Press.
Legrand, Lucien. 1990. *Unity and Plurality: Mission in the Bible*. Trans. Robert R. Barr. Maryknoll, N.Y.: Orbis.
Lehmann, Arno. 1957. *Die Kunst der Jungen Kirchen*. 2nd ed. Berlin: Evangelische Verlagsanstalt.
——. 1969. *Christian Art in Africa and Asia*. Trans. Erich Hopka et al. St. Louis: Concordia.
Lehmann, Hartmut. 2008. "The Mobilization of God's Pious Children in the Era of the French Revolution and Beyond." *Pietismus und Neuzeit* 34: 189–98.
Livingstone, David. 1858. *Dr. Livingstone's Cambridge Lectures*. Ed. William Monk. Cambridge, U.K.: Deighton, Bell and Co.

Llull, Ramon. 1985. *Selected Works of Ramon Llull (1232–1316)*. Ed. and trans. Anthony Bonner. 2 vols. Princeton, N.J.: Princeton University Press.

——. 1993. *Doctor Illuminatus: A Ramon Llull Reader*. Ed. and trans. Anthony Bonner, with Eve Bonner, trans. Princeton, N.J.: Princeton University Press.

Love, Rick. 2000. *Muslims, Magic and the Kingdom of God: Church Planting among Folk Muslims*. Pasadena, Calif.: William Carey Library.

Lowe, Chuck. 1998. *Territorial Spirits and World Evangelisation: A Biblical, Historical and Missiological Critique of Strategic-Level Spiritual Warfare*. Fearn, U.K.: Mentor/OMF.

Loyola, Ignatius. 1970. *Constitutions of the Society of Jesus [by] Saint Ignatius of Loyola*. Trans. George E. Ganss. St. Louis: Institute of Jesuit Sources.

Luzbetak, Louis J. 1988. *The Church and Cultures: New Perspectives in Missiological Anthropology*. Maryknoll, N.Y.: Orbis.

MacKenzie, John M. 1990. "David Livingstone: The Construction of the Myth." In *Sermons and Battle Hymns: Protestant Popular Culture in Modern Scotland*, ed. Graham Walker and Tom Gallagher, 24–42. Edinburgh: Edinburgh University Press.

——. 2003. "Missionaries, Science, and the Environment in Nineteenth-Century Africa." In *The Imperial Horizons of British Protestant Missions, 1880–1914*, ed. Andrew Porter, 106–30. Grand Rapids: Eerdmans.

MacMullen, Ramsay. 1997. *Christianity and Paganism in the Fourth to Eighth Centuries*. New Haven, Conn.: Yale University Press.

Macnicol, Nicol. 1928. "Christianity and Hinduism." In *The Christian Life and Message in Relation to Non-Christian Systems of Thought and Life*. Jerusalem meeting of the International Missionary Council. Vol. 1: 3–42. New York: International Missionary Council.

Malbon, Elizabeth Struthers. 2000. *In the Company of Jesus: Characters in Mark's Gospel*. Louisville: Westminster John Knox.

Maluleke, Tinyiko Sam. 2000. "The Quest for Muted Black Voices in History: Some Pertinent Issues in (South) African Mission Historiography." *Missionalia* 28, no. 1: 41–61.

——. 2005. "The Next Phase in the Vernacular Bible Discourse: Echoes from Hammanskraal." *Missionalia* 33, no. 2: 355–74.

Marguerat, Daniel. 2002. *The First Christian Historian: Writing the "Acts of the Apostles."* Trans. Ken McKinney, Gregory J. Laughery, and Richard Bauckham. SNTSMS 121. Cambridge: Cambridge University Press.

Markus, R. A. 1997. *Gregory the Great and His World*. Cambridge: Cambridge University Press.

Martínez, Alejandro. 2010. "Evangelization, Visual Technologies, and Indigenous Responses: The South American Missionary Society in the Paraguayan Chaco." *IBMR* 34, no. 2: 83–86.

Masuzawa, Tomoko. 2005. *The Invention of World Religions: Or, How European Universalism Was Preserved in the Language of Pluralism*. Chicago: University of Chicago Press.

Matthey, Jacques. 2006. "Editorial." *IRM* 95, no. 376–77: 3–6.

Maughan, Steven. 1996. "'Mighty England Do Good': The Major English Denominations and Organisation for the Support of Foreign Missions in the Nineteenth Century." In *Missionary Encounters: Sources and Issues*, ed. Robert A. Bickers and Rosemary Seton, 11–37. Richmond, U.K.: Curzon.

Maxwell, David. 2006. "Writing the History of African Christianity: Reflections of an Editor." *Journal of Religion in Africa* 36, no. 3–4: 379–99.

Maxwell, Ian Douglas. 2001. "Civilization or Christianity? The Scottish Debate on Mission Methods, 1750–1835." In *Christian Missions and the Enlightenment*, ed. Brian Stanley, 123–40. Grand Rapids: Eerdmans.

Mbiti, John S. 1986. *Bible and Theology in African Christianity*. Nairobi: Oxford University Press.

McClintock, Wayne. 1988. "Sociological Critique of the Homogeneous Unit Principle." *IRM* 77, no. 305: 107–16.

McCormick, Richard A. 1979. "Human Rights and the Mission of the Church." In *Liberation Theologies in North America and Europe*, ed. Gerald H. Anderson and Thomas F. Stransky, 37–50. Mission Trends, no. 4. New York: Paulist.

McGavran, Donald A. 1955. *The Bridges of God: A Study in the Strategy of Missions*. New York: Friendship.

——. 1962. "The God Who Finds and His Mission." *IRM* 51, no. 203: 303–16.

——. 1970. *Understanding Church Growth*. Grand Rapids: Eerdmans.

McKnight, Scot. 1991. *A Light among the Gentiles: Jewish Missionary Activity in the Second Temple Period*. Minneapolis: Fortress.

McNamara, Jo Ann Kay. 1996. *Sisters in Arms: Catholic Nuns through Two Millennia*. Cambridge, Mass.: Harvard University Press.

Meeks, Wayne A. 1983. *The First Urban Christians: The Social World of the Apostle Paul*. New Haven, Conn.: Yale University Press.

Merritt, Catherine Winn, and Eric J. Sterling. 2009. "The Collision of Two Cultures: Chinua Achebe's *Things Fall Apart* and Christianity's Coming to Nigeria." In *Mother Tongue Theologies: Poets, Novelists, Non-Western Christianity*, ed. Darren J. N. Middleton, 47–60. Eugene, Ore.: Pickwick.

Miller, Donald E., and Tetsunao Yamamori. 2007. *Global Pentecostalism: The New Face of Christian Social Engagement*. Berkeley: University of California Press.

"Mission Studies as Intercultural Theology and Its Relationship to Religious Studies." 2008. *Mission Studies* 25, no. 1: 103–8.

Momigliano, Arnaldo. 1966. "Gibbon's Contribution to Historical Method." In *Studies in Historiography*, 40–55. New York: Harper & Row.

Montgomery, Laura M. 1993. "Short-Term Medical Missions: Enhancing or Eroding Health?" *Missiology* 21, no. 3: 333–41.

——. 2007. "Reinventing Short-Term Medical Missions to Latin America." *Journal of Latin American Theology* 2, no. 2: 84–103.

Mooney, Catherine M. 2009. "Ignatian Spirituality, A Spirituality for Mission." *Mission Studies* 26, no. 2: 192–213.

Müller, Karl. 1987. *Mission Theology: An Introduction*. With contributions by Hans-Werner Gensichen and Horst Rzepkowski. Trans. Francis Mansfield. Nettetal: Steyler Verlag.

Musk, Bill. 1988. "Dreams and the Ordinary Muslim." *Missiology* 16, no. 2: 163–72.

Myers, Bryant L. 1999. *Walking with the Poor: Principles and Practices of Transformational Development*. Maryknoll, N.Y.: Orbis.

Neely, Alan. 1996. "Images: Mission and Missionaries in Contemporary Fiction and Cinema." *Missiology* 24, no. 4: 451–78.

——. 1999. "Saints Who Sometimes Were: Utilizing Missionary Hagiography." *Missiology* 27, no. 4: 441–57.

Netland, Harold A. 2001. *Encountering Religious Pluralism: The Challenge to Christian Faith and Mission*. Downers Grove, Ill.: InterVarsity.

Newbigin, Lesslie. 1978. *The Open Secret: Sketches for a Missionary Theology*. Grand Rapids: Eerdmans.

——. 1986. *Foolishness to the Greeks: The Gospel and Western Culture*. Grand Rapids: Eerdmans.

——. 1987. "Can the West Be Converted?" *IBMR* 11, no. 1: 2–7.

——. 1989. *The Gospel in a Pluralist Society*. Grand Rapids: Eerdmans.

——. 1991. *Truth to Tell: The Gospel as Public Truth*. Grand Rapids: Eerdmans.

——. 1995. *The Open Secret: An Introduction to the Theology of Mission*. Rev. ed. Grand Rapids: Eerdmans.

Nida, Eugene A. 1960. *Message and Mission: The Communication of the Christian Faith*. New York: Harper.

——. 1964. *Toward a Science of Translating: With Special Reference to Principles and Procedures Involved in Bible Translating*. Leiden: Brill.

Nobili, Roberto de. 2000. *Preaching Wisdom to the Wise: Three Treatises by Roberto de Nobili, S.J., Missionary and Scholar in 17th Century India*. Trans. Anand Amaladass and Francis X. Clooney. St. Louis: Institute of Jesuit Sources.

Nock, A. D. 1933. *Conversion: The Old and the New in Religion from Alexander the Great to Augustine of Hippo*. London: Oxford University Press.

Noll, Mark A. 1998. "The Potential of Missiology for the Crises of History." In *History and the Christian Historian*, ed. Ronald A. Wells, 106–23. Grand Rapids: Eerdmans.

Norton, H. Wilbert, Sr. 1993. "The Student Foreign Missions Fellowship over Fifty-five Years." *IBMR* 17, no. 1: 17–21.

Oborji, Francis Anekwe. 2006. *Concepts of Mission: The Evolution of Contemporary Missiology*. Maryknoll, N.Y.: Orbis.

Oddie, Geoffrey A. 2003. "Constructing 'Hinduism': The Impact of the Protestant Missionary Movement on Hindu Self-Understanding." In *Christians and Missionaries in India: Cross-Cultural Communication since 1500*, ed. Robert Eric Frykenberg, 155–82. Grand Rapids: Eerdmans.

——. 2006. *Imagined Hinduism: British Protestant Missionary Constructions of Hinduism, 1793–1900*. Thousand Oaks, Calif.: Sage.

O'Donnell, Kelly, ed. 1992. *Missionary Care: Counting the Cost for World Evangelization*. Pasadena, Calif.: William Carey Library.

——, ed. 2002. *Doing Member Care Well: Perspectives and Practices from Around the World*. Pasadena, Calif.: William Carey Library.

O'Donnell, Kelly, and Michèle Lewis O'Donnell, eds. 1988. *Helping Missionaries Grow: Readings in Mental Health and Missions*. Pasadena, Calif.: William Carey Library.

Okure, Teresa. 2009. "The Church in the Mission Field: A Nigerian / African Response." In *Edinburgh 2010: Mission Then and Now*, ed. David A. Kerr and Kenneth R. Ross, 59–73. Oxford: Regnum.

Okyerefo, Michael Perry Kweku. 2010. "Christianising Africa: A Portrait by Two African Novelists." *Studies in World Christianity* 16, no. 1: 63–81.

O'Loughlin, Thomas. 2000. *Celtic Theology: Humanity, World and God in Early Irish Writings*. New York: Continuum.

——. 2008. "'Celtic Spirituality': A Case Study in Recycling the Christian Past for Present Needs." In *"With Wisdom Seeking God": The Academic Study of Spirituality*, ed. Una

Agnew, Bernadette Flanagan, and Greg Heylin, 143–61. Studies in Spirituality, supp. 15. Leuven: Peeters.

O'Malley, John W. 1993. *The First Jesuits*. Cambridge, Mass.: Harvard University Press.

Ong, Walter J. 1982. *Orality and Literacy: The Technologizing of the Word*. London: Routledge.

Onyinah, Opoku. 2006. "God's Grace, Healing and Suffering." *IRM* 95, no. 376–77: 117–27.

Orobator, Agbonkhianmeghe E. 2005. *From Crisis to Kairos: The Mission of the Church in the Time of HIV/AIDS, Refugees and Poverty*. Nairobi: Paulines Publications Africa.

Origen. 1998. "Letter to Gregory." In *St. Gregory Thaumaturgus: Life and Works*, trans. Michael Slusser, 190–92. Fathers of the Church 98. Washington, D.C.: Catholic University of America Press.

Pachuau, Lalsangkima. 2000. "Missiology in a Pluralistic World: The Place of Mission Study in Theological Education." *IRM* 89, no. 355: 539–55.

——. 2002. "Engaging the 'Other' in a Pluralistic World: Toward a Subaltern Hermeneutics of Christian Mission." *Studies in World Christianity* 8, no. 1: 63–80.

Pachuau, Lalsangkima, and Max L. Stackhouse, eds. 2007. *News of Boundless Riches: Interrogating, Comparing, and Reconstructing Mission in a Global Era*. 2 vols. Delhi: ISPCK.

Padilla, C. René. 1982. "The Unity of the Church and the Homogeneous Unit Principle." *IBMR* 6, no. 1:23–30.

Pagden, Anthony. 1982. *The Fall of Natural Man: The American Indian and the Origins of Comparative Ethnology*. Cambridge, U.K.: Cambridge University Press.

Parker, Michael. 1998. *The Kingdom of Character: The Student Volunteer Movement for Foreign Missions (1886–1926)*. Lanham, Md.: American Society of Missiology and University Press of America.

Parrinder, Edward Geoffrey. 1954. *African Traditional Religion*. London: Hutchinson's University Library.

Parshall, Phil. 1983. *Bridges to Islam: A Christian Perspective on Folk Islam*. Grand Rapids: Baker.

——. 2003. *Muslim Evangelism: Contemporary Approaches to Contextualization*. Rev. ed. of *New Paths in Muslim Evangelism: Evangelical Approaches to Contextualization*. Waynesboro, Ga.: Gabriel.

Peel, J. D. Y. 2000. *Religious Encounter and the Making of the Yoruba*. Bloomington: Indiana University Press.

Pelikan, Jaroslav. 2005. *Whose Bible Is It? A History of the Scriptures through the Ages*. New York: Viking.

Pernoud, Régine. 2006. *Martin of Tours: Soldier, Bishop, and Saint*. Trans. Michael J. Miller. San Francisco: Ignatius.

Pesch, Rudolf. 1982. "Voraussetzungen und Anfänge der urchristlichen Mission." In *Mission im Neuen Testament*, ed. Karl Kertelge, 11–70. QD 93. Freiburg: Herder.

Phan, Peter C. 2003. "Crossing the Borders: A Spirituality for Mission in Our Times from an Asian Perspective." *SEDOS Bulletin* 35, no. 1–2: 8–19.

——. 2008. "World Christianity and Christian Mission: Are They Compatible? Insights from the Asian Churches." *IBMR* 32, no. 4: 193–200.

Pickett, J. Waskom. 1933. *Christian Mass Movements in India: A Study with Recommendations*. New York: Abingdon.

Piggin, Stuart. 1984. *Making Evangelical Missionaries 1789–1858: The Social Background, Motives and Training of British Protestant Missionaries to India*.Appleford, Abingdon, U.K.: Sutton Courtenay Press.

Pike, Kenneth L. 1967. *Language in Relation to a Unified Theory of the Structure of Human Behavior*. 2nd rev. ed. The Hague: Mouton.

Pinnock, Clark H. 1992. *A Wideness in God's Mercy: The Finality of Jesus Christ in a World of Religions*. Grand Rapids: Zondervan.

Pliny the Younger. 1975. *Letters and Panegyricus*. Vol. 2. Trans. Betty Radice. Loeb Classical Library. Cambridge, Mass.: Harvard University Press.

Pohl, Christine D. 2003. "Biblical Issues in Mission and Migration." *Missiology* 31, no. 1: 3–15.

Porter, Andrew N. 1985. "'Commerce and Christianity': The Rise and Fall of a Nineteenth-Century Missionary Slogan." *Historical Journal* 28, no. 3: 597–621.

——. 2004. *Religion versus Empire? British Protestant Missionaries and Overseas Expansion, 1700–1914*. Manchester, U.K.: Manchester University Press.

Porterfield, Amanda. 1997. *Mary Lyon and the Mount Holyoke Missionaries*. New York: Oxford University Press.

Priest, Robert J., Terry Dischinger, Steve Rasmussen, and C. M. Brown. 2006. "Researching the Short-Term Mission Movement." *Missiology* 34, no. 4: 431–50.

Purcell, William F. 2004. "Contested Translations: The Gospel versus Foreign Missionaries in John Munonye's *Obi*." *Christianity and Literature* 54, no. 1: 15–29.

Putney, Clifford. 2001. *Muscular Christianity: Manhood and Sports in Protestant America, 1880–1920*. Cambridge, Mass.: Harvard University Press.

Rahner, Karl. 1966. "Christianity and the Non-Christian Religions." In *Theological Investigations*. Trans. Karl-H. Kruger. Vol. 5: 115–34. Baltimore: Helicon.

Ramachandra, Vinoth. 1999. *Faiths in Conflict? Christian Integrity in a Multicultural World*. Downers Grove, Ill.: InterVarsity.

Rees, Daniel, ed. 1997. *Monks of England: The Benedictines in England from Augustine to the Present Day*. London: SPCK.

Renault, François. 1994. *Cardinal Lavigerie: Churchman, Prophet and Missionary*. Trans. John O'Donohue. London: Athlone.

Richebächer, Wilhelm. 2003. "*Missio Dei*: The Basis of Mission Theology or a Wrong Path?" *IRM* 92, no. 367: 588–605.

Richter, Michael. 1999. *Ireland and Her Neighbors in the Seventh Century*. New York: St. Martin's.

Rives, James B. 2007. *Religion in the Roman Empire*. Malden, Mass.: Blackwell.

Riyad, Umar. 2002. "Rashid Rida and a Danish Missionary: Alfred Nielsen (d. 1965) and Three *Fatwas* from *al-Manar*." *Islamochristiana* 28: 87–107.

Robert, Dana L. 1993. "Evangelist or Homemaker? Mission Strategies of Early Nineteenth-Century Missionary Wives in Burma and Hawaii." *IBMR* 17, no. 1: 4–12.

——. 1997. *American Women in Mission: A Social History of Their Thought and Practice*. Macon, Ga.: Mercer University Press.

——. 2006. "World Christianity as a Women's Movement." *IBMR* 30, no. 4: 180–88.

——, ed. 2008. *Converting Colonialism: Visions and Realities in Mission History, 1706–1914*. Grand Rapids: Eerdmans.

Rohrer, James R. 2006. "Biography as Missiology: A Reflection on the Writing of Missionary Lives." *Taiwan Journal of Theology* 28: 175–212.

Romero, Oscar A. 1985. *Voice of the Voiceless: The Four Pastoral Letters and Other Statements*. Trans. Michael J. Walsh. Maryknoll, N.Y.: Orbis.
Ross, Andrew C. 1994. *A Vision Betrayed: The Jesuits in Japan and China, 1542–1742*. Maryknoll, N.Y.: Orbis.
——. 2002. *David Livingstone: Mission and Empire*. London: Hambledon and London.
Rowbotham, Judith. 2002. "Ministering Angels, Not Ministers: Women's Involvement in the Foreign Missionary Movement, *c*. 1860–1910." In *Women, Religion and Feminism in Britain, 1750–1900*, ed. Sue Morgan, 179–95. Houndmills, Basingstoke, Hampshire: Palgrave Macmillan.
Roxborogh, John. 1996. Review of *Philosophy, Science, and Theology of Mission in the 19th and 20th Centuries*, vol. 1, by Jan A. B. Jongeneel. *Missiology* 24, no. 1: 127–28.
Ruokanen, Miikka. 1992. *The Catholic Doctrine of Non-Christian Religions, According to the Second Vatican Council*. Leiden: Brill.
Russell, James C. 1994. *The Germanization of Early Medieval Christianity: A Sociohistorical Approach to Religious Transformation*. New York: Oxford University Press.
Saayman, Willem. 2009. "David Bosch—Some Personal Reflections." *Mission Studies* 26, no. 2: 214–28.
Sanneh, Lamin. 1989. *Translating the Message: The Missionary Impact on Culture*. Maryknoll, N.Y.: Orbis.
——. 1995. "Global Christianity and the Re-education of the West." *Christian Century* 112 (July 19–26): 715–18.
——. 1999. *Abolitionists Abroad: American Blacks and the Making of Modern West Africa*. Cambridge, Mass.: Harvard University Press.
——. 2008. *Disciples of All Nations: Pillars of World Christianity*. New York: Oxford University Press.
Satterthwaite, Philip E. 1993. "Acts against the Background of Classical Rhetoric." In *The Book of Acts in Its First Century Setting*, ed. Bruce W. Winter and Andrew D. Clarke. 1:337–79. Grand Rapids: Eerdmans.
Schenkel, Albert F. 1995. *The Rich Man and the Kingdom: John D. Rockefeller, Jr., and the Protestant Establishment*. Minneapolis: Fortress.
Schleiermacher, Friedrich. 1988. *Brief Outline of Theology as a Field of Study*. Trans. Terrence N. Tice. Lewiston, N.Y.: Edwin Mellen.
Schlenther, Boyd Stanley. 1997. *Queen of the Methodists: The Countess of Huntingdon and the Eighteenth-Century Crisis of Faith and Society*. Durham, U.K.: Durham Academic Press.
Schmidlin, Joseph. 1931. *Catholic Mission Theory*. Ed. and trans. Matthias Braun. Techny, Ill.: Mission Press.
Schmidt, Mette. 2007. "An Ecumenical Miracle—An Arabic Satellite Channel Devoted to Christian Unity in a Torn Region." *IRM* 96, no. 382–83: 288–92.
Schnabel, Eckhard J. 2004. *Early Christian Mission*. 2 vols. Downers Grove, Ill.: InterVarsity.
Schoepflin, Rennie B. 2005. "Making Doctors and Nurses for Jesus: Medical Missionary Stories and American Children." *Church History* 74, no. 3: 557–90.
Schreiter, Robert J. 1985. *Constructing Local Theologies*. Maryknoll, N.Y.: Orbis.
——. 1992. *Reconciliation: Mission and Ministry in a Changing Social Order*. Maryknoll, N.Y.: Orbis.
——. 1996. "Reconciliation as a Model of Mission." *Neue Zeitschift für Missionswissenschaft* 50, no. 4: 243–50.

——. 1997a. *The New Catholicity: Theology between the Global and the Local*. Maryknoll, N.Y.: Orbis.
——. 1997b. "Reconciliation." In *Dictionary of Mission: Theology, History, Perspectives*, ed. Karl Müller et al., 379–82. Maryknoll, N.Y.: Orbis.
——. 1998. *The Ministry of Reconciliation: Spirituality and Strategies*. Maryknoll, N.Y.: Orbis.
Schroeder, Roger. 2000. "Women, Mission, and the Early Franciscan Movement." *Missiology* 28, no. 4: 411–24.
Schubert, Esther. 1991. "Personality Disorders and the Selection Process for Overseas Missionaries." *IBMR* 15, no. 1: 33–36.
——. 1999. A Suggested Prefield Process for Mission Candidates. *Journal of Psychology and Theology* 27, no. 2: 87–97.
Schultze, Andrea. 2004. "Writing of Past Times: An Interdisciplinary Approach to Mission History." In *European Traditions in the Study of Religion in Africa*, ed. Frieder Ludwig and Afe Adogame, in coop. with Ulrich Berner and Christoph Bochinger, 323–28. Wiesbaden: Harrassowitz.
Schütte, Josef Franz. 1985. *Valignano's Mission Principles for Japan*. Vol. 1, part 2. Trans. John J. Coyne. St. Louis: Institute of Jesuit Sources.
Scott, Jamie S. 2008a. "Missions and Film." *IBMR* 32, no. 3: 115–20.
——. 2008b. "Missions in Fiction." *IBMR* 32, no. 3: 121–18.
Scott, Jamie S., and Gareth Griffiths, eds. 2005. *Mixed Messages: Materiality, Textuality, Missions*. New York: Palgrave Macmillan.
Sebastian, Mrinalini. 2003. "Reading Archives from a Postcolonial Feminist Perspective: Native Bible Women and the Missionary Ideal." *Journal of Feminist Studies in Religion* 19, no. 1: 5–25.
Selles, Johanna M. 2006. "The Role of Women in the Formation of the World Student Christian Federation." *IBMR* 30, no. 4: 189–94.
Selvanayagam, Israel. 2004. "Interfaith Dialogue." In *A History of the Ecumenical Movement, Vol. 3 1968–2000*, ed. John Briggs, Mercy Amba Oduyoye, and Georges Tsetsis, 149–74. Geneva: World Council of Churches.
Selwyn, Jennifer D. 2004. *A Paradise Inhabited by Devils: The Jesuits' Civilizing Mission in Early Modern Naples*. Aldershot, U.K.: Ashgate.
Semple, Rhonda Anne. 2003. *Missionary Women: Gender, Professionalism and the Victorian Idea of Christian Mission*. Woodbridge, U.K.: Boydell.
Senior, Donald, and Carroll Stuhlmueller. 1983. *The Biblical Foundations for Mission*. Maryknoll, N.Y.: Orbis.
Seton, Rosemary. 1996. "'Open Doors for Female Labourers': Women Candidates of the London Missionary Society, 1875–1914." In *Missionary Encounters: Sources and Issues*, ed. Robert A. Bickers and Rosemary Seton, 50–69. Richmond, U.K.: Curzon.
Sharkey, Heather J. 2004. "Arabic Antimissionary Treatises: Muslim Responses to Christian Evangelism in the Modern Middle East." *IBMR* 28, no. 3: 98–104.
——. 2008. "Muslim Apostasy, Christian Conversion, and Religious Freedom in Egypt." In *Proselytization Revisited: Rights Talk, Free Markets and Culture Wars*, ed. Rosalind I. J. Hackett, 139–66. London: Equinox.
Sharpe, Eric J. 1965. *Not to Destroy but to Fulfill: The Contribution of J. N. Farquhar to Protestant Missionary Thought in India before 1914*. Uppsala: Gleerup.
Shelley, Michael T. 1999. "Temple Gairdner of Cairo Revisited." *Islam and Christian-Muslim Relations* 10, no. 3: 261–78.

Shenk, Wilbert R. 1983. *Henry Venn—Missionary Statesman*. Maryknoll, N.Y.: Orbis.
Showalter, Nathan D. 1998. *The End of the Crusade: The Student Volunteer Movement for Foreign Missions and the Great War*. Lanham, Md.: Scarecrow.
Simpson, Donald. 1997. "Missions and the Magic Lantern." *IBMR* 21, no. 1: 13–15.
Singh, Maina Chawla. 2005. "Women, Mission, and Medicine: Clara Swain, Anna Kugler, and Early Medical Endeavors in Colonial India." *IBMR* 29, no. 3: 128–33.
Sittser, Gerald L. 2007. "Protestant Missionary Biography as Written Icon." *Christian Scholar's Review* 36, no. 3: 303–21.
Skreslet, Stanley H. 1997. "Networking, Civil Society, and the NGO: A New Model for Ecumenical Mission." *Missiology* 25, no. 3: 307–19.
——. 1999. "Impending Transformation: Mission Structures for a New Century." *IBMR* 23, no. 1: 2–6.
——. 2003. "Doctoral Dissertations on Mission: Ten-Year Update, 1992–2001." *IBMR* 27, no. 3: 98–133.
——. 2006a. "Configuring Missiology: Reading Classified Bibliographies as Disciplinary Maps." *Mission Studies* 23, no. 2: 171–201.
——. 2006b. *Picturing Christian Mission: New Testament Images of Disciples in Mission*. Grand Rapids: Eerdmans.
——. Forthcoming. "Missiology." *New Westminster Dictionary of Christian Theology*. Louisville: Westminster John Knox.
Smalley, William A. 1991. *Translation as Mission: Bible Translation in the Modern Missionary Movement*. Macon, Ga.: Mercer University Press.
——. 1993. "Doctoral Dissertations on Mission: Ten-Year Update, 1982–1991." *IBMR* 17, no. 3: 97–100.
Smith, Edwin W. 1929. *The Secret of the African*. London: Student Christian Movement.
Smith, George. 1881. *The Life of Alexander Duff, D.D., LL.D.* London: Hodder and Stoughton.
Smith, Jane I. 1998. "Christian Missionary Views of Islam in the Nineteenth and Twentieth Centuries." *Islam and Christian-Muslim Relations* 9, no. 3: 357–73.
——. 1999. "Islam and Christendom: Historical, Cultural, and Religious Interaction from the Seventh to the Fifteenth Centuries." In *The Oxford History of Islam*, ed. John L. Esposito, 304–45. Oxford: Oxford University Press.
Smith, Wilfred Cantwell. 1981. *Towards a World Theology: Faith and the Comparative History of Religion*. Philadelphia: Westminster.
Sobrino, Jon. 2003. *Witnesses to the Kingdom: The Martyrs of El Salvador and the Crucified Peoples*. Maryknoll, N.Y.: Orbis.
Søgaard, Viggo. 1993. *Media in Church and Mission: Communicating the Gospel*. Pasadena, Calif.: William Carey Library.
Sorrell, Roger D. 1988. *St. Francis of Assisi and Nature: Tradition and Innovation in Western Christian Attitudes toward the Environment*. Oxford: Oxford University Press.
Speer, Robert E. 1904. *Missions and Modern History: A Study of the Missionary Aspects of Some Great Movements of the Nineteenth Century*. 2 vols. New York: Fleming H. Revell.
——. 1928. "What Is the Value of the Religious Values of the Non-Christian Religions?" In *The Christian Life and Message in Relation to Non-Christian Systems of Thought and Life*. Jerusalem meeting of the International Missionary Council. Vol. 1: 345–67. New York: International Missionary Council.

Spencer, Stephen, ed. 2008. *Mission and Migration: Papers Read at the Biennial Conference of the British and Irish Association for Mission Studies at Westminster College, Cambridge, July2–5, 2007*. Calver, U.K.: Cliff College Publishing.

Spicq, Ceslas. 1994. *Theological Lexicon of the New Testament*. Ed. and trans. James D. Ernest. 3 vols. Peabody, Mass.: Hendrickson.

Spindler, Marc R. 1995. "The Biblical Grounding and Orientation of Mission." In *Missiology: An Ecumenical Introduction*, ed. F. J. Verstraelen et al., 123–43. Grand Rapids: Eerdmans.

Stackhouse, Max L. 1988. *Apologia: Contextualization, Globalization, and Mission in Theological Education*. With Nantawan Boonprasat-Lewis et al. Grand Rapids: Eerdmans.

——. 2005. "Missions: Missionary Activity." *ER* 9: 6068–76.

Standaert, Nicholas. 2001. "Social Organization of the Church." In *Handbook of Christianity in China,* Vol. 1: 635–1800, ed. Nicholas Standaert, 456–61. Leiden: Brill.

Stanley, Brian. 1998. "The Legacy of Robert Arthington." *IBMR* 22, no. 4: 166–71.

——, ed. 2001. *Christian Missions and the Enlightenment*. Grand Rapids: Eerdmans.

——. 2003. "Where Have Our Mission Structures Come From?" *Transformation* 20, no. 1: 39–46.

——. 2009. *The World Missionary Conference, Edinburgh 1910*. Grand Rapids: Eerdmans.

Stanley, John R. 2010. "Establishing a Female Medical Elite: The Early History of the Nursing Profession in China." In *Pioneer Christian Women: Gender, Christianity, and Social Mobility*, ed. Jessie G. Lutz, 274–91. Bethlehem, Pa.: Lehigh University Press.

Stark, Rodney. 1996. *The Rise of Christianity: A Sociologist Reconsiders History*. Princeton, N.J.: Princeton University Press.

Steer, Roger. 2004. "'Without Note or Comment': Yesterday, Today, and Tomorrow." In *Sowing the Word: The Cultural Impact of the British and Foreign Bible Society, 1804–2004*, ed. Stephen Batalden, Kathleen Cann, and John Dean, 63–80. Sheffield, U.K.: Sheffield Phoenix.

Sterk, Andrea. 2010a. "Mission from Below: Captive Women and Conversion on the East Roman Frontier." *Church History* 79, no. 1: 1–39.

——. 2010b. "'Representing' Mission from Below: Historians as Interpreters and Agents of Christianization." *Church History* 79, no. 2: 271–304.

Stipe, Claude E. 1980. "Anthropologists versus Missionaries: The Influence of Presuppositions." *Current Anthropology* 21, no. 2: 165–79.

Stoneman, Timothy H. B. 2007. "Preparing the Soil for Global Revival: Station HCJB's Radio Circle, 1949–1959." *Church History* 76, no. 1: 114–55.

Strengholt, Jos M. 2008. *Gospel in the Air: 50 Years of Christian Witness through Radio in the Arab World*. Zoetermeer: Boekencentrum.

Sugirtharajah, R.S. 2001. *The Bible and the Third World: Precolonial, Colonial and Postcolonial Encounters*. Cambridge: Cambridge University Press.

Sulpicius Severus. 1995. "The Life of St. Martin of Tours." Trans. F.R. Hoare. In *Soldiers of Christ: Saints and Saints' Lives from Late Antiquity and the Early Middle Ages*, ed. Thomas F. X. Noble and Thomas Head, 1–29. University Park: Pennsylvania State University Press.

Sundkler, Bengt. 1948. *Bantu Prophets in South Africa*. London: Lutterworth.

Svelmoe, William Lawrence. 2008. *A New Vision for Missions: William Cameron Townsend, the Wycliffe Bible Translators, and the Culture of Early Evangelical Faith Missions, 1896–1945*. Tuscaloosa: University of Alabama Press.

Taber, Charles R. 1991. *The World Is Too Much with Us: "Culture" in Modern Protestant Missions*. Macon, Ga.: Mercer University Press.

Tacitus. 1937. *The Annals of Tacitus*. Vol. 4. Trans. John Jackson. Loeb Classical Library. Cambridge, Mass.: Harvard University Press.

Tan, Jonathan Y. 2004. "*Missio Inter Gentes*: Towards a New Paradigm in the Mission Theology of the Federation of Asian Bishops' Conferences (FABC)." *Mission Studies* 21, no. 1: 65–95.

Taylor, William D., ed. 1997. *Too Valuable to Lose: Exploring the Causes and Cures of Missionary Attrition*. Pasadena, Calif.: William Carey Library.

Temperley, Howard. 1991. *White Dreams, Black Africa: The Antislavery Expedition to the River Niger, 1841–1842*. New Haven, Conn.: Yale University Press.

Tennent, Timothy C. 2002. *Christianity at the Religious Roundtable: Evangelicalism in Conversation with Hinduism, Buddhism, and Islam*. Grand Rapids: Baker.

——. 2005. "The Challenge of Churchless Christianity: An Evangelical Assessment." *IBMR* 29, no. 4: 171–77.

——. 2006. "Followers of Jesus (*Isa*) in Islamic Mosques: A Closer Examination of C-5 'High-Spectrum' Contextualization." *International Journal of Frontier Missions* 23, no. 3: 101–15.

——. 2010. *Invitation to World Missions: A Trinitarian Missiology for the Twenty-first Century*. Grand Rapids: Kregel.

Tew, C. Delane. 2006. "Baptist Missionary Funding: From Societies to Centralization." *Baptist History and Heritage* 41, no. 2: 55–67.

Theissen, Gerd. 1978. *Sociology of Early Palestinian Christianity*. Trans. John Bowden. Philadelphia: Fortress.

Thomas, Norman E., ed. 2003. *International Mission Bibliography, 1960–2000*. Lanham, Md.: Scarecrow Press.

Thorne, Susan. 1999. *Congregational Missions and the Making of an Imperial Culture in Nineteenth-Century England*. Stanford, Calif.: Stanford University Press.

Tippett, Alan R. 1974. "Research Method and the Missiological Process at the School of World Mission." In *The Means of World Evangelization: Missiological Education*, ed. Alvin Martin, 498–504. South Pasadena, Calif.: William Carey Library.

——. 1987. *Introduction to Missiology*. Pasadena, Calif.: William Carey Library.

Togarasei, Lovemore. 2009. "The Shona Bible and the Politics of Bible Translation." *Studies in World Christianity* 15, no. 1: 51–64.

Travis, John [pseudonym]. 1998. "The C1 to C6 Spectrum: A Practical Tool for Defining Six Types of 'Christ-centered Communities Found in the Muslim Context.'" *Evangelical Missions Quarterly* 34, no. 4: 407–8.

Tucker, Ruth A. 1999. "Biography as Missiology: Mining the Lives of Missionaries for Cross-Cultural Effectiveness." *Missiology* 27, no. 4: 429–40.

Turner, Harold W. 1967. *History of an African Independent Church: The Church of the Lord (Aladura)*. 2 vols. Oxford: Clarendon Press.

Ukpong, Justin S. 1987. "What Is Contextualization?" *Neue Zeitschrift für Missionswissenschaft* 43, no. 3: 161–68.

United Bible Societies. "Statistical Summary of Languages with the Scriptures." *www.ubs-translations.org/about_us*.

United Nations. "The World's Most Translated Document." *http://www.un.org/events/humanrights/2007/worldtransdoc.shtml*.

Ustorf, Werner. 2000. *Sailing on the Next Tide: Missions, Missiology, and the Third Reich*. Frankfurt am Main: Peter Lang.

——. 2001. "Rethinking Missiology." In *World Christianity Reconsidered: Questioning the Questions of Ecumenism and Missiology; Contributions for Bert Hoedemaker*, ed. Anton Houtepen and Albert Ploeger, 67–78. IIMO Research Publications 57. Zoetermeer: Meinema.

——. 2008. "The Cultural Origins of 'Intercultural Theology.'" *Mission Studies* 25, no. 2: 229–51.

Vadakumpadan, Paul. 2006. *Missionaries of Christ: A Basic Course in Missiology*. Shillong, India: Vendrame Institute, Sacred Heart Theological College.

Vähäkangas, Mika. 2010. "The Future of Missiologies." In *Walk Humbly with the Lord: Church and Mission Engaging Plurality*, ed. Viggo Mortensen and Andreas Østerlund Nielsen, 217–29. Grand Rapids: Eerdmans.

Van der Meer, Erwin. 2001. "Reflections on Spiritual Mapping." *Africa Journal of Evangelical Theology* 20, no. 1: 47–70.

Verkuyl, J. 1978. *Contemporary Missiology: An Introduction*. Trans. and ed. Dale Cooper. Grand Rapids: Eerdmans.

Verstraelen, F. J., A. Camps, L. A. Hoedemaker, and M. R. Spindler, eds. 1995. *Missiology: An Ecumenical Introduction; Texts and Contexts of Global Christianity*. With the assistance of J. D. Gort. Grand Rapids: Eerdmans.

Volf, Miroslav. 1996. *Exclusion and Embrace: A Theological Exploration of Identity, Otherness, and Reconciliation*. Nashville: Abingdon.

Wacker, Grant. 2001. *Heaven Below: Early Pentecostals and American Culture*. Cambridge, Mass.: Harvard University Press.

Walls, Andrew F. 1991. "Structural Problems in Mission Studies." *IBMR* 15, no. 4: 146–55.

——. 1993. "Missions." *Dictionary of Scottish Church History and Theology*, 567–94. Downers Grove, Ill.: InterVarsity.

——. 1994. "Thomas Fowell Buxton, 1786–1844: Missions and the Remedy for African Slavery." In *Mission Legacies: Biographical Studies of Leaders of the Modern Missionary Movement*, ed. Gerald H. Anderson et al., 11–17. Maryknoll, N.Y.: Orbis.

——. 1996. *The Missionary Movement in Christian History: Studies in the Transmission of Faith*. Maryknoll, N.Y.: Orbis.

——. 1997. "Old Athens and New Jerusalem: Some Signposts for Christian Scholarship in the Early History of Mission Studies." *IBMR* 21, no. 4: 146–53.

——. 1999. "In Quest of the Father of Mission Studies." *IBMR* 23, no. 3: 98–105.

——. 2001. "The Eighteenth-Century Protestant Mission Awakening in Its European Context." In *Christian Missions and the Enlightenment*, ed. Brian Stanley, 22–44. Grand Rapids: Eerdmans.

——. 2002a. *The Cross-Cultural Process in Christian History: Studies in the Transmission and Appropriation of Faith*. Maryknoll, N.Y.: Orbis.

——. 2002b. "Missiology." *Dictionary of the Ecumenical Movement*. 2nd ed., 781–83. Geneva: World Council of Churches.

——. 2003. "Missions and Historical Memory: Jonathan Edwards and David Brainerd." In *Jonathan Edwards at Home and Abroad: Historical Memories, Cultural Movements, Global Horizons*, ed. David W. Kling and Douglas A. Sweeney, 248–65. Columbia: University of South Carolina Press.

——. 2004. "Geoffrey Parrinder (*1910) and the Study of Religion in West Africa." In *European Traditions in the Study of Religion in Africa*, ed. Frieder Ludwig and Afe

Adogame, in cooperation with Ulrich Berner and Christoph Bochinger, 207–15. Wiesbaden: Harrassowitz.

Wang, Jiali. 1997. "The House Church Movement: A Participant's Assessment." *Word and World* 17, no. 2: 175–12.

Ward, William. 1817. *A View of the History, Literature, and Religion of the Hindoos: Including a Minute Description of Their Manners and Customs, and Translations from Their Principal Works*. 3rd ed. 2 vols. Serampore, India: Mission Press.

Warneck, Gustav. 1892–1903. *Evangelische Missionslehre. Ein missionstheoretischer Versuch*. 5 vols. in 3. Gotha: F. A. Perthes.

——. 1906. *Outline of a History of Protestant Missions from the Reformation to the Present Time*. 3rd English ed. Ed. George Robson. New York: Fleming H. Revell.

Weber, Charles W. 2001. "Mission Strategies, Anthropologists, and the Harmon Foundation's African Film Projects: Presenting Africa to the Public in the Inter-War Years, 1920–1940." *Missiology* 29, no. 2: 201–23.

Welz, Justinian Ernst von. 1969. *Justinian Welz: Essays by an Early Prophet of Mission*. Trans. James A. Scherer. Grand Rapids: Eerdmans.

Wenger, Etienne. 1998. *Communities of Practice: Learning, Meaning, and Identity*. Cambridge: Cambridge University Press.

Wessels, Anton. 2002. "In Memoriam Johannes Verkuyl." *Exchange* 31, no. 1: 81–93.

Whaling, Frank. 1981. "A Comparative Religious Study of Missionary Transplantation in Buddhism, Christianity and Islam." *IRM* 70, no. 280: 314–33.

Whiteman, Darrell L. 1983. *Melanesians and Missionaries: An Ethnohistorical Study of Social and Religious Change in the Southwest Pacific*. Pasadena, Calif.: William Carey Library.

——. 2008. "Integral Training Today for Cross-Cultural Mission." *Missiology* 36, no. 1: 5–16.

Williams, C. Peter. 1980. "'Not Quite Gentlemen': An Examination of 'Middling Class' Protestant Missionaries from Britain, c. 1850–1900." *Journal of Ecclesiastical History* 31, no. 3: 301–15.

——. 1990. *The Ideal of the Self-Governing Church: A Study in Victorian Missionary Strategy*. Leiden: Brill.

——. 1993. "'The Missing Link': The Recruitment of Women Missionaries in Some English Evangelical Missionary Societies in the Nineteenth Century." In *Women and Missions, Past and Present: Anthropological and Historical Perceptions*, ed. Fiona Bowie, Deborah Kirkwood, and Shirley Ardener, 43–69. Providence, R.I.: Berg.

——. 2000. "'Not Transplanting': Henry Venn's Strategic Vision." In *The Church Missionary Society and World Christianity, 1799–1999*, ed. Kevin Ward and Brian Stanley, 147–72. Grand Rapids: Eerdmans.

Wilson, J. Christy, Jr. 1979. *Today's Tentmakers: Self-Support—An Alternative Model for Worldwide Witness*. Wheaton, Ill.: Tyndale House.

Wimber, John. 1986. *Power Evangelism*. With Kevin Springer. San Francisco: Harper & Row.

Winter, Ralph D. 1996. "Missiological Education for Lay People." In *Missiological Education for the Twenty-first Century: The Book, the Circle, and the Sandals; Essays in Honor of Paul E. Pierson*, ed. J. Dudley Woodberry, Charles E. Van Engen, and Edgar J. Elliston, 169–85. Maryknoll, N.Y.: Orbis.

Winter, Ralph D., and Steven C. Hawthorne, eds. 1981. *Perspectives on the World Christian Movement: A Reader*. Pasadena, Calif.: William Carey Library.

Wood, Ian. 2001. *The Missionary Life: Saints and the Evangelisation of Europe, 400–1050*. Harlow, U.K.: Longman.
Wood, Vanessa. 2008. "The Part Played by Chinese Women in the Formation of an Indigenous Church in China: Insights from the Archive of Myfanwy Wood, LMS Missionary." *Women's History Review* 17, no. 4: 597–610.
Woodberry, J. Dudley. 2008. "Power and Blessing: Keys for Relevance to a Religion as Lived." In *Paradigm Shifts in Christian Witness: Insights from Anthropology, Communication, and Spiritual Power*, ed. Charles E. Van Engen, Darrell Whiteman, and J.Dudley Woodberry, 98–105. Maryknoll, N.Y.: Orbis.
Woods, Leonard. 1966. "The Ordination Sermon." In *Pioneers in Mission: The Early Missionary Ordination Sermons, Charges, and Instructions; A Source Book on the Rise of American Missions to the Heathen*, ed. R. Pierce Beaver, 257–78. Grand Rapids: Eerdmans.
World Council of Churches. 1967. *The Church for Others and the Church for the World*. Geneva: World Council of Churches.
World Missionary Conference, 1910 [IV]. N.d. [1910]. *Report of Commission IV: The Missionary Message in Relation to Non-Christian Religions*. Edinburgh: Oliphant, Anderson & Ferrier.
World Missionary Conference, 1910 [V]. N.d. [1910]. *Report of Commission V: The Training of Teachers*. Edinburgh: Oliphant, Anderson & Ferrier.
Wuthnow, Robert. 2009. *Boundless Faith: The Global Outreach of American Churches*. Berkeley: University of California Press.
Xi, Lian. 2010. *Redeemed by Fire: The Rise of Popular Christianity in Modern China*. New Haven, Conn.: Yale University Press.
Xin, Yalin. 2008. "Inner Dynamics of the Chinese House Church Movement: The Case of the Word of Life Community." *Mission Studies* 25, no. 2: 157–84.
Xu, Yihua. 2009. "Birth, Growth, and Decline of the Chinese Student Volunteer Movement for the Ministry in 20th Century China." In *Christian Mission and Education in Modern China, Japan, and Korea: Historical Studies*, ed. Jan A. B. Jongeneel et al., 65–80. Frankfurt am Main: Peter Lang.
Yamamori, Tetsunao. 1987. *God's New Envoys: A Bold Strategy for Penetrating "Closed Countries."* Portland, Ore.: Multnomah.
Yamamori, Tetsunao, and Kenneth A. Eldred, eds. 2003. *On Kingdom Business: Transforming Missions through Entrepreneurial Strategies*. Wheaton, Ill.: Crossway.
Yates, Timothy. 1994. *Christian Mission in the Twentieth Century*. Cambridge: Cambridge University Press.
Yohn, Susan M. 2002. "'Let Christian Women Set the Example in Their Own Gifts': The 'Business' of Protestant Women's Organizations." In *Women and Twentieth-Century Protestantism*, ed. Margaret Lamberts Bendroth and Virginia Lieson Brereton, 213–35. Urbana: University of Illinois Press.
Yong, Amos. 2005. "A P(new)matological Paradigm for Christian Mission in a Religiously Plural World." *Missiology* 33, no. 2: 175–91.
——. 2008. *Hospitality and the Other: Pentecost, Christian Practices, and the Neighbor*. Maryknoll, N.Y.: Orbis.

Index

PREVIOUSLY PUBLISHED IN
THE AMERICAN SOCIETY OF MISSIOLOGY SERIES

The American Society of Missiology Series, published in collaboration with Orbis Books, seeks to publish scholarly works of high merit and wide interest on numerous aspects of missiology—the study of Christian mission in its historical, social, and theological dimensions. Able presentations on new and creative approaches to the practice and understanding of mission will receive close attention from the ASM Series Committee.

1. *Protestant Pioneers in Korea*, Everett Nichols Hunt Jr.
2. *Catholic Politics in China and Korea,* Eric O. Hanson
3. *From the Rising of the Sun,* James M. Phillips
4. *Meaning Across Cultures*, Eugene A. Nida and William D. Reyburn
5. *The Island Churches of the Pacific*, Charles W. Forman
6. *Henry Venn,* Wilbert Shenk
7. *No Other Name?* Paul F. Knitter
8. *Toward a New Age in Christian Theology,* Richard Henry Drummond
9. *The Expectation of the Poor,* Guillermo Cook
10. *Eastern Orthodox Mission Theology Today,* James J. Stamoolis
11. *Confucius, the Buddha, and the Christ,* Ralph Covell
12. *The Church and Cultures*, Louis J. Luzbetak, SVD
13. *Translating the Message,* Lamin Sanneh
14. *An African Tree of Life*, Thomas G. Christensen
15. *Missions and Money* (second edition), Jonathan J. Bonk
16. *Transforming Mission,* David J. Bosch
17. *Bread for the Journey,* Anthony J. Gittins, CSSp
18. *New Face of the Church in Latin America,* Guillermo Cook
19. *Mission Legacies,* edited by Gerald H. Anderson, Robert T. Coote, Norman A. Horner, and James M. Phillips
20. *Classic Texts in Mission and World Christianity*, edited by Norman E. Thomas
21. *Christian Mission: A Case Study Approach,* Alan Neely
22. *Understanding Spiritual Power,* Marguerite G. Kraft

23. *Missiological Education for the 21st Century: The Book, the Circle, and the Sandals,* edited by J. Dudley Woodberry, Charles Van Engen, and Edgar J. Elliston
24. *Dictionary of Mission: Theology, History, Perspectives,* edited by Karl Müller, SVD, Theo Sundermeier, Stephen B. Bevans, SVD, and Richard H. Bliese
25. *Earthen Vessels and Transcendent Power: American Presbyterians in China, 1837–1952,* G. Thompson Brown
26. *The Missionary Movement in American Catholic History, 1820–1980,* Angelyn Dries, OSF
27. *Mission in the New Testament: An Evangelical Approach,* edited by William J. Larkin Jr. and Joel W. Williams
28. *Changing Frontiers of Mission,* Wilbert Shenk
29. *In the Light of the Word: Divine Word Missionaries of North America,* Ernest Brandewie
30. *Constants in Context: Theology of Mission for Today,* Stephen B. Bevans, SVD, and Roger Schroeder, SVD
31. *Changing Tides: Latin America and Mission Today,* Samuel Escobar
32. *Gospel Bearers, Gender Barriers: Missionary Women in the Twentieth Century,* edited by Dana L. Robert
33. *Church: Community for the Kingdom,* John Fuellenbach, SVD
34. *Mission in Acts: Ancient Narratives for a Postmodern Context,* edited by Robert L. Gallagher and Paul Hertig
35. *A History of Christianity in Asia: Volume I, Beginnings to 1500,* Samuel Hugh Moffett
36. *A History of Christianity in Asia: Volume II, 1500–1900,* Samuel Hugh Moffett
37. *A Reader's Guide to Transforming Mission,* Stan Nussbaum
38. *The Evangelization of Slaves and Catholic Origins in Eastern Africa,* Paul Vincent Kollman, CSC
39. *Israel and the Nations: A Mission Theology of the Old Testament,* James Chukwuma Okoye, CSSp
40. *Women in Mission: From the New Testament to Today,* Susan Smith
41. *Reconstructing Christianity in China: K. H. Ting and the Chinese Church,* Philip L. Wickeri

42. *Translating the Message: The Missionary Impact on Culture* (second edition), Lamin Sanneh
43. *Landmark Essays in Mission and World Christianity*, Robert J. Gallagher
44. *The World Mission in the Wesleyan Spirit*, Darryll L. Whiteman and Gerald H. Anderson
45. *Miracles, Missions & American Pentecostalism*, Gary B. McGee
46. *The Gospel among the Nations: Christian Mission in a Pluralistic World*, Robert A. Hunt
47. *Mission and Unity: Lessons from History, 1792–2010,* Norman E. Thomas
48. *Mission and Culture: The Louis J. Luzbetak Lectures*, Stephen B. Bevans